GREEK

AND

ROMAN

COMEDY

E D I T E D   B Y

S H A W N   O ' B R Y H I M

With contributions by

George Fredric Franko

Timothy J. Moore

Shawn O'Bryhim

S. Douglas Olson

 UNIVERSITY OF TEXAS PRESS, AUSTIN

GREEK
AND
ROMAN
COMEDY

TRANSLATIONS
AND INTERPRETATIONS
OF FOUR
REPRESENTATIVE PLAYS

This book has been supported by an endowment dedicated to classics and the ancient world, funded by grants from the National Endowment for the Humanities and the Gladys Krieble Delmas Foundation, the James R. Dougherty, Jr. Foundation, and the Rachael and Ben Vaughan Foundation, and by gifts from Mark and Jo Ann Finley, Lucy Shoe Meritt, Anne Byrd Nalle, and other individual donors.

Library of Congress Cataloging-in-Publication Data

Greek and Roman comedy : translations and interpretations of four representative plays / edited by Shawn O'Bryhim ; with contributions by George Fredric Franko . . . [et al.].— 1st ed.
        p.   cm.
    Includes bibliographical references and index.
    ISBN 0-292-76054-X (cloth : alk. paper) — ISBN 0-292-76055-8 (pbk. : alk. paper)
    1. Classical drama (Comedy)—Translations into English.   2. Classical drama (Comedy)—History and criticism.   I. O'Bryhim, Shawn, 1960–   II. Franko, George Fredric.

PA3629 .G74   2001
880'21—dc09
                                                                    00-064879

CONTENTS

PREFACE

Every year several new translations of ancient tragedy appear. If not for the relatively few translations of ancient comedy, the general reader might think that the Greeks and Romans were humorless wrecks, obsessed with death and disaster. Nothing could be further from the truth. The ancients had a robust sense of humor that encompassed everything from politics to sexuality. The scarcity of new translations of ancient comedies may stem from any number of factors, including the erroneous belief that what is serious is by definition more worthwhile than what is humorous. It is my hope that this book will dispel this misconception.

Although this volume will be of interest to the general reader, it is meant primarily as a textbook for university students in basic courses on classical civilization, classical literature in translation, Great Books, English, and theater. I have taught several of these courses over the years and have been frustrated by the lack of a text that contains representative works of all extant comic playwrights and includes introductions to each author and essays on their plays. My only recourse has been to instruct my students to buy several different texts in order to cover these authors, which is very costly and inadequate for our needs. Hence the impetus for this book.

Four scholars of ancient comedy have contributed to this volume. Since every comic playwright whose work survives is represented here, the reader can form a fairly good picture of the types of comedy that were produced in Greece and Rome from the fifth to the second century B.C. It is not our intention to present the "greatest hits" of ancient comedy or those works that are most easily produced on stage. On the contrary, we chose these plays because they are representative of each author's corpus. The inclusion of *Lysistrata,* for example, would have been a mistake, because it is not representative of Aristophanes' work and would give the reader an inaccurate picture of Aristophanic comedy. The substitution of Menander's *Samia* for *Dyskolos* would have required substantial additions by the translator because of its fragmentary state, thus making it more of an adaptation than a translation.

Some readers favor loose translations that border on adaptations. However, the creation of modernized versions of these plays runs contrary to the philosophy behind our translations: they should be smooth and readable, but should stay as close to the ideas and tone of the text as possible. As a result, they will be usable twenty years from now, when older adaptations filled with ephemeral slang will have been replaced by newer adaptations filled with ephemeral slang. And while all translations are, by nature, adaptations, very loose ones can often mislead those who wish to understand the culture in which the originals were written. In an attempt to avoid this, the translators have followed a few general guidelines in preparing their translations: avoid anachronisms; remain true to the original; translate all songs and significant changes of meter into verse; and include the bare minimum of stage directions. Stage directions are not found in the ancient manuscripts, so only exits, entrances, and a few directions that are absolutely necessary have been included here. Cues imposed by translators can act as a straitjacket upon imagination and creativity; their absence frees each reader to determine how each play might have taken shape on stage.

Since ancient comedies are sometimes inextricably bound to the time in which they were written, the best way to understand these translations is to read the elements of each section in the order in which they appear. The introduction includes information about the author and the category into which his comedy falls. A plot summary at the end of the introduction provides the background necessary to understand the events and characters discussed in the essay, which concentrates on an important theme in the play. After reading these sections, the reader will be in a better position to fully enjoy the translation and to appreciate the artistry of the author of the play. However, the format is very flexible, thus allowing the book to be used in several ways. The reader can concentrate on just a couple of authors, gain a general understanding of ancient comedy by reading all of the introductory chapters in order, or simply read the plays in isolation.

One word of caution: relatively few ancient comedies survive. There were other authors who probably wrote significantly different—and perhaps better—plays than the ones presented here, but their works have been lost. Therefore, to know the plays in this book is not to know all there is about ancient comedy. This is only an introduction to the genre. Some of the plays in this book are incomplete; sometimes substantial elements are missing, and other times just a few lines. In such cases, the translators have supplied what they deemed necessary to make the plays comprehensible to the modern reader. These additions are contained within brackets and in most cases are guesses based upon a few surviving words or letters. Other interpretations are possible and are encouraged.

SHAWN O'BRYHIM, Arcadia, Indiana, January 24, 2000

GREEK

AND

ROMAN

COMEDY

ARISTOPHANES AND ATHENIAN OLD COMEDY

S. DOUGLAS OLSON

INTRODUCTION

The Development of Old Comedy

OFFICIAL performances of comedies began in Athens at the City Dionysia festival in 487 or 486 B.C. and at the Lenaia festival sometime around 442 B.C.[1] The origins of the genre are obscure, and will most likely always remain so. According to the fourth-century philosopher Aristotle in his *Poetics,* comedy was originally performed in Athens by "volunteers" rather than by professional actors in a state-sponsored contest (1449b1–2); the genre grew out of "introductions to phallic songs," i.e., from material associated with events like the Rural Dionysia that we see take place onstage at *Acharnians* lines 237–79 (1449a11–13). Aristotle suggests that the Greek word *komoidia* ("comedy"), the second part of which certainly means "song," is derived either from *kóme,* an (originally non-Athenian?) term for a rural village, or from *kómos,* "a drunken band of revelers" (*Poetics* 1448a35–38). The notion that at least some of the roots of Athenian Old Comedy must be sought in informal, local festival traditions also finds support in a number of vase paintings from late-sixth-century Athens that depict groups of men dressed up as animals, as Aristophanic and other early comic choruses often are.[2]

In addition, Aristotle notes that Athens' neighbor Megara claimed that comedy had been invented there (1448a30–32), and the occasional sneering references to unsophisticated Megarian humor in Aristophanes (e.g., *Acharni-*

1. The best discussion of the festivals and what is known of them is A. Pickard-Cambridge, *The Dramatic Festivals of Athens* (2d ed., rev. J. Gould and D. M. Lewis; Oxford, 1968), 25–42 (Lenaia), 57–101 (City Dionysia).

2. See G. M. Sifakis, *Parabasis and Animal Choruses* (London, 1971), esp. 71–93.

3

ans lines 738–39, 822; *Wasps* 57) and elsewhere (Ecphantides fr. 3 K-A; Eupolis fr. 261 K-A) suggest that in the fifth century there was some awareness of the existence of another old local comic tradition. Perhaps more important, Aristotle twice associates the origin of comedy with the work of the Sicilian poet Epicharmos, who probably dates to the early fifth century, although Aristotle would place him a generation or so earlier (1448a32–34, 1449a5–7). Epicharmos' plays have been preserved only in unrevealing and generally very tiny fragments, but Aristotle reports that he and his even more obscure contemporary Phormis were the first to give comedy a plot (1449a5–6). What little survives of his plays suggests that they featured not only actors but a chorus, and makes clear that their author was fond of mythological parody. That verbal reports and eventually copies of plays by Epicharmos and perhaps also Phormis and others made their way to Athens seems likely, just as we know that a century or so later Athenian comedies were read and even performed in the cities of the Greek West.[3]

On the most straightforward reading of the evidence, one might conclude that acquaintance with the texts of these Sicilian comedies, and perhaps with a crude Megarian comic theater, led one or more individuals in Athens to think of drawing on local processional and performance traditions to write their own comic dramas. As time passed, work of this sort became more and more sophisticated, until someone suggested that a program of comedies be added to the dramatic competition at the City Dionysia, where tragedy had been performed for a generation or so. It must nonetheless be conceded that this is a largely hypothetical reconstruction, which may be wrong in some (or even most) of its particulars.

The Production of the Plays

We are better—although still imperfectly—informed about the comic competitions in the second half of the fifth century, when Aristophanes and his older contemporaries were active. The official Athenian year began in midsummer, and one of the first duties of two of the city's chief annual officers (or "archons") was to decide which poets would compete in the dramatic festivals at the Lenaia festival (in January) and the City Dionysia (in April). For tragic poets, the City Dionysia, which large numbers of foreign visitors attended, seems to have been a more prestigious venue than the Lenaia, which was a largely intra-Athenian affair; for comic poets, no such difference is apparent.

3. See O. Taplin, *Comic Angels* (Oxford, 1993), 1–54.

We do not know how the archons' decisions were made, although the poet's reputation was probably important. A passage in Plato's *Laws* suggests that samples of the proposed play (or, for tragedy, the proposed set of plays) were read in the archon's presence (817d).

For each festival, five comic and three tragic poets were awarded a chorus, which is to say that responsibility for the expenses involved in producing their play or plays was assigned to a wealthy man known as the *choregus* (literally "chorus leader"). This was an expensive but prestigious office and, like many similar duties, such as outfitting and maintaining the city's warships, was carried out on something approximating a rotating basis among Athens' wealthiest (or "liturgical") class. The playwright was allowed three principal actors, who varied their costumes (and presumably their voices) to take on the different parts in his play or plays. All parts were played by men, in padded "female" costumes if necessary. The most important of the actors (the "protagonist") was chosen by the archon and assigned to the playwright, probably by lot; the protagonist plays Dikaiopolis in *Acharnians*. The second and third actors (the "deuteragonist" and "tritagonist") were probably selected by the poet himself, although we have no solid information on this point. In addition, the poet was free to bring any number of mutes (or at least any number the *choregus* would agree to pay for) onstage, and comic poets on occasion use a fourth actor who speaks only a few lines; in *Acharnians,* a fourth actor probably plays the Herald, Dikaiopolis' daughter, one of the Megarian "pussies," and Lamachos' servant.[4] Specialized dancers could be hired also, and although none appear in *Acharnians,* they are featured in other Aristophanic comedies, including *Wasps* and *Lysistrata.* In addition to a chorus and a protagonist (and thus the right to produce a play), poets were awarded pay from the state (see Aristophanes, *Frogs* line 367), and although we have no idea how much this was, it must have been enough to provide a comfortable level of personal support in the months leading up to the dramatic competition or competitions.

Already by the mid-fifth century, theatrical producing was a complicated and difficult undertaking (compare Aristophanes' comments on this point at *Knights* line 512–44), and while some playwrights did everything themselves, professional chorus-trainers known as *chorodidaskaloi* ("chorus-teachers") or *didaskaloi* ("teachers") were apparently common. The fact that poets could present plays at both festivals—if they were able to persuade each of the two rel-

4. See D. M. MacDowell, "The Number of Speaking Actors in Old Comedy," *Classical Quarterly,* n.s., 44 (1994): 325–35.

evant archons to grant them a chorus, as Aristophanes often did in the early
years of his career—also meant that there might be a large number of con-
flicting demands on the time of the most talented and successful individuals. In
addition, some playwrights must have recognized that they simply did not have
a gift for the fine points of theatrical production. Many of Aristophanes' comedies were accordingly produced "through" either Kallistratos (who was responsible not only for *Acharnians* but for *Banqueters* and *Babylonians,* the poet's
two other earliest comedies) or Philonides, which presumably means that Aristophanes entrusted them with the day-to-day business of getting his works
onstage. We know that other comic poets did the same thing on occasion, and
we have so little information on this point that there is no reason to believe that
the practice was uncommon.

Both comedies and tragedies were performed in the Theater of Dionysos,
which lies in the middle of the south slope of Athens' Acropolis. We know relatively little about the physical structure of the theater in Aristophanes' time
beyond what can be deduced from the text of his comedies and the tragedies of
his contemporaries Sophocles and Euripides. The theater's seating capacity was
probably about 17,000, which meant that it could hold a substantial percentage of the city's adult male citizen population (perhaps 30,000 in the 420s B.C.).
The seats were stone benches without padding or backs and were arranged in
a series of semicircular rows facing the stage. The Priest of Dionysos and certain other priests, the archons, and eventually the city's generals, were provided front-row seating, and a special section of seats, probably in the center
and near the front of the theater, was reserved for members of the city's Council. Foreigners and boys were certainly allowed to attend performances of both
comedies and tragedies; most likely women could as well, but the point has
been hotly debated. An admission fee was charged, but it appears to have been
relatively low, and by the beginning of the fourth century the state granted all
citizens enough money to buy seats and perhaps pay for other festival expenses
as well.

Between the first row of seats and the stage was a large open area known
as the *orchestra* (or "dancing area"), which could be entered from passageways
on the left and right. The members of the chorus are generally confined to this
area, although they interact freely with the actors on the stage. A permanent
altar stood in the *orchestra* and is often used by the actors for sacrifice and sup-
plication scenes. Most of the action in Aristophanes' plays, however, takes
place on the stage, which in this period seems to have been made of wood and
raised slightly above the *orchestra,* to which it was connected by a few central

steps. At the back of the stage was a wall (the *scaenae frons*) approximately one story high, with a large permanent central door, which is used in *Acharnians* to represent Euripides' house. One or two side-doors could be added if a playwright wished; *Acharnians* is most easily staged with two (one representing Lamachos' house, the other Dikaiopolis'), but other stagings are possible. Behind the central door was a moveable platform (the *ekkuklema*), which could be rolled out to represent interior scenes; in *Acharnians* it is used to bring Euripides onstage. The back of the *scaenae frons* was fitted with ladders leading to an upper platform, allowing actors to stand on the roofs of the houses, as Dikaiopolis' wife is told to do during the phallic procession in *Acharnians*. There was also a theatrical crane (the *mechane*), used in tragedy to allow gods or heroes to "fly" onstage from behind the *scaenae frons*. Aristophanes makes no use of the crane in *Acharnians,* although he does elsewhere, most often to poke fun at Euripidean tragedy, which uses it constantly. Stage-paintings were used to indicate the setting, but we know next to nothing else about them.

The costuming for Aristophanes' plays is on occasion quite elaborate, as in the case of the richly dressed Ambassadors, the Persian emissary Bushel-of-Lies, and Lamachos with his plumes and armor in *Acharnians*.[5] More often, the playwright's characters are dressed like average residents of Athens and its environs, and wear a rough woolen outer robe (or *himation*), a short woolen inner garment (or *chiton*), and a pair of heavy shoes (or *embades*). All characters wore masks that covered the front of the face and wigs that covered the top and back of the head. Perhaps the most important thing to be said about these masks is that they seemed normal to ancient audiences, who expected them on theatrical characters of all sorts. Modern producers of Aristophanic comedies are therefore in general ill-advised to use masks, despite their apparent "authenticity," when staging plays for audiences unaccustomed to this convention. Comic characters were also fitted with a considerable amount of padding on their bellies and buttocks, and male characters wore large phalluses that hung out of their clothing in full view and could be made to stand upright to indicate sexual excitement. Once again, this would all have seemed unremarkable to a fifth-century audience.

Formally, the comedies staged by Aristophanes and his contemporaries were part of a festival in honor of Dionysos, god of wine and theater, but the playwrights were also engaged in an intense competition to take first place in

5. For an exhaustive discussion of this aspect of the comedies, see L. M. Stone, *Costume in Aristophanic Comedy* (Salem, N.H., 1984).

the balloting that followed the performances. Shortly before the festival began, the names of potential judges from each of the ten "tribes" into which the Athenian people were divided were inscribed on individual pieces of broken pottery or the like and sealed in ten urns. The qualifications to serve probably had nothing to do with intelligence or critical expertise, but concerned whether a man was a member in good standing of his tribe and would agree to attend all performances of the category for which he proposed to serve as judge. When the contest was about to begin, the urns were placed in the theater and one name drawn from each. These men were the judges and were required to swear that they would be impartial; whether they always were is impossible to tell, but seems unlikely. At the end of the contest, each judge, doubtless influenced not only by the general public reaction to the plays in the theater but by the comments and requests of his friends and neighbors, ranked the poets and deposited his ballot in an urn; whether the same men voted on both comedy and tragedy is unknown. The archon in charge of the festival drew five ballots from the urn; the results were tabulated; and the winner was announced and crowned with ivy in the theater.

This system of judging contains just enough odd, random elements that it is easy to believe that inappropriate decisions were rendered on occasion; Sophocles' *Oedipus the King,* for example, took second place, and the first (now lost) version of Aristophanes' *Clouds* took third, much to the author's disgust. In neither case, however, do we know the quality of the other works on the program, and the system worked well enough to be retained for many years; the judges' collective verdicts seem to have been accepted as a legitimate expression of the voice of the Athenian people.

Aristophanes and His Rivals

The earliest Athenian comic poets whose names we know are Susarion (said to have invented the genre, whatever that may mean); Chionides, who won the first contest at the City Dionysia in the early 480s B.C. and wrote plays entitled *Heroes, Beggars,* and *Persians or Assyrians;* and Magnes, who won eleven times at the City Dionysia and to whom titles including *Frogs, Dionysos, Lydians,* and *The Female Grass-Cutter* are attributed. Very little else is known of any of these men, and some of Magnes' titles may be late scholarly conjectures based on a remark by Aristophanes at *Knights* lines 522–24 about the behavior of his choruses. The next generation of comic playwrights included Krates, who Aristotle says was the first to advance beyond crude personal slander to plots of a more general interest (*Poetics* 1449b7–9) and who probably won three times at the City

Dionysia, and Kratinos, whose popularity is apparent in the fact that he took the prize six times at the City Dionysia (for the last time probably in 423 B.C., when his *Wine-flask* defeated *Clouds*) and three times at the Lenaia. Large numbers of fragments but no complete plays survive by both men.

Aristophanes was born most likely in the early 440s B.C. and died in 388 or shortly thereafter. Beyond that, we know little about his personal life and origins; how much truth there is in Plato's portrait of him in the *Symposium* is anyone's guess, but a substantial degree of scepticism seems called for. His father's name was Philippos (literally "Horse-lover"), and he was attached to the local Athenian administrative district (or "deme") of Kydathenaion. Although deme affiliations originally indicated place of residence, they were then passed on from father to son, so that the fact that Aristophanes was legally "from Kydathenaion" tells us nothing certain about where he and his family lived and thus potentially about their political and social sympathies.

Acharnians lines 652–54 suggest that the poet had some substantial personal connection to and was perhaps for a while even a resident of the nearby island of Aigina, where his family may have been alloted land in 431 B.C., when the original, pro-Spartan population of the place was expelled as a security measure, but that as well tells us nothing certain about his socioeconomic status. A more important clue is Aristophanes' obviously high degree of literacy, which—when combined with the fact that children were educated privately in fifth-century Athens, so that the poor often received little or no formal education—makes it likely that his family was at least moderately well-to-do. That conclusion finds further support in an inscription dating from the beginning of the fourth century (*IG* II² 2343) that gives the names of a group of probably wealthy and well-born men involved in a cult of Herakles in Aristophanes' deme of Kydathenaion. One of these men bears the name Allgod (Greek *Amphitheos*), which is otherwise very rare but is shared by a character in *Acharnians;* another is called Philonides and is easily identified with the man who served as one of Aristophanes' theatrical producers (see above); and a third is named Simon and may be the individual referred to as a cavalry commander and opponent of Aristophanes' archenemy Kleon at *Knights* line 242 (424 B.C.).

One can thus make a reasonable case that Aristophanes was somehow connected with these men, particularly since we know he had the support of an otherwise obscure group of patrons early in his career (see below) and that the chorus of his first play, *Banqueters,* was made up of a company of men who had just concluded a feast in a temple of Herakles (*Banqueters* testimonium iii K-A). That Aristophanes was himself a Knight (i.e., a member of the second of

Athens' four formal economic classes), or that he at least had strong personal or familial connections with the Knights, thus seems likely, given not only his father's name but the flattering reference to these men in the opening verses of *Acharnians* and the fact that they make up the chorus in his comedy of 424 B.C. Beyond this we know only that he had three sons, Philippos II, Araros, and Nikostratos (or Philetairos?), all of whom wrote comedies, and that at one point, probably late in life, he served as a member of Athens' administrative Council. As this was an alloted rather than an elective office, that fact as well tells nothing about his social, economic, or political status or his interests.

Aristophanes was recognized in antiquity as one of the three greatest masters of the Old Comedy (the others being his contemporaries Eupolis and Kratinos), and approximately forty plays were attributed to him in antiquity. Eleven of those plays (*Acharnians, Knights, Clouds, Wasps, Peace, Birds, Lysistrata, Women at the Thesmophoria, Frogs, Assemblywomen,* and *Wealth,* in the order in which they appear to have been performed)[6] survive complete or almost complete in manuscripts, as do almost one thousand fragments preserved either in quotations by later authors or (less often) on scraps of papyrus. The earliest play to be preserved entire is *Acharnians,* which was performed at the Lenaia festival in early 425 B.C., when the poet was in his early to mid-twenties and had already staged two comedies, *Banqueters* (427 B.C.) and *Babylonians* (City Dionysia, 426 B.C.). Aristophanes refers several times to the earliest stages of his career, and although the precise significance of these passages has been debated, the basic outlines of this part of his professional history can be recovered with a reasonable degree of certainty.

As Stephen Halliwell has shown, comic poets in the late fifth century probably worked both with and for one another on occasion,[7] and remarks Aristophanes makes at *Wasps* lines 1018−20 suggest that as a young man he looked at and commented on the work of others; precisely how substantial his contributions to these plays were cannot be determined from the passage, despite its boastful tone. *Clouds* lines 528−31 make it clear that at some time, most likely in early 428 B.C., Aristophanes showed a script of *Banqueters* to a group of presumably older and influential men, who are most likely to be identified with the individuals associated with the Kydathenaion cult of Herakles mentioned

6. In fact, the surviving *Clouds* appears to be an incompletely revised version of the original play and probably dates to sometime in the mid-410s B.C.

7. See S. Halliwell, "Authorial Collaboration in the Athenian Comic Theatre," *Greek, Roman, and Byzantine Studies* 30 (1989): 515−28.

above and who arranged for it to be accepted for one of the festivals and produced by Kallistratos, despite the poet's youth and apparently without his name
being known at first. An ancient comment on *Clouds* line 529 tells us that *Banqueters* took second place, but the play must have been a success, since Aristophanes was awarded choruses for *Babylonians* at the City Dionysia in 426 B.C.
and *Acharnians* at the Lenaia in 425 B.C., and probably for a Lenaia play in 426
as well (compare *Acharnians* lines 1150–55). We do not know what sort of reception *Babylonians* received, except from Kleon, who attempted to create legal trouble for its author on account of its contents, although there are reasons
for thinking that the Athenian people generally approved of it (see the essay that
follows).

By the end of the 420s B.C., at any rate, when he cannot have been much
over thirty, Aristophanes was one of the most important and popular figures in
the Theater of Dionysos, having had at least nine plays performed at either the
Lenaia or the City Dionysia[8] and having taken first place a minimum of two
times (with *Acharnians* and *Knights*) and quite possibly several more.[9]

Some Characteristics of Aristophanic Comedy

Most of Aristophanes' comedies are constructed of standard elements, which
the playwright uses time and time again. The first and in some ways most important of these is the hero's grand and improbable plan, which sets the plot in
motion; thus in *Acharnians* Dikaiopolis arranges a separate peace with Sparta for
himself and his family, while elsewhere in the Aristophanic corpus heroes fly up
to Heaven on a dungbeetle to complain to Zeus about the effects of the Peloponnesian War (in *Peace*), go off to the land of the birds and found a new city
there (in *Birds*), organize a sex strike among the city's women to force the men
into peace negotiations with Sparta (in *Lysistrata*), or descend to the Under-

8. I.e. (in chronological order), *Banqueters;* the Lenaia play of 426 B.C.; *Babylonians; Acharnians; Knights* (Lenaia, 424 B.C.); a Lenaia play in 423 B.C. (see *Wasps* 1037–42); *Clouds* (City
Dionysia, 423 B.C.); *Wasps* (Lenaia, 422 B.C.); and *Peace* (City Dionysia, 421 B.C.). The lost
Farmers and *Merchantships* were probably performed in this period as well, although whether
they are the unidentified Lenaia plays of 426 and 423 B.C. is another question. It is possible that
the *Proagon* with which Philonides took first place at the Lenaia in 422 B.C. was written by Aristophanes as well; see D. M. MacDowell's commentary on *Wasps* (Oxford, 1971), Hypothe-
sis I.34.

9. We know that *Clouds* was a great failure and that *Banqueters, Wasps,* and *Peace* took second place; how the other plays fared is uncertain, but Aristophanes' continuing ability to be
awarded choruses strongly suggests that the majority of them did well.

world to fetch a dead poet (in *Frogs*). The hero's plan is generally met with op-position, frequently expressed in a great debate (or *agon*) like Dikaiopolis' de-fense of his separate peace before the chorus and Lamachos in *Acharnians*. In the end, he is at least nominally successful in doing what he wants, and much of the second half of the play illustrates the consequences of his plan, often (as in *Acharnians*) by means of a series of visitors, who complain to him or praise him for what he has done. In the end, he exits as part of a triumphal procession.

The action among the characters onstage in Aristophanes' comedies is re-peatedly interrupted by the chorus, which enters only after the hero's plan is underway and remains present in the orchestra for the rest of the play. In the first half of the action, the chorus is sometimes opposed to the hero's plan, as in *Acharnians,* where the chorus members threaten to attack Dikaiopolis and later call in Lamachos as their ally. By the end, however, they are in general firmly on his side and form the core of the celebratory group that accompanies him out. Most of the chorus' lines are sung rather than spoken, and it is clear that they engaged in elaborate dance numbers, about which we know little. The most important of the chorus' songs is the *parabasis* (or "stepping forward"), which occurs in the middle of the play at a point when the stage is empty of characters and which consists of a direct and often pointed address to the audi-ence that often takes up topics only peripherally related to the action of the play. The Aristophanic *parabasis* has a complex, fixed metrical structure and is probably a traditional element common to all Athenian comedies of the late fifth century. Aristophanes abandons it in his two final surviving plays, *Assem-blywomen* and *Wealth,* which are generally regarded as Middle rather than Old Comedy and in which the role of the chorus is restricted in other ways as well.

Aristophanic humor is made up of very diverse material, much of which remains obviously and immediately appealing today, although a few aspects of some plays may strike modern readers as incomprehensible or offensive. The subject of every comedy is, in one way or another, the city of Athens, and the poet's larger themes and many of his individual jokes are intensely political. Some of the individual jokes are directed against particular people and can be difficult to appreciate without an intimate knowledge of who was who in late-fifth-century Athens; indeed, even specialists in Aristophanic poetry cannot make sense of all of them. The poet's general view of life in a political society, on the other hand, requires little translation or explanation for the twenty-first-century reader and can be broadly described as a combination of profound cynicism with an unreasonable, exuberant hopefulness. Everyone in power is corrupt and everyone else (except the hero) is a fool, but the possibility that the world might be made radically better is nonetheless always to the fore. This new and better world is not necessarily better for everyone, but it certainly is for the hero, and one of his greatest pleasures is to mock his enemies, who are in the end excluded from everything good. That this is by modern standards bad behavior seems not to be to the point.

One fundamental characteristic of Aristophanic humor is thus its profoundly political nature. A second is the extraordinary mix of literary and social styles apparent in the words and behavior of the playwright's creatures. On the one hand, Aristophanes' characters are fascinated with contemporary tragedy and in particular Euripides, who is actually represented onstage in *Acharnians* and again in *Women at the Thesmophoria* in 411 and *Frogs* in 405 B.C. That tragedy (or at least Euripidean tragedy) is in some sense ridiculous is taken for granted in *Acharnians:* Euripides dresses and behaves in a ludicrous fashion, talks nonsense, and is fixated on writing about beggars and cripples. When he wants to be at his most persuasive, however, Dikaiopolis disguises himself as the tragic Telephos, insists that "comedy knows what's right, too" (i.e., as tragedy is automatically assumed to do), and uses a modified version of the arguments advanced by the Euripidean hero to defend his peace treaty to the chorus and the audience.[10] Elsewhere in the play, on the other hand, Dikaiopolis and the other characters speak in a highly colloquial style and use a large amount of obscenity. The scene in which the hero and his Megarian visitor discuss what should be done with the two young "pussies" the latter has brought to sell, for example, is raunchy by modern standards, but there can be little doubt that this raunchiness is an important part of what made Aristophanes' comedies appealing.

In other ways as well the poet relies on what we would today call relatively simple forms of humor: his characters trade insults, assault one another physically, and revel in basic sensual pleasures, including eating, drinking, and sex. That this was all typical of late-fifth-century Old Comedy seems likely, but Aristophanes was clearly a master of the genre, and much of the genius of his plays consists in the way he combines a variety of influences and styles to create brilliant literary and dramatic wholes.

10. See the first part of the essay that follows.

THE POLITICS OF COMEDY
AND THE PROBLEM OF
THE RECEPTION OF
ARISTOPHANES' *ACHARNIANS*

ACHARNIANS was performed at the Lenaia festival in Athens in 425 B.C. and took first place in the balloting that came at the end, defeating Kratinos' *Storm-tossed* and Eupolis' *New Moons,* neither of which has been preserved. There can be little doubt that the original audience consisted mostly of average democrats, to whom the play must have appealed in some important way, since a majority of their representatives voted to award it the prize. This may at first be surprising, for the opening scenes in *Acharnians* in particular present Athens' government as controlled not by the people themselves (as state ideology would have had it) but by a group of corrupt insiders, whose malfeasance is made possible by the stupidity of the rest of the population. Rather than correct this situation, the poet's hero gives up, severs himself from the state, and spends most of the play thumbing his nose at anyone who disagrees with his decision. On the face of it, therefore, *Acharnians* seems blatantly insulting to average democrats. It must nonetheless have pleased them, and the possibility that this is an accident is eliminated by the fact that one year later *Knights,* in which the people are represented by an imbecilic old man whose affairs are run for him by his conniving slaves, took first place as well.

Almost all of Aristophanes' surviving comedies are, in a very basic sense, political, in that they are set in contemporary Athens and offer detailed criticisms of the state of public affairs there. The schemes the poet's heroes devise to convert the city into a better place to live, however, are utterly impractical in real-world terms, so that it is impossible to understand the comedies as straightforward proposals for political or social reform. In addition, although the historical Aristophanes must have had political convictions, and although the hero in *Acharnians* is clearly to be identified with the author in some important way (see below), the opinions expressed by the playwright's characters cannot necessarily be identified with his own. Aristophanes almost certainly always had one eye set on winning the prize at the festival in which he was competing and therefore had little choice but to appeal to what he took to be popular tastes and prejudices, presumably repressing some of his own feelings in order to do so. The apparent inconsistency between the playwright's portrayal of the Athenian people as idiots and his desire to be awarded first place by their representatives thus poses a fundamental question: how can *Acharnians* have been approved by an audience that would not, on the face of it, seem likely to have been sympathetic to many of its most basic assertions? The essay that follows is an attempt to answer that question.

Dikaiopolis and Athens

By 425 B.C., Athens and Sparta were the two leading Greek powers in the eastern Mediterranean world and had been locked for about six years in a nasty war of attrition, commonly referred to as the Peloponnesian War. The origins of this conflict are traced in detail by the contemporary historian Thucydides, who describes a number of incidental causes, including a trade embargo imposed by Athens on her pro-Spartan neighbor Megara, to which Aristophanes refers in *Acharnians* and again in *Peace* a few years later. Thucydides nonetheless insists that the "truest cause" of the hostilities—although the one least mentioned openly—was that the Spartans became afraid of the widespread commercial and military empire Athens had built up in the years following the Persian invasion of Greece in 480–479 B.C. and decided to put an end to it (Thuc. 1.23.6).

Sparta in the late fifth century was a formidable military power, which preferred to support narrow, oligarchic governments in other cities and exercised a firm and often brutal control over many of its Peloponnesian neighbors. On land, the Peloponnesian forces were far superior to the Athenians and their allies, and when war broke out in 431 B.C. the Spartans adopted a strategy of invading the enemy's countryside every summer, destroying farmsteads and crops, and then withdrawing again into their own territory. One of the first areas damaged in this way was the rural district of Acharnai (Thuc. 2.19.2), whose inhabitants make up the chorus of embittered old peasant-farmers in the Aristophanic comedy that bears their name. Athens for its part was a radically democratic state, in which all important offices were filled by lot or election and the people's Council, Assembly, and law courts reigned supreme. The allies who made up Athens' empire were nominally free and independent states, and were in general under the control of democratic governments. All attempts at secession from the empire were nonetheless brutally suppressed, and every year at the time of the City Dionysia the allies were required to bring a tribute payment which made their subject-status clear. In military terms, Athens was primarily a naval power, and at the urging of her leading statesman, Perikles, the city had adopted at the outbreak of the war a strategy of relying on her fleet and the tribute-payments and trade resources of the Empire.

Rather than confronting the Spartans and their allies when they invaded, and risking almost certain defeat, the Athenians forfeited their countryside, brought the rural population within the city's walls, and waited out the attacks. The Spartans calculated that the damage done in their raids would either quickly wear out the willingness of the Athenians to resist or force the enemy to come out into the field with their land forces and suffer a terrible defeat (Thuc. 2.20). There can be little doubt that many average Athenian citizens—and especially farmers who did not normally live within the city's walls—suffered terribly during these years. Indeed, Thucydides tells us that during the first invasion there was considerable dissent within the city, with many citizens—and especially the Acharnians, who made up a sizeable percentage of the population, and the young, who had never seen the Athenian countryside ravaged—eager to go out and fight, to the extent that Perikles was forced to suspend regular meetings of the Assembly to keep from being forced into military action (Thuc. 2.21.2–22.1). This state of affairs is reflected in *Acharnians,* where the chorus members are outraged that Dikaiopolis has made a private peace despite the fact that their farms have been ruined, and the hero himself is a displaced farmer whose vines have been cut and who (at the beginning of the play, at least) wants only to get back to his old, easy life in the country. Despite the Spartans' calculations, the Athenians did not give in but hung on stubbornly year after year, even after a terrible plague (doubtless caused in part by overcrowding and the resulting unsanitary conditions) struck the city and killed a substantial portion of the population, including Perikles in 429 B.C. Indeed, despite occasional blunders Athens' democratic government proved remarkably resilient and resourceful throughout the early years of the Peloponnesian War, and after Perikles died his place was taken by a wealthy leather-tanner named Kleon, who, like him, argued that the city had no choice but to continue to pursue the war as aggressively as possible or risk losing the power she had struggled for several generations to obtain.

As *Acharnians* begins, Dikaiopolis presents himself as a thoroughly isolated figure, the only citizen who cares enough about Athens' public affairs and what he, at least, takes to be the universal good of peace to come to a meeting of the Assembly on time. No one else is willing to abandon the private pleasure of gossiping in the marketplace until forced to do so, and when the Assembly officers at last appear, hours late, they put their bad attitude on immediate display by elbowing and shoving to get to the best seats. Discussing the arrangements necessary to bring about an end to the war—which ought, as Dikaiopolis sees it, to be their highest priority—concerns them not at all. Indeed, the city's public authorities seem actively hostile to the idea of peace, since they have denied Allgod the expense money he needs to travel to Sparta to arrange an armistice, and the moment he begins to complain, the Herald has him dragged out of the Assembly-place as a troublemaker. Nor is this situation unique, for Dikaiopolis makes it clear that things are always this way. He has accordingly come resolved not to allow business to proceed as usual; today he will do whatever is necessary to get the question of peace put on the agenda.

The opening action of *Acharnians* thus leaves little doubt that Athens' public affairs are in an unhappy and irrational state, and what happens in the rest of the scene reveals what the problem is. The first speaker allowed to address the Assembly is an anonymous Ambassador recently returned from an eleven-year mission to Persia, in the course of which he has—despite his complaints—had a wonderful time, traveling in great luxury, eating huge meals, and drinking undiluted wine from beautiful and expensive cups, all the while drawing two drachmas a day (at least twice the average daily wage) from the public treasury. As Dikaiopolis points out, the Ambassadors have been making fools of everyone else by pretending to engage in public service while living in luxury and being paid for it, and it is unsurprising that they have no interest in seeing the war come to an end. Thus when the Persian emissary Bushel-of-Lies makes the incomprehensible announcement "*Iartamanexarxanapissonasatra,*" the Ambassador claims that this can be translated to mean that the Great King is sending enormous quantities of gold to support the war effort. In fact, as Dikaiopolis quickly establishes, this is nonsense; no gold is coming and the Athenian people are fools if they allow themselves to be convinced that it is.

The next speaker, Theoros, has spent the winter being paid to get drunk with another prominent barbarian, King Sitalkes of Thrace, and offers a series of tall tales about the devotion this new ally feels toward Athens' people and the benefits he is likely to bestow. Unfortunately, the only thing the Odomantian mercenaries Sitalkes has sent accomplish is to steal the ingredients for Dikaiopolis' next meal, which amounts to saying that whatever inflated wages they are paid will come out of the mouths of average Athenians.

As his words and behavior throughout this scene make clear, Dikaiopolis knows that a democratic state ought to be run for the good of its citizens, so that he is frustrated with the current state of affairs but initially still quite public-minded. Peace—and with it the freedom for the people to return to the countryside and their farms—is what Athens needs, and Dikaiopolis is eager to have the topic brought up in the Assembly. Nor will there be any problem with obtaining an armistice from the Spartans, once positive action on the matter has been taken by the people, since Allgod has been approved by the gods to fetch an agreement. Dikaiopolis' confrontations with the Ambassadors and Theoros and his inability to get the question of peace taken up for debate nonetheless reveal that accomplishing anything so sensible in Athens is impossible. The city's leaders are unanimously dedicated to self-interest, while the rest of the citizens are unable to detect the (utterly transparent) fraud going on around them, even when it is pointed out to them. Despite his initial good intentions, the only option the hero has left is to give up his interest in public life, and that is what he does after the Assembly officials provide another example of their selfish attitude by inviting Bushel-of-Lies into the City Hall to share a publicly subsidized meal, leaving everyone else outside in the cold. "The rest of you can go right on acting like idiots," Dikaiopolis declares, but now that his last, desperate attempt to function within political society has failed, he will not. Instead, he digs into his pocket, gives Allgod the expense-money required to arrange a truce for himself and his family alone, and severs his ties to Athenian public life.

In the opening scenes of *Acharnians,* the conflict with Sparta is a stupid, ugly fact, from which anyone not earning an inflated wage as an ambassador or the like would naturally want to be free. As the play's original audience was well aware, however, Athens and Sparta had real, long-standing disputes, most recently the repeated Peloponnesian ravaging of the Attic countryside. To argue that this war ought to be brought to an end immediately on the ground that war is, by definition, bad for almost everyone involved, would thus appear to be a patently facile approach to a complicated concrete problem. It is precisely this objection that Dikaiopolis is forced to confront when the chorus appears onstage, and his response is to prove that they have misunderstood matters completely. In the Acharnians' eyes, Dikaiopolis' willingness to conclude a separate peace with the enemy makes him the foulest of all possible traitors, and they are prepared to stone him to death in an act of collective retribution. Only by defending the Spartans can the hero defend himself, and to prepare for this great and terrible undertaking he goes off to the house of the tragic playwright Euripides to borrow a set of rags originally worn by Telephos.

Telephos was a legendary king of Mysia, an area near Troy, and was the subject of a Euripidean tragedy performed in perhaps 438 B.C.; Aristophanes himself may have seen the play as a young man and refers to and quotes from it repeatedly in his comedies.[1] The play is preserved only in fragments (many of them quoted by the ancient commentators on *Acharnians*), and our knowledge of the exact sequence of events in it is sketchy. All the same, enough can be recovered to make basic sense of the way Aristophanes put the Euripidean text to work for his own purposes. Telephos was Greek by birth but had been banished by his father and had settled in Mysia, where he married the wife of the previous king and thus became king himself. In a battle with Greek forces involved in an abortive preliminary attack on the area, he was wounded by the hero Achilleus and, when the wound failed to get better, consulted Apollo, the god of prophecy, who told him that he could only be healed by "the one that had injured him." Telephos dressed in rags and made his way to Argos, where the Greeks had gathered in anticipation of a renewed attack on Troy, and entered the house of the chief commander, Agamemnon. His intent was apparently to pass himself off as a ruined Greek soldier, wait until Achilleus arrived, and beg him to touch the wound.

At this point, a quarrel broke out among the Greek commanders, probably having to do with whether revenge ought to be taken on the Mysians and their king. Despite his seemingly low status, the disguised Telephos spoke up, arguing that "Telephos" actions were justified because he had been acting in self-defense, and insisting that the Greeks would have done the same or worse under similar circumstances. Not surprisingly, he was recognized and fled to a temple of Apollo for sanctuary, taking with him Agamemnon's child, Orestes (replaced in *Acharnians* by the chorus' beloved charcoal basket), whom he threatened to kill if his own life was not spared. In the end Telephos was for-

---

1. For the Euripidean *Telephos* and Aristophanes' treatment of it in this play, see H. P. Foley, "Tragedy and Politics in Aristophanes' *Acharnians*," *Journal of Hellenic Studies* 108 (1988): 33–47; M. J. Cropp in C. Collard, M. J. Cropp, and K. H. Lee, *Euripides: Selected Fragmentary Plays,* vol. I (Warminster, 1995), 17–52 (with extensive bibliography).

given, perhaps as a result of arguments made by Odysseus, and was healed (although not by Achilleus himself but by contact with the hero's spear, which had actually done the wounding) and gave the Greeks crucial advice they needed to make their way to Troy. Dikaiopolis claims that he needs a set of rags so as to appear as pitiful as possible to the chorus and win their sympathy, while Aristophanes is clearly intent on satirizing Euripidean drama generally by insisting that the tragedian likes to bring ill-dressed, fast-talking, crippled heroes onstage because he himself prefers to wear dirty clothes, hates to leave the house, and is full of pretentious, wordy nonsense. The reason Aristophanes' hero needs the rags of Telephos in particular, however, is that the Mysian king was a brilliant orator and Dikaiopolis wants to make the same arguments in defense of the Spartans and himself.

Dikaiopolis begins his speech by insisting that he is no partisan of the Spartans, since his vines too have been cut during their invasions. Indeed, he claims to wish the enemy only the worst: "I wish Poseidon would send an earthquake and knock their houses down around their ears." All the same, he argues that the Spartans' behavior ought not to be the issue, for they merely responded in a reasonable fashion to a series of provocations from the Athenians themselves. Trouble began, Dikaiopolis says, when some marginal individuals "mixed in with the rest of us like counterfeit coins" began denouncing goods produced in Megara as enemy contraband and having them auctioned off, presumably pocketing a reward in return for these displays of allegedly good citizenship. Nothing might have come of that, but a few young drunks then kidnapped a Megarian whore, and the Megarians responded by kidnapping two Athenian whores.[2] Unfortunately, this second set of whores belonged to Perikles' mistress, Aspasia (a real historical person), and Perikles became so angry that he barred the Megarians from Athens' ports and marketplaces, threatening them with starvation. When the Megarians asked the Spartans to intervene to get Perikles' decree repealed, the Athenians refused, leaving the Spartans little choice but to go to war. After all, as Dikaiopolis (quoting a line taken directly from the Euripidean Telephos' defense of his people's willingness to take up arms against the Greeks) points out, the Athenians would have done the same or worse in re-

2. This part of Dikaiopolis' speech appears to be a parody of the historian Herodotus' account of the mythological origin of the great conflict between East and West that culminated in the Persians' decision to invade Greece at the beginning of the fifth century; see D. Sansone, "The Date of Herodotus' Publication," *Illinois Classical Studies* 10 (1985): 1–9.

sponse to even a much more trivial wrong, such as the kidnapping of a puppy-dog from the tiny allied island of Seriphos. The fact that the Spartan invasions have done average Athenians a considerable amount of painful damage is thus true but beside the point. Not only is the war about little more than "three professional cocksuckers," but responsibility for it must be traced to Athens itself and in particular to the self-serving behavior of a few bad but influential citizens, abetted by a general local pigheadedness. The whole thing is a blunder, and Dikaiopolis is right to have gotten out of it.

Half the chorus is convinced by these arguments, while the other half becomes even more outraged, not so much by what Dikaiopolis says as because a beggar (which is what the hero's disguise makes him appear to be) has dared to speak this way. They accordingly summon Lamachos, giving Dikaiopolis a chance to offer what amounts to the second (and conclusive) part of his defense. Lamachos was a real Athenian, who served repeatedly as one of the city's ten general military commanders (an elective annual office), although it is unclear whether he actually held that position in 426/5 B.C. He was also relatively poor, at least for someone actively involved in Athenian public life, where the well-to-do tended to dominate, and was thus an easy target for charges of attempted war-profiteering. When Lamachos appears onstage in *Acharnians,* he is brilliantly arrayed in full military costume, including a helmet topped with a large and obviously quite expensive plume. After he too denounces Dikaiopolis for speaking badly of the city despite being a beggar, the hero responds by calling his opponent an example of the very thing that drove him to make a private peace in the first place. Lamachos and other arrogant young men, Dikaiopolis insists, have spent the war years seeking out paid public positions and running about the world on official embassies, as a result of which they have grown rich overnight. Decent, hardworking citizens like the chorus, on the other hand, serve in the battle-ranks and get no appointments or privileges whatsoever, a point the chorus themselves confirm.

Lamachos' defense of this peculiar state of affairs (the reality of which he never attempts to deny) is that he and his fellow officials have been duly elected, so that Dikaiopolis' criticisms amount to an assault on Athenian democracy. Naturally, the hero will have none of this: if Lamachos and his ilk have been chosen for plum positions over and over again, it is because the people are fools (literally "three cuckoo-birds"), and his opponent is devoted not to democracy itself but to the possibility of earning a wage. Lamachos' response is to stalk off, insisting he will never give up waging war on the Peloponnesians, and this brings the debate to an abrupt end. The entire chorus now declares itself convinced: Dikaiopolis is right, the contemporary democracy is a disaster, and all one can reasonably do is wash one's hands of it.

Dikaiopolis' New World

As Dikaiopolis makes clear in his opening monologue, his life before he concludes his peace with Sparta consists of a large number of pains, balanced by relatively few pleasures: "The number of good things that have happened to me is small, really small—maybe four. But my sufferings? Hah! Sand-zillions of them!" The specific focus of the hero's initial remarks is on events in the Odeion and the Theater of Dionysos, where the dramatic and musical offerings over the last few years have dismayed and disgusted him. All the same, the rest of Dikaiopolis' existence appears to be equally miserable. Politically, he is isolated. He is the only Athenian citizen who cares about peace, i.e., the only one who understands that the way the city is run benefits no one except a small class of corrupt insiders, but every time he raises his voice in the Assembly he is either silenced or ignored, and nothing he says or does has any effect on how public business is conducted.

Dikaiopolis' political misery is compounded by the fact that the war has driven him off his land and into the city, where he lives in the garbage piles alongside the fortification walls, and as he sits in the Assembly-place waiting for his fellow citizens to appear, he stares off into the distance and longs for his farm. This physical dislocation has brought with it economic dislocation as well, for the hero complains that in the countryside he had everything he needed and was never forced to resort to the cash-economy. Now he must buy olive oil, vinegar, and charcoal, and is poor enough to fret about the loss of a few heads of garlic to the Odomantians.[3] The city's political insiders, meanwhile, draw obscenely high daily wages from the public treasury and eat and drink to their hearts' content, allegedly as part of their official duties. To add insult to injury, many of these people are either of dubious nationality (meaning that they ought to be disqualified from playing a part in the city's politics) or sexual perverts (which for Athenians in the classical period meant especially adult men who enjoyed being penetrated by other adult men, and brought with it disqualification from public office).

3. See S. D. Olson, "Dicaeopolis' Motivations in Aristophanes' *Acharnians,*" *Journal of Hellenic Studies* 111 (1991): 200–203.

Dikaiopolis' new world of peace represents a systematic reversal of most of the unfortunate characteristics of the old. Because he is effectively the only citizen of his new state (or, better put, is himself identical with the state),[4] there is no longer any danger that he will be outvoted by fools or taken advantage of by scoundrels, for everything is his and his word is law. Malicious abusers of the legal system like the anonymous Informer and Nikarchos are accordingly beaten and expelled rather than being allowed to dominate the political process, while Lamachos, who used to play at being a military commander without entering the field, is forced to stand guard over a mountain pass during a snowstorm and wounded in the fighting that ensues. In addition, once he has made peace, Dikaiopolis returns immediately to the countryside, where he celebrates a rural festival of Dionysos, and the urban cash-economy he resented so bitterly disappears: the Megarian trades his daughter for a little salt and garlic, the Boiotian exchanges the huge variety of goods he has brought for a sycophant, and when Lamachos' servant dares to offer money for an eel and some thrushes, he is turned down flat.

Whereas Dikaiopolis was previously excluded from everything good, he now has unlimited access to sensual pleasures of every sort, and the second half of the play amounts to an extended celebration of the joys of abundant food and wine and of an aggressive male heterosexuality.[5] The final scenes accordingly draw an extended and elaborate contrast between the fate of the hero and that of his opponent. Dikaiopolis goes off to a party at the house of the priest of Dionysos, where every sort of dainty waits, and appears at the end of the play drunk and accompanied by a pair of naked (and presumably young and beautiful) prostitutes, with whom he is about to go off to bed. Lamachos, on the other hand, is forced to pack for a military campaign while Dikaiopolis loads up his basket for dinner, and is then brought onstage, cold, miserable, and groaning with pain, and carried off to the doctor's.

In one sense, Dikaiopolis' new world is a perfect place, a sort of anti-Athens in which there is peace rather than war and where the good control all power and privileges, while the bad get what they deserve. Although it is true that the hero is successful only because he abandons his initial concern for the state as a

---

4. In line with ancient political practice, the women, children, and slaves who belong to Dikaiopolis' household are understood to be residents but not citizens of his new state.

5. See J. Henderson, *The Maculate Muse: Obscene Language in Attic Comedy,* 2d ed. (New York and Oxford, 1991), 57–62.

whole and becomes as selfish as everyone else, the dark side of his behavior in the second half of the play ought not to be exaggerated.[6] It seems extremely unlikely, first of all, that the audience is supposed to see Dikaiopolis as taking improper advantage of the personal troubles of the Megarian, for whose (admittedly unfortunate) situation there is no trace of sympathy anywhere in the text.[7] In fact, the Megarian is a buffoon, who is happy to sell his daughters (and seems to think he has accomplished something clever by doing so), while they in turn are happy to be sold. Although Dikaiopolis gets a wonderful bargain, there is no reason to think we are expected to condemn him for it. So too, if the Boiotian agrees to take an Informer in exchange for all his goods, that is his business and there is no point in worrying about whether he has been treated "fairly."

Nor can the fact that Dikaiopolis shows no interest in giving the bridegroom a bit of peace to allow him to stay home with his wife rather than serve with the army be made to count against his characterization elsewhere as a partisan of heterosexual fertility. When the bride makes what amounts to the same request, after all, the hero grants it, pointing out that she can scarcely be charged with responsibility for the origin or continuation of the war, whereas her husband, as an adult male citizen, can and therefore deserves no sympathy. The blind and ruined farmer, finally, is a figure in some ways reminiscent of Dikaiopolis at the beginning of the action, and the hero's refusal to grant him a bit of peace with which to anoint his eyes appears reprehensible at first glance. Immediately after this, the farmer identifies himself as Sharpeyes (Greek "Derketes") of Phyle, which is a joke in and of itself. Given that the name is rare, however, and that we know a real contemporary Athenian bore it, the most likely interpretation of the scene is that the real Sharpeyes of Phyle was an outspoken supporter of the war, whose sudden onstage eagerness for peace after he suffers a bit of personal damage justly earns him Dikaiopolis' contempt. If that is true, there is once again no reason to censure the hero for the way he treats his visitor.[8]

---

6. See the eminently sensible discussion of this point by C. Carey, in "The Purpose of Aristophanes' *Acharnians*," *Rheinisches Museum* 136 (1993): 245–63.

7. Despite Foley (above, note 1); N. R. E. Fischer, "Multiple Personalities and Dionysiac Festivals: Dicaeopolis in Aristophanes' *Acharnians*," *Greece and Rome* 40 (1993): 31–47; G. Compton-Engle, "From Country to City: The Persona of Dicaeopolis in Aristophanes' *Acharnians*," *Classical Journal* 94 (1999): 369, 373.

8. See D. M. MacDowell, "The Nature of Aristophanes' *Akharnians*," *Greece and Rome* 30 (1983): 158–60.

There are thus no substantial grounds for making Dikaiopolis out to be a bad or vicious character, and no reason to condemn his new world on that account. There can nonetheless be no disputing the fact that he is extraordinarily selfish; indeed, the chorus say he is so pleased with what he has got that he has no intention of sharing it with anyone, and complain that he is making his neighbors miserable with the sounds and smells of his celebration. That the hero opts for radical self-interest after separating himself from the rest of the city cannot, in one sense, be taken as a criticism of him, for the other characters in the play have been acting this way all along. Why should Dikaiopolis alone be miserable, if everyone else is either having a good time or content to be made an ass of? Although the hero's behavior is in one way understandable and perhaps justifiable, however, it is also true that his disgust with his fellow citizens in the opening scene is driven precisely by his realization that they lack an interest in the common good; that he ultimately chooses to go them one better by arranging a private peace with Sparta does not make his behavior admirable.

Thus whatever the audience is to make of Dikaiopolis' actions within the dramatic context of *Acharnians,* it is not obviously supposed to take him as a model for its own behavior or as an expression of what Aristophanes himself takes to be right. That problem leads directly to the question of the relationship between the hero and the poet and thus to the problem with which we began: the political message and effect of the play.

Dikaiopolis, Aristophanes, and Athens

As noted at the very beginning of this essay, Dikaiopolis is Aristophanes' creature rather than Aristophanes himself, and the actions and opinions of the two cannot necessarily be identified with one another; indeed, there is no reason why a playwright should not invent a hero whose attitudes and behavior he disapproves of entirely. In the case of *Acharnians,* however, the existence of some more substantial relationship between author and character is suggested by a series of remarks Dikaiopolis makes just before he goes off to borrow his rags from Euripides and then again at the beginning of his Telephos-speech, as well as by what the chorus say about their poet in their great central speech (the *parabasis*).

Just before he sets off for Euripides' house, Dikaiopolis unexpectedly announces that he had some trouble with Kleon "on account of last year's comedy," and notes that he was dragged before the city's Council, denounced in abusive terms there and almost destroyed. Up to this point, Dikaiopolis has been presented as an old peasant-farmer who attends theatrical and musical performances but drops no hint that he produces them. Now it is clear that he has for a moment taken on the character of the author of the play.[9] So too after Dikaiopolis has put on his Telephos-disguise and come back to address the chorus, he abruptly begins to speak to the audience instead, noting that he is in the middle of staging a comedy and insisting that this time Kleon will not be able to accuse him of slandering Athens in the presence of foreigners, since this is the Lenaia festival, at which only permanent residents of Athens are present (i.e., as opposed to the City Dionysia, when official representatives of the allied states and many other foreigners were in attendance). Once again, the hero appears to speak with the voice of the author of the play in which he is a character, and he goes on a few lines later to ask the audience to remember that he is attacking specific individuals rather than the state as a whole when he describes the local origins of the war with Sparta, for he does not wish to face the same charges a second time.

After the chorus announces that Dikaiopolis has convinced them all of the rightness of his decision to make a private peace, finally, they turn to the audience and say that their poet has decided to speak out on his own behalf, since his enemies have slandered him with the charge of making a mockery (literally "a comedy") of the city and treating the people outrageously. In fact, they insist, he has done the Athenians a great deal of good by teaching them not to be taken in by the flattering words of foreigners and by showing them what sort of democracies exist in the allied states (or, depending on how one translates the Greek, "how our democratic government treats the allies").[10]

These passages are most easily interpreted as references to the same set of events, and ancient comments (or "scholia") preserved in the margins of some of our manuscripts tell us that the play Dikaiopolis mentions is Aristophanes' *Babylonians,* which was staged at the City Dionysia in 426 B.C. and is preserved in a few small fragments.[11] The plot of *Babylonians* appears to have involved a

9. Since *Babylonians* and *Acharnians* were both produced by Kallistratos, it is possible that he was the one attacked by Kleon, although one would expect the poet who wrote the words pronounced onstage to be held legally responsible for them.

10. The connections between the poet and his hero in the *parabasis* in particular are carefully explored by A. M. Bowie in "The Parabasis in Aristophanes: Prolegomena, *Acharnians,*" *Classical Quarterly,* n.s., 32 (1982): 27–40, followed by T. K. Hubbard, *The Mask of Comedy: Aristophanes and the Intertextual Parabasis* (Cornell, 1991), 41–59.

11. For attempts to reconstruct the action in *Babylonians,* see G. Norwood, "The *Babylonians* of Aristophanes," *Classical Philology* 25 (1930): 1–10; D. Welsh, "The Chorus of Aristophanes' *Babylonians,*" *Greek, Roman, and Byzantine Studies* 24 (1983): 137–50.

visit made by Dionysos, god of wine, natural fertility, and theater, to Athens (see fr. 75 K-A); it followed a standard pattern of Dionysiac myth, in which the god arrives in a place, encounters resistance from local authorities, and defeats them.[12] Aristophanic comedies with titles in the plural are inevitably named after the chorus (as *Acharnians* is), and the cult of Dionysos is elsewhere routinely associated with the exotic East; Norwood therefore argued that the god must have appeared in Athens accompanied by a band of Babylonian followers (see fr. 81 K-A).[13] Be that as it may, we know that the chorus in the play was thrown into a mill to work (fr. 71 K-A; cf. fr. 74 K-A) and thus reduced to slavery of the most painful and degrading sort. The Babylonians also seem to have been tattooed (see frr. 90; 99 K-A), but an ancient comment on a fragment of the play tells us that someone who saw them in the mill was puzzled and astonished, and identified one of them with the people of Samos, who had all had an Athenian owl tattooed on their foreheads after an unsuccessful attempt to revolt from the empire in 440 (fr. 71 K-A).[14] It is impossible to say whether this is merely a silly remark by an ignorant bystander, or whether the chorus represented both a group of Babylonians and the Athenian allied states, although the allies probably figured somehow in the action (see below).

Dionysos as well, at any rate, was apparently arrested and taken off for trial, at which point some of Athens' leading politicians asked him for a pair of drinking cups, presumably as a bribe in return for his freedom (fr. 75 K-A; cf. fr. 68 K-A). Indeed, the scholia to *Acharnians* tell us that in *Babylonians* Aristophanes abused not only Kleon but Athenian office-holders of all sorts, including those who were chosen by lot; the people appear to have behaved like fools again (fr. 67 K-A); and somewhere in the text the origin of the Peloponnesian War was blamed on local political corruption (fr. 84 K-A). The chorus' remarks in the *parabasis* of *Acharnians* suggest that representatives of the allied states spoke, perhaps as accusers at Dionysos' trial, and proved as corrupt as all other Aristophanic politicians. In the end the god must have freed both himself and the chorus (see fr. 77 K-A) and taken revenge on his enemies, and Dikaiopolis' approving reference in his opening monologue to having seen Kleon vomit up five

12. The best-known example of the pattern is Euripides' *Bacchants* (405 B.C.).

13. Norwood (above, note 11). Contrast Welsh (above, note 11), who argues (on tenuous historical grounds) that there may instead be an allusion to a contemporary Babylonian commander who attempted to assist the Athenians in the East but was badly treated in return.

14. Tattooing of this sort was normally reserved for runaway slaves, and the political implications of the punishment are clear.

talents of silver may be a reference to a scene at the end of *Babylonians*. The
scholia to *Acharnians* tell us that Kleon's reaction to *Babylonians* was to bring Aristophanes before Athens' Council (which, under certain circumstances, had
the power of indictment), arguing that the poet had brought disgrace on the city
in the presence of her subjects, who ought instead, presumably, to be taught to
fear and respect her. Dikaiopolis' remarks leave little doubt that the Council
rejected the charges. All the same, Aristophanes speaks of Kleon with undis-
guised loathing in most of his early comedies and seems to have felt intense personal hostility toward him, probably due in substantial part to this incident.

    Although Dikaiopolis and Aristophanes cannot automatically be identified
with one another, there are clear signals within the text that the hero and the
poet (at least as he chooses to present himself) are to be understood as closely
connected figures.[15] Indeed, the author's conflict with Kleon may well have provided the model for Dikaiopolis' confrontation with Lamachos, while the nasty
fate that ultimately befalls Lamachos is easily interpreted as Aristophanes' own
wish for his enemy. The problem is to decide how far this identification should
be pressed, and the likelihood that it is not intended to be systematic is suggested by the chorus' comments in the *parabasis* on a recent Spartan offer of
peace if Athens would only return Aigina to its original inhabitants. This pro-
posal ought to be rejected, the chorus insists, because their poet would have to
be given up as well, the implication being that he or his family had personal connections to the place. This is obviously a joke, but the crucial point is that the
author of the play is presented as opposing a quick and easy end to the conflict
with Sparta. Indeed, the chorus has just proudly quoted the Persian king to the
effect that their poet's advice will make whichever side he abuses more likely to
defeat its enemies in war. Although Dikaiopolis has had enough of the fighting,
the author of *Acharnians* apparently has not, and there is no reason to think that
he endorses his hero's decision to seek an independent peace, particularly since
it is based on a patently cockeyed view of recent political history and would be
impossible for anyone living in the real world to imitate. Nor has the poet yet
decided to withdraw from public life, as Dikaiopolis does, for although Kleon's
attack gave him a considerable scare, in the end no damage was done, so that the

    15. Note also how Dikaiopolis at the end of the play asks to be carried off in triumph to
the judges (i.e., not just of the drinking contest but of the dramatic festival as well) and to King
Archon (who, Aristotle tells us, oversaw the dramatic contests at the Lenaia). This point is
carefully explored by Bowie (above, note 10), followed by Hubbard (above, note 10).

people as he has experienced them have at least a bit of sense and are not the complete fools his hero encounters in the Assembly.

The identification between Dikaiopolis and the poet is thus a limited one, and one important aspect of it expires the moment the hero makes his peace with Sparta. In the opening scene of *Acharnians,* Dikaiopolis seems to want the best for his fellow citizens and accordingly attempts to alert them to the outrages going on in Athenian public life, although he finally gives up in disgust at the blindness of everyone else and separates himself from the city. So too, according to the chorus in the *parabasis,* their poet's goal with his comedies is to make the Athenian people happier, better, and more successful, which is to say that his plays have a fundamentally educational purpose. The alleged proof of this is that, before his plays were staged, the Assembly was routinely taken in by foreign ambassadors who addressed it with flowery poetic language, whereas now, the implication is, his exposure of this sort of thing means that such tricks are doomed to fail. What makes their poet's benevolent intentions difficult to appreciate is that he works through abuse, i.e., by rubbing the people's collective nose in their shortcomings so that they will be less likely to repeat them in the future. Kleon's claim that Aristophanes ought to be prosecuted for what was said and done onstage in *Babylonians* clearly turned on an insistence that to heap ridicule on Athens and her people, particularly in the presence of the allies, amounted to an act of political disloyalty, which showed that the poet felt no concern for the commonwealth. In the *parabasis* in *Acharnians,* on the other hand, the chorus claims that their poet is the one concerned about the city, whereas his opponent is a coward, liar, and pervert. Flattery and bribes in the form of wages for sitting on juries and the like (which is what Kleon has to offer) do not make the city stronger, although they offer the people a temporary illusion of happiness. What Athens needs is someone with the nerve to tell the people the ugly truth about their lives, and the paradoxical result will be not only that they will become far happier and more successful, but that the allies will come bearing their tribute with greater alacrity than before, eager to witness what amounts to a political miracle.

The opening scene in *Acharnians,* in which all the alleged failures of the Athenian democracy are put on public view and mocked in a relentless, brutal fashion, thus amounts to an illustration of the fundamental nature of Aristophanic comedy and poses the city a stark but necessary choice. To the extent that Dikaiopolis' new world can be regarded as a good thing (see above), it represents what the city as a whole could (at least allegedly) have by rejecting Kleon, La-

machos, and the misery and defeat that will inevitably hound them and that
bring Lamachos limping and wailing onstage in the final scene of the play. Much
more important, the hero's decision to turn his back on his fellow citizens
when he fails to stir the Assembly out of its torpor amounts to a none too subtle
(if perhaps not altogether serious) threat from the poet himself. Up to this
point, he has been (like his hero) a committed citizen, who has run great personal risks to serve Athens as best he can, by alerting the people to what is being done to them under the guise of a democracy. If no one is going to pay him
any attention (i.e., if charges of the sort Kleon has made are going to be taken
seriously), he may as well stop behaving so recklessly. He has done his best and
has gotten nothing but grief for it. The rest of the city can go to hell, for all he
cares, if they prefer to be led around by the nose by self-serving professional
deceivers; he will concentrate on taking care of himself and will end up both
much happier than everyone else and totally unsympathetic to their complaints.
The alternative is for the people to show they understand and appreciate the
nature of his comedies and thus his public services, and the best way to do that
is by voting for *Acharnians* to take the prize. That is exactly what the Athenian
audience in 425 B.C. did, and the choice would seem to have been sensible, if
the comedy offered a telling and productive analysis of the day-to-day conduct
of Athenian political life. In fact, it does not, and the problem of why Aristophanes' play was awarded the prize is more complicated than this.

The basic political argument of *Acharnians* is that everyone in the city with
any power is corrupt and that the people could put a stop to this by paying
more attention to what is going on around them and acting more responsibly
(see above). Beyond that, the drama offers little in the way of concrete policy
proposals, except for the suggestion in the *parabasis* that the Spartan offer of
peace in return for restoring the Aiginetans (probably never taken seriously in
Athens) be rejected, a vague appeal a little later to the "good old days" of
Marathon (which amounts to nothing in practical terms), and the repeated implication throughout the play (easily dismissed as the result of personal spite)
that Kleon ought to be removed from all positions of public responsibility. Democracies are inevitably cumbersome things, and Athens' made its share of mis-
takes in the early years of the Peloponnesian War. It is nonetheless true that the
city's political system included elaborate safeguards against the abuse of public
power, in that all annual magistrates underwent an audit of their personal and
political affairs when they left office. The image presented of the state in the
opening scene of *Acharnians* in particular is thus so exaggerated and so lacking
in specifics that, were one to take the political argument implicit in the action

seriously, one would have little choice but to condemn the play as a whole as irresponsible and ultimately unconstructive. Although *Acharnians* was awarded the prize by a democratic audience despite taking numerous nasty swipes at the democracy, therefore, the chorus' defense of their poet as a selfless exposer of the truth will not do as an explanation of this seemingly paradoxical fact, because his play is not what they imply it is. I suggest instead that the key to making sense of the positive popular verdict passed on *Acharnians* is to be found in what we know about the reception of *Babylonians*.

From what we can tell from Dikaiopolis' remarks in *Acharnians* and the scholia, Kleon argued before the Council that the portrait of Athenian public life presented in *Babylonians* was simultaneously so hostile and so far removed from the truth that staging the play in the presence of the city's allies amounted to an act of political treachery. That Kleon (who was by this time a seasoned political veteran with impeccable democratic credentials) was entirely wrong about the larger implications of the plot of *Babylonians* (which had been written by someone most likely in his twenties, who can have had no substantial political experience whatsoever) is not self-evident. Indeed, the play apparently branded everyone who held any sort of office in Athens as corrupt, and the people seem to have been presented as idiots and justice as openly up for sale (see above). The fact that the Council declined to bring an indictment of the playwright nonetheless suggests that it rejected Kleon's interpretation of the significance of the comedy. The implication is that *Babylonians* looked very different to different groups of democrats, depending upon the position they occupied within the city: average citizens had no problem with what the comedy had to say, whereas the democracy's most important leader loathed it. While we do not know what Kleon thought of *Acharnians,* it requires no great stretch of the historical imagination to think he was no happier with it than he had been with *Babylonians*. There is some reason to think he prosecuted Aristophanes again afterward on a different ground.[16]

A substantial number of average Athenians, on the other hand, apparently approved of the play, since their representatives voted to award it the prize. *Acharnians* thus most likely evoked the same sort of divided response among

16. On the most likely reading of the scholia to *Acharnians* line 378, Kleon's second prosecution of Aristophanes involved a claim that the poet was not a legitimate Athenian citizen, although this may be nothing more than an ancient scholar's deduction from the allusion to the poet's connections with Aigina at *Acharnians* lines 652–54. The history of Aristophanes' conflict with Kleon has been traced most recently by I. C. Storey in "*Wasps* 1284–91 and the Portrait of Kleon in *Wasps*," *Scholia* 4 (1995): 7–11 (with extensive bibliography).

Athenian democrats that we know *Babylonians* did, and the obvious conclusion is that ordinary people were content to watch comedies in which the state was portrayed as in a terrible mess and in which they themselves were presented as fools, provided that they were simultaneously allowed to affirm, by applauding the play and voting to award it the prize, that they were victims of their leaders and alleged allies and deserved nothing like the sufferings they had recently endured.[17] Not surprisingly, arguments of this sort outraged politically prominent individuals like Kleon, who faced the difficult task of managing the city's affairs on a day-to-day basis, and that outrage (and the attempt at indictment it spawned) played directly into the hands of the poet, who could misrepresent it as anger at the fact that a public-minded citizen had dared expose corrupt political schemes to public scrutiny.

Despite the chorus' claims in the *parabasis,* therefore, *Acharnians* in its own way panders just as shamelessly to its audience as it accuses Kleon of doing. The early 420s B.C. had not been happy years in Athens, and *Acharnians* takes the anger of ordinary citizens at that fact as its dramatic and rhetorical starting point. Indeed, the most brilliant literary and social maneuver in the play is the way in which it allows an audience made up of average democrats, who collectively exercised absolute authority over the state, to affirm not only that "everyone in power is corrupt" but that they are all individually victims, who bear no responsibility for the troubles they have got in recent years and who would in fact have been better off had they not been so stupid as to be taken in by those who claimed to be their friends. Contrary to initial appearances, the fact that *Acharnians* was awarded the prize in the popular balloting at the Lenaia in 425 B.C. makes perfect sense: the play appealed to a democratic audience not despite but because of the nasty picture it painted of the contemporary city.

17. See J. Henderson, "Comic Hero versus Political Elite," in A. H. Sommerstein et al., eds., *Tragedy, Comedy, and the Polis. Papers from the Greek Drama Conference, Nottingham 18–20 July 1990* (Bari, 1993), 307–19.

SELECT BIBLIOGRAPHY

Useful modern commentaries in English on *Acharnians:*

Rennie, R. *The Acharnians of Aristophanes.* London, 1909.

Sommerstein, A. H. *The Comedies of Aristophanes,* vol. 1: *Acharnians.* Warminster, 1980.

Starkie, W. J. M. *The Acharnians of Aristophanes.* London, 1909; reprint New York, 1979.

I am producing a new critical text and commentary on the play for Oxford University Press; projected publication date 2003.

Standard handbooks in English on Aristophanes and his work:

Dover, K. J. *Aristophanic Comedy.* Berkeley and Los Angeles, 1972.

MacDowell, D. M. *Aristophanes and Athens.* Oxford, 1995.

Other recent work in English on *Acharnians* and closely related topics:

Bowie, A. M. "The Parabasis in Aristophanes: Prolegomena, *Acharnians.*" *Classical Quarterly,* n.s., 32 (1982): 27–40.

Carey, C. "The Purpose of Aristophanes' *Acharnians.*" *Rheinische Museum* 136 (1993): 245–63.

Compton-Engle, G. "From Country to City: The Persona of Dicaeopolis in Aristophanes' *Acharnians.*" *Classical Journal* 94 (1999): 359–73.

Edmunds, L. "Aristophanes' *Acharnians.*" *Yale Classical Studies* 26 (1980): 1–41.

Fischer, N. R. E. "Multiple Personalities and Dionysiac Festivals: Dicaeopolis in Aristophanes' *Acharnians.*" *Greece and Rome* 40 (1993): 31–47.

Foley, H. P. "Tragedy and Politics in Aristophanes' *Acharnians.*" *Journal of Hellenic Studies* 108 (1988): 33–47.

Forrest, W. G. "Aristophanes' *Acharnians.*" *Phoenix* 17 (1963): 1–12.

Henderson, J. "The *Demos* and the Comic Competition." In J. J. Winkler and F. Zeitlin, eds., *Nothing to Do with Dionysos? Athenian Drama in Its Social Context,* 271–313. Princeton, 1990.

———. *The Maculate Muse: Obscene Language in Attic Comedy,* 2d ed. New York and Oxford, 1991.

———. "Comic Hero versus Political Elite." In A. H. Sommerstein et al., eds., *Tragedy, Comedy, and the Polis. Papers from the Greek Drama Conference, Nottingham 18–20 July 1990,* 307–19. Bari, 1993.

Hubbard, T. K. *The Mask of Comedy: Aristophanes and the Intertextual Parabasis,* 41–59. Cornell, 1991.

MacDowell, D. M. "The Nature of Aristophanes' *Akharnians.*" *Greece and Rome* 30 (1983): 143–62.

Olson, S. D. "Dicaeopolis' Motivations in Aristophanes' *Acharnians.*" *Journal of Hellenic Studies* 111 (1991): 200–203.

Whitman, C. H. *Aristophanes and the Comic Hero* (Martin Classical Lectures XIX), 59–80. Cambridge, Mass., 1964.

A Note on the Translation

Aristophanes' language is quite colloquial and often explicitly sexual, and I have made no effort to disguise these characteristics. The comedies are also full of wordplay of various sorts, and I have generally attempted to translate these, although in a few cases I have (like most translators) thrown up my hands in despair and let the point pass. Dialects pose a special problem but must be dealt with somehow, inevitably at the cost of offending someone. Since this text is intended for an American audience, I represent the Megarian as speaking as if he were from the rural South, and the Boiotian as sounding as if he were from a working-class area of New Jersey or New York. That these are crude linguistic stereotypes carrying with them a bundle of frequently inaccurate cultural and political prejudices is entirely appropriate, for Aristophanes' Megarian and Boiotian are Athenian caricatures of residents of those areas rather than a real Megarian and Boiotian brought magically onstage. For the patently absurd paratragic language used by Euripides, as well as by the chorus on occasion, I offer a vaguely Elizabethan dialect intended to sound like a cross between a parody of the King James Bible and cut-rate Shakespeare.

My translation is based on Hall and Geldart's 1906 Oxford edition of Aristophanes, which despite its many faults is adequate for this purpose.

ACHARNIANS

DIKAIOPOLIS, *an old farmer*

A HERALD

TWO SKYTHIAN POLICEMEN, *(mute parts)*

ALLGOD, *an Athenian citizen*

TWO AMBASSADORS, *recently returned from Persia*

BUSHEL-OF-LIES, *the "Eye" (or special agent) of the Persian king*

THEOROS, *another ambassador, recently returned from King Sitalkes of Thrace*

THE CHORUS, *twenty-four old farmers from the rural district of Acharnai*

DIKAIOPOLIS' DAUGHTER

DIKAIOPOLIS' WIFE, *(mute part)*

EURIPIDES' SLAVE

EURIPIDES, *a tragic playwright*

LAMACHOS, *a military commander*

A MEGARIAN

TWO GIRLS, *the Megarian's daughters*

A POLITICAL INFORMER

A BOIOTIAN

ISMENIAS, *the Boiotian's slave or assistant (mute part)*

NIKARCHOS, *a professional informer*

LAMACHOS' SLAVE

SHARPEYES OF PHYLE, *a farmer*

A BEST MAN

A BRIDESMAID, *(mute part)*

A MESSENGER

LAMACHOS' FRIENDS, *(mute parts)*

TWO NAKED GIRLS, *(mute parts)*

VARIOUS SLAVES, *(mute parts)*

SCENE: Three doors are visible. The one in the center will represent Euripides' house; the one to the right will represent Dikaiopolis' house; and the one to the left will repre-

sent Lamachos' house. The stage is otherwise bare. An altar (a permanent fixture of the theater) stands in the middle of the Chorus' dancing area.

Dikaiopolis, dressed in plain, inexpensive clothes and carrying a small sack containing a few heads of garlic and perhaps some other items of cheap, coarse food, comes onstage from the wing and sits on the ground facing the audience. After a few minutes of silent fidgeting, he begins to speak. At first he appears to be only another spectator in the theater and comments on musical and dramatic performances over the course of the last year or so. After a few verses, however, he reveals that the dramatic setting is the Assembly-place in Athens and the time is dawn.

DIKAIOPOLIS: You can't imagine how many heartaches I've had! The number of good things that've happened to me is small, really small—maybe four. But my sufferings? Hah! Sand-zillions of them! Let's see—what pleasure have I had worth mentioning? I guess I know one sight that warmed my heart—those five bars of silver Kleon puked up![1] *That* made me smile, all right, and the Knights[2] earned my friendship by making it happen: "a deed worthy of Greece"[3]! But then I suffered something tragic, when I was sitting there stupidly expecting Aeschylus,[4] and the herald said "Bring your chorus out, *Theognis*."[5] Imagine how *that* shook me up! On the other hand, I liked it when Dexitheos followed Moschos on and performed a Boiotian piece—although then this year I was so horrified when Chairis came out to sing a soprano song, that I nearly passed out.[6] But ever since I was little and got soap in my eyes at bathtime, I've never wanted to cry as much as I do today! The Assembly's scheduled to start at dawn, but the meeting place here is deserted, and everyone else is hanging out in the marketplace gos-

1. Kleon was the leading democratic politician in Athens in this period and a bitter personal and political enemy of Aristophanes. Whether he was actually forced to "disgorge" a bribe during the previous year, or whether Dikaiopolis is referring to events in a recent comedy, perhaps in *Babylonians,* is unclear.

2. The Knights were men wealthy enough to be able to outfit a horse for war, and their politics were probably generally conservative. In Aristophanes' comedy of 424 B.C., they serve as the chorus and are relentlessly hostile to Kleon.

3. A quotation from Euripides' *Telephos* (see Introduction).

4. The greatest Athenian playwright of the first half of the fifth century B.C.; his tragedies were being revived in this period.

5. A tragic poet, attacked again later in the play; see note 18.

6. Dexitheos, Moschos, and Chairis were all well-known contemporary lyre players and singers, although we know little more about them than what Dikaiopolis says here.

siping and running every which way, trying to avoid getting roped into attendance.[7] Not even the Executive Officers are here yet! Oh, no! They'll come late, and then, of course, they'll all rush down front in a big crowd, pushing and shoving, trying to get the best seats. But as for peace? They couldn't care less! "Alas, my city!"[8] As for *me*, on the other hand, I'm always the first one to get here and sit down, and then—since I'm alone— I groan, and yawn, and stretch, and fart, and get bored, and doodle, and pull out some of my pubic hairs, and count up my debts. And all the while I'm staring off toward my farm, longing for peace and thinking how much I hate the city and how I'd like to be back in my home-district, where you never heard "Buy your charcoal here!" or "Get your vinegar!" or "Olive oil for sale!" Where I come from, they didn't even know what "buy and sell" meant; the land produced everything by itself, and there wasn't any of this constant "Buy! Buy! Buy!" So the upshot is, I've come today prepared to shout and interrupt and harass the speakers, if anyone tries to discuss *anything* except peace. But here come the Executive Officers, at noon right on the dot. Didn't I predict this? It's exactly what I said would happen: every one of them is trying to elbow his way up to the front!

The Herald enters from the wing, accompanied by several Thracian bowmen.

HERALD: *(to the imaginary men entering the Assembly-place)* Move forward! Move, so you're inside the area that's been purified!

Allgod enters from the wing.[9]

ALLGOD: Did anybody speak yet?
HERALD: Who wishes to address the Assembly?
ALLGOD: Me! I do.
HERALD: And who are you?
ALLGOD: I'm Allgod.
HERALD: You mean . . . you're not a human being?
ALLGOD: Well no, I'm an immortal. You see, the original Allgod was a child of Demeter and Triptolemos.[10] And Keleos was descended from him, and

7. A rope smeared with purple dye was used to herd people out of the Agora and to the Assembly-place; anyone who tried to avoid it and had his clothes stained was subject to a fine.

8. Probably a quotation from a lost tragedy.

9. Allgod was a real Athenian, probably known to Aristophanes (see introduction). His name in Greek is Amphitheos, literally "God on both sides" or the like.

10. Demeter was worshiped at a site near Athens known as Eleusis. According to the nor-

he married my grandmother, whose name was Phainarete. And then Phainarete had Lukinos, and I'm Lukinos' son—which means I'm immortal. And
the result is that the gods have given me—and me only—authority to
make peace with the Spartans. But, even though I'm immortal, gentlemen,
I don't have any money for travel expenses, because the Executive Officers
won't give me any.

HERALD: Bowmen!

The Bowmen step forward and drag Allgod off.

ALLGOD: Triptolemos and Keleos! Are you going to let this happen?

DIKAIOPOLIS: *(leaping to his feet and addressing the Executive Officers)* Gentlemen, you're not being fair to the Assembly, having this guy arrested! He
wanted to arrange a peace treaty for us! We could have put our shields into
storage!

HERALD: Stay in your seat and shut up!

DIKAIOPOLIS: By Apollo, I will *not!* Not unless you put peace on the agenda!

HERALD: Let the Ambassadors from the King come forward!

DIKAIOPOLIS: What king? I've had it up to here with these ambassadors and
their crazy costumes and their bullshit!

HERALD: Silence!

Two Ambassadors dressed in exotic Eastern clothing enter from the wing.

DIKAIOPOLIS: Yikes! Where'd you get those clothes?!

AMBASSADOR: You sent us off to the Great King at a salary of two drachmas
per day eleven years ago—

DIKAIOPOLIS: Now *that's* money wasted!

AMBASSADOR: —and we had a terrible time of it. We suffered immensely,
traveling through the plains of the River Kaister on top of fancy little Persian wagons, parasols over our heads, enjoying all sorts of delicious good-
ies . . . I mean, we were almost at death's door.

DIKAIOPOLIS: Meanwhile, *I* was safe at home—on top of the garbage piles
by the city walls!

AMBASSADOR: And whenever we stopped for the night, they forced us to
drink wine out of crystal goblets and gold bowls. We were absolutely for-
bidden to mix any water in with it—

---

mal version of the myth, Triptolemos was a prince there when Demeter visited. She taught
him how to sow crops, and he spread the knowledge throughout the world.

DIKAIOPOLIS: City of Athens! Don't you see that these ambassadors are
making fools out of us?

AMBASSADOR: —because, you see, as far as the barbarians are concerned,
only someone who eats and drinks huge amounts is a real man.

DIKAIOPOLIS: We Athenians, on the other hand, prefer cocksuckers and
queers!

AMBASSADOR: Finally, after traveling for three years, we reached the royal
palace. But the King had taken an expeditionary force and gone off to
Crappadocia, and he spent the next eight months shitting on the Golden
Hills.

DIKAIOPOLIS: Really? So how long did it take him to get his asshole closed
up again?

AMBASSADOR: He finished that around the time of the full moon, and then
he came home and started to entertain us. He regularly served us whole
baked oxen.

DIKAIOPOLIS: Oh, who's ever heard of whole baked oxen? What a bunch of
nonsense!

AMBASSADOR: He also served us a bird three times as big as Kleonymos[11];
they call it a "robin."

DIKAIOPOLIS: So that's why *you* were a-robbin' *us* of two drachmas a day!

AMBASSADOR: But now we're back, and we have with us Bushel-of-Lies, the
Eye of the King.

DIKAIOPOLIS: Hah! I wish a bird would peck this eye out! And yours too,
Mr. Ambassador!

HERALD: Let the Eye of the King come forward!

*Bushel-of-Lies, dressed in exotic Eastern clothing, including a pair of trousers, and with
a large fake eye attached to the front of his costume, enters from the wing. He is trailed
by two attendants.*

DIKAIOPOLIS: My god, sir, that's a nasty face you're making at me! Are you
looking for something? A harbor, maybe?[12] And what's with the sack down
below?[13]

AMBASSADOR: All right, Bushel-of-Lies, give the Athenians the message
from the King!

11. A prominent Athenian politician; he was apparently grossly overweight.

12. Greek ships often had large eyes painted on their front, presumably to help them "see"
their way through the sea.

13. The Greeks did not wear pants and thought of them as a bizarre barbarian affectation.

BUSHEL-OF-LIES: *Iartamanexarxanapissonasatra.*

AMBASSADOR: Does everybody understand what he's saying?

DIKAIOPOLIS: By Apollo, *I* certainly don't.

AMBASSADOR: He says the King's going to send you gold. Hey you! Say the word "gold" louder and clearer!

BUSHEL-OF-LIES: You no will be getting any gold, Ionian[14] butt-fucks.

DIKAIOPOLIS: Unfortunately, *that's* pretty clear!

AMBASSADOR: Wait, wait—what's he saying?

DIKAIOPOLIS: What's he saying? He says us Ionians are a bunch of butt-fucks, if we're expecting any gold from barbarians!

AMBASSADOR: No, no, no! He's saying "buckets"! "Fucking BUCKETS of gold!"

DIKAIOPOLIS: What do you mean, "buckets"? You're full of shit. Get out of here; I'll cross-examine this guy myself.

The Ambassadors exit into one of the wings. Dikaiopolis holds up his fist in a threatening fashion.

All right, you—now keep what I've got here in mind and tell me straight out, so I don't have to dye you a nice exotic crimson: Is the Great King going to send us any gold, or not?

Bushel-of-Lies and his attendants shake their heads "No."

Are these Ambassadors trying to make fools of us?

Bushel-of-Lies and his attendants nod their heads "Yes."

These guys nodded their heads "Yes" in Greek, which means they must be from *here!*[15] As a matter of fact, I recognize one of the "eunuchs"—it's Kleisthenes[16] son of Siburtios!

Dikaiopolis steps up to one of Bushel-of-Lies' attendants and yanks off his beard.

---

14. The Ionians were one of the main ethnic and linguistic subgroups among the Greeks and included the Athenians, who claimed to inhabit the original Ionian mother-city but nonetheless regarded being called "Ionians" as insulting.

15. In fact, the Greeks nodded their head back to say "No," forward to say "Yes," and if Dikaiopolis is not merely talking nonsense to intimidate his enemies, the Persians may have done things differently.

16. An Athenian citizen who was for some reason beardless, a fact Aristophanes takes to mean he deliberately shaved his cheeks so as to resemble a boy and be able to play the boy's traditionally passive role in male-male sexual relations.

Why, you reckless asshole, with your shaved cheeks! Have you come here wearing a big beard and a eunuch's costume, you monkey, just to put on a little show for us? *(turning to the other attendant)* And who's this over here? Am I wrong, or is it Straton? [17]

HERALD: Shut up and sit down again! The City Council invites the Eye of the King to dinner at the Town Hall.

Bushel-of-Lies and his attendants exit into one of the wings.

DIKAIOPOLIS: It's enough to make you throw up! So I'm supposed to cool my heels out here, am I? And meanwhile, nothing ever prevents *them* from having a good time! Well, I'm going to do something very important— but sort of frightening. Where's Allgod?

Allgod, who has quietly returned at some point during the scene, steps forward.

ALLGOD: Here I am.

DIKAIOPOLIS: *(holding out a small bag of money)* Look—I want you to take these eight drachmas and arrange a peace treaty with the Spartans, but only for *me,* plus my wife and kids. *(to the audience)* And the rest of you can go right on sending out ambassadors and acting like idiots.

Allgod takes the money and runs off into the wing. Theoros, dressed in expensive clothes, enters from the other wing.

HERALD: Let Theoros come forward and report on his mission to King Sitalkes!

THEOROS: Here I am!

DIKAIOPOLIS: Yet another bullshit-artist given the floor!

THEOROS: We wouldn't have been in Thrace so long—

DIKAIOPOLIS: Of course not—not if you weren't being paid so much!

THEOROS: —except that a snowstorm buried the whole country and the rivers froze solid.

DIKAIOPOLIS: That must have been right around the time when Theognis was putting on one of his tragedies here! [18]

THEOROS: I spent my time getting drunk with Sitalkes, and he turned out to be extraordinarily fond of our city. In fact, he's so much in love with you, that he kept putting graffiti up all over the place that said "The Athenians are cute." And as for his son—the one we made an Athenian citizen?—

17. Another beardless Athenian, mentioned along with Kleisthenes in *Knights* in 424 B.C.
18. Theognis' plays were notoriously "frigid," i.e., stiff and strained, and thus lifeless.

well, his favorite activity is eating those two-faced sandwiches we serve at our festivals, and he was always begging his father to help out his adopted country. So Sitalkes solemnly swore he'd come to our aid "with such a big army," he said, "that the Athenians will think it's a swarm of locusts approaching!"

DIKAIOPOLIS: I'll be damned if I believe anything you've said so far—except maybe the part about the locusts.

THEOROS: And here they are! Of all the Thracian tribes, he's sent you the one that's most dangerous in war!

DIKAIOPOLIS: At least we'll find out if *this* is true.

HERALD: Let the Thracians that Theoros brought come forward!

A group of barbarian mercenary soldiers, carrying bows and Thracian half-moon shields, and with conspicuously circumcised penises, enter from the wing.

DIKAIOPOLIS: What in hell is this?

THEOROS: An army of Odomantians.

DIKAIOPOLIS: What do you mean, "Odomantians"? What's going on? Who trimmed these Odomantians' dicks?[19]

THEOROS: For just two drachmas a day per man, they'll reduce Boiotia to ruins!

Several of the Thracians step away from the group, begin to poke about, and eventually discover and rummage through Dikaiopolis' bag.

DIKAIOPOLIS: Two drachmas a day? For these guys with their foreskins whacked off? That wouldn't make the rowers in the fleet very happy—and they're the ones who keep the city safe![20] *(noticing what's being done to his bag)* Hey! Help! I'm being ruined! The Odomantians have stolen my garlic! Put that down!

THEOROS: Stay back, you idiot! Once they've had a bite of garlic, they're ready to fight![21]

DIKAIOPOLIS: Executive Officers, are you going to let this happen to me—in my own country? And at the hands of *barbarians?* Well . . . I forbid you

19. The Greeks did not practice circumcision and regarded it as another distinctly "barbarian" trait.

20. Athens was a primarily naval power, and her ships were manned in large part by average citizens who were paid a modest daily wage (probably one-half drachma in this period).

21. Fighting cocks were fed garlic before a match to increase their fierceness; the idea is extended to the Odomantians.

to let the Assembly consider hiring these Thracians. A drop of rain hit me! It's a sign from Zeus—he wants the Assembly to adjourn!

HERALD: Let the Thracians go away and be present again tomorrow! The Executive Officers declare the Assembly adjourned.

The Thracians and Theoros exit into one of the wings, followed by the Herald.

DIKAIOPOLIS: Oh, poor me! What a nice garlic salad I lost! But here's Allgod, back from Sparta.

Allgod enters from the other wing on the run, carrying three small wineskins and a libation bowl.

Good morning, Allgod.

ALLGOD: There's not going to be anything good about it until I get to stop running! I'm trying to get away from the Acharnians!

DIKAIOPOLIS: What's the matter?

ALLGOD: I was hurrying here with the drink-offerings for your peace, when some old Acharnians smelled them—a bunch of ancient geezers, tough as maple wood or oak,[22] hard-bitten Marathon veterans.[23] And they all screamed out "You son-of-a-bitch! Is that peace-offerings you're bringing, when our grapevines have been cut down?" And they started picking up stones and stashing them in their robes. So I tried to get away, but they kept chasing me and screaming.

DIKAIOPOLIS: Let them scream. Have you got the peace-offerings?

ALLGOD: I do indeed; samples of three different kinds, right here. These *(holding out one of the wineskins)* are good for five years; take them and have a taste.

Dikaiopolis sniffs at the first wineskin without trying the contents.

DIKAIOPOLIS: Yuck!

ALLGOD: What's the matter?

22. The rural district of Acharnai still had a considerable amount of woods in the late fifth century, and peasant-farmers from the area supplemented their income by cutting wood and producing charcoal for sale in town or (if they lacked access to timber but had a strong back) by carrying baskets of charcoal produced by others in from the countryside, as the chorus members later on say they did when they were younger.

23. Marathon was the site of one of Athens' most glorious military victories, over an invading Persian force in 490 B.C. Very few if any real Marathon veterans were probably alive in 425, although Aristophanes may have known some in his youth.

DIKAIOPOLIS: I definitely don't like these; they smell like the pitch we use on warships.

ALLGOD: *(holding out the second wineskin)* Well then, take these ten-year ones; try them.

DIKAIOPOLIS: *(after taking a sniff)* Oooh! These stink too! They've got an odor of embassies to different cities, with the gradual destruction of our allies mixed in.

ALLGOD: *(holding out the third wineskin)* But these are good for thirty years by land and sea.

DIKAIOPOLIS: *(taking a sniff)* Ahhh! Festivals of Dionysos! Now *these* smell like nectar and ambrosia,[24] and not having to keep an eye out for a notice to buy yourself some rations![25] *(He pours a bit of wine from the third wineskin into the libation bowl and tastes it.)* And in my mouth, they say "Go wherever you want!" I'll take *these,* and after I pour an offering with them *(he dumps a small quantity of wine on the ground),* I'll drink the rest of the cup *(he does so)* and say "To hell with the Acharnians!" And now that I'm finished with the war and free of my other troubles, I think I'll go in and celebrate the Rural Dionysia.[26]

ALLGOD: And I think *I'll* try to get away from the Acharnians!

Dikaiopolis enters the door on the right, carrying the third wineskin and the libation bowl. Allgod runs into the wing with the other two skins. Seconds later, the Chorus members, dressed in rough peasants' clothes, hobble onstage, accompanied by a piper. The song that follows—like most of the Chorus' parts throughout the play—can easily be divided among the individual Acharnians.

CHORUS:
Follow this way! Chase him! Chase him!
Cross-examine all wayfarers!
For we owe it to our city
to arrest this miscreant!
Tell me you who sit there watching:
where'd he turn, the peacemaker?

24. The food of the gods.

25. Athenian foot-soldiers were expected to buy their own rations (normally three days' worth to start) before going out on campaign.

26. A fertility festival carried out once a year in the Athenian countryside, from which Dikaiopolis has been barred by the war. The procession that follows is one of our most important sources for the details of the ceremony.

Damn! He's gone! Somehow we've lost him!
Curse the fact we've grown so old!
In my youth I carried charcoal;
no one ever outraced *me.*
Then I would have caught that bastard;
he would not have slipped away!
Now my legs are dried and shriveled;
Muscles here has got a limp.
Still, we have to try to chase him
or he'll take us for old fools,
since, by God, he's made a treaty
with my deadly enemies.
In revenge for my poor farmland
I would love to stab them deep!
Jab a spear in! That would stop them
trampling on my precious vines!
For the moment, though, our duty
is to chase a local villain.
He'll be sorry, since I'll never
tire of pelting him with stones!

DIKAIOPOLIS: (*from offstage*) Silence! Preserve holy silence!

CHORUS:

Shut your mouths, there! Did you hear that?
Him! It's him, the man we seek!
Everybody hide now! Quickly!
Here he comes to sacrifice!

The Chorus crouches down to the side. Dikaiopolis emerges from the house, holding an earthenware pot, and makes his way to the altar in the orchestra. He is accompanied by his Daughter, who is carrying a flat basket loaded with sacrificial cakes; his Wife; and two slaves, who hold a pair of carrying poles on which is balanced a wooden model of a large erect penis.

DIKAIOPOLIS: Silence! Preserve holy silence! Basket-bearer, move forward a little! (*to one of the slaves*) Xanthias, set the phallus up straight! All right, daughter, put the basket down so we can make the preliminary sacrifice.

DAUGHTER: (*after doing what she has been told*) Mother, hand me that ladle so I can pour some sauce over this cake.

DIKAIOPOLIS: Excellent! Perfect! (*stretching out his hands in prayer*) O lord

Dionysos, if this procession and this sacrifice that my household and I are making find favor in your eyes, let me enjoy good fortune as I celebrate the Rural Dionysia—now that I've been released from military service—and let my thirty-year peace turn out well for me. All right, my pretty girl, do a pretty job of carrying that basket, and give everyone a nasty look. He'll be a lucky man who marries you and gets a hard-on, and then produces a batch of little skunks whose farts are just as nasty as their mother's! Move forward now! And keep your eyes peeled as you pass through the crowd, so no one steals any of your jewelry. Xanthias, you two need to hold the phallus straight up and stay right behind the basket-bearer. I'll walk in back and sing the ritual song. And as for you, wife, your job is to watch me from the roof. *(Everyone takes position.)* Forward . . . *march!*

The procession begins to circle the orchestra.

Hail dear Phallus, friend of Bacchos,
drinking comrade, nighttime prowler,
adulterer and pederast!
In the sixth year now I greet you
here at last in my home district,
having made peace for myself and
gotten free of war and troubles
and old general Lamachos.
How much sweeter, sweeter, Phallus,
is to catch a Thracian slave-girl
stealing wood from my estate, and
pin her arms and throw her down and
spread her legs and come inside her!
That is sweet, O Phallus, Phallus!

(to the audience)

If you join our drinking party, tomorrow morning we'll cure your hang-over with a bowl of peace! And you can put your shield into storage over the fireplace!

The Chorus stands up and rushes the procession.

CHORUS:
Him! It's him! Right there! It's him!
Stone him! Stone him! Stone him! Stone him!

Hit him! Hit him! Hit the bastard!
Quickly! Stone him! Stone him! Stone him!

The Chorus hurls a wild shower of stones in Dikaiopolis' direction.

DIKAIOPOLIS:

Herakles! What's going on here? Hey, you'll break the sacred pot!

CHORUS:

You're the one our stones are aimed at, you fucking son-of-a-bitch!

DIKAIOPOLIS:

What's the crime that I've been charged with, oldest of Acharnian sirs?

CHORUS:

Can you ask this? You're disgusting!
What a loathsome, shameless traitor,
who alone of all our people
made peace with the enemy!
Can you look us in the eye?

DIKAIOPOLIS:

But you don't know why I made peace! Let me make my case to you!

CHORUS:

Listen to you? No! You'll *die* now,
buried to your neck in stones!

DIKAIOPOLIS:

Not before you've heard me out! Just wait a minute, gentlemen!

CHORUS:

No, I *won't* wait!
Shut your mouth, pal!
You're much worse than
that damn Kleon,
whom I'll soon chop
up for shoes!

I'm not going to listen to any long speeches from somebody like you, who made peace with the Spartans! I'm going to *punish* you!

DIKAIOPOLIS: Gentlemen, please! Leave the Spartans out of it, and concentrate on whether or not I was right to make peace.

CHORUS: "Right"? How can you even say that word, when you've made a treaty with people who don't respect altars or honesty or oaths?

DIKAIOPOLIS: Look, I know we're very angry with the Spartans, but I'm convinced they're not responsible for all our troubles.

CHORUS: Not responsible for all of them, you bastard? You have the nerve to say that sort of thing to my face, and then you expect me to spare your life?

DIKAIOPOLIS: Not for *all* of them! No, no! Not for *all* of them! In fact, I could give you a list right now of all sorts of matters where the *Spartans* are the ones who've been wronged!

CHORUS: This is horrible! My heart! Are you actually prepared to make a speech in defense of our enemies?

DIKAIOPOLIS: I am, in fact! And on the off-chance I can't convince a majority of you I'm right, I'm willing to speak with my head over a chopping block!

CHORUS: What are we saving our stones for, gentlemen? Why don't we just turn this guy into a bloody rag?

DIKAIOPOLIS: It's like something inside you is on fire! Won't you listen to me? Please! Listen to me, Acharnians!

CHORUS: No, we *won't* listen.

DIKAIOPOLIS: Well then, I'm in trouble.

CHORUS: I'll be *goddamned,* if I'm going to listen to *you!*

The Chorus fill their hands with the stones hidden in the folds of their robes, and raise them in a threatening fashion.

DIKAIOPOLIS: No! Don't, Acharnians!

CHORUS: Prepare to die!

DIKAIOPOLIS: If I do, you'll be sorry! Because I'll take revenge by killing what you love best! I'm holding some of your people hostage, and I'm going to get them and slaughter them!

Dikaiopolis enters the house.

CHORUS: Uh-oh, neighbors! What's he threatening us Acharnians with? You don't suppose he's got somebody's kid locked up inside? And if he doesn't, why's he acting so confident?

Dikaiopolis comes out of the house, carrying a charcoal-basket in one hand and a sword in the other.

DIKAIOPOLIS: Go ahead, stone me if you want to—because then I'll murder this little basket here! And that way we'll find out which of you loves charcoal! [27]

27. See note 22.

CHORUS: Damn! We've had it! That charcoal's from my village! Don't do it! No, no! Please don't! No!

DIKAIOPOLIS: I think I'll kill him anyway—so go ahead and scream! Why should I listen to you?

CHORUS: You wouldn't ruin somebody who loves charcoal as much as I do, would you? Especially since we're both the same age?

DIKAIOPOLIS: Well, *you* wouldn't listen to *me* just now!

CHORUS:
All right, make your speech for Sparta!
Go ahead, if that's your pleasure!
Say exactly what you want to!
For I'll never be a traitor
to my friend the charcoal-basket!

DIKAIOPOLIS: Drop your stones on the ground, please!

CHORUS: *(complying)* There you go—they're on the ground! Now *you* lower that sword!

DIKAIOPOLIS: Let's make sure there aren't any other stones hidden in your clothing!

CHORUS:
(doing a wild, twirling dance)
Look, I'm shaking and I'm twirling!
Now no more excuses! Please, friend!
Put your sword down! See me shaking!

Dikaiopolis sets the sword and basket down.

DIKAIOPOLIS: You had to stop shouting eventually anyway, and now some charcoal from Mount Parnes nearly died, all on account of the stupidity of its neighbors! Why, this basket was so frightened it shat charcoal dust all over me, like a squid shooting out ink! It's horrible, when a man's heart has turned so sour that he throws stones and screams and refuses to listen to a balanced argument—especially when I'm willing to make my speech for the Spartans with my head over a butcher's block, "although I'm quite fond of my life."[28]

CHORUS:
(in a mock-tragic style)
Why then, O thou most wretched creature
Dost thou not thy

28. Probably a quotation from a lost tragedy.

block fetch forth here?
I would with eagerness
hear thy great speech.
Still, as thou hast thyself laid the rule down,
bring forth the wood and
then offer thy defense.

Dikaiopolis steps forward to the altar in the middle of the orchestra.

DIKAIOPOLIS: All right—here's the chopping block, and I'm the guy who's going to speak, however unimpressive I may look. And don't worry, I'm not going to be confrontational; I'll just make what seems to me a reasonable argument on behalf of the Spartans. I'll admit, though—I'm terrified, since I understand what peasant-farmers are like: they're just delighted if some gas-bag says nice things about them and their city, whether he tells the truth or not. And so they don't notice when they're being sold out! I also know how our old men feel: all they're looking for is a chance to do something nasty with their ballots. Plus I remember what Kleon did to me because of the comedy I put on last year: he dragged me into the Council-chamber, and slandered me, and gave me a tongue-job with his lies, and yelled, and beat me up, until I nearly died from getting mixed up with his dirty behavior.[29] So this time I want to get dressed up in the most pitiful costume I can find before I make my speech.

CHORUS:
Why dost thou twist and scheme and try delays?
For all I care ask
Hieronymos[30] for
Hades' gloomy
dark-haired magic cap![31]
Like Sisyphos[32] unfold thy plans, for
now's no occasion
for excuses.

DIKAIOPOLIS: It's time to get my courage up and go visit Euripides. *(He steps up to the central door and knocks.)* Slave! Slave!

29. For Aristophanes' conflict with Kleon over *Babylonians,* his comedy from the previous year, see the introduction.
30. A contemporary tragic and dithyrambic poet, but the point of the allusion is unclear.
31. The mythological cap of darkness made whoever wore it invisible.
32. A great mythological trickster.

Euripides' Slave opens the door.

EURIPIDES' SLAVE: What is it?

DIKAIOPOLIS: Is Euripides home?

EURIPIDES' SLAVE: Well . . . he is and he isn't, if you know what I mean.

DIKAIOPOLIS: You mean he *is* home, but he *isn't* home?

EURIPIDES' SLAVE: That's it exactly, old man! His *mind's* off someplace else, collecting verses, but *he's* upstairs, writing a tragedy!

DIKAIOPOLIS: What a lucky fellow Euripides is, if he's got a servant who can come up with answers like that! But go tell him to get out here!

EURIPIDES' SLAVE: I'm afraid that's really impossible.

DIKAIOPOLIS: Do it anyway—because I'm not going to go away, I'll just keep on knocking.

The Slave goes into Euripides' house and closes the door. Dikaiopolis knocks again.

DIKAIOPOLIS: Euripides! Sweet little Euripides! Pay attention to me, "if ever thou listeneth to anyone"![33] It's *me* that's calling you! Dikaiopolis of Cholleidai!

EURIPIDES: *(sticking his head out of an upstairs window)* I have no time for this!

DIKAIOPOLIS: Well then, have yourself rolled out.

EURIPIDES: I cannot.

DIKAIOPOLIS: Do it anyway!

EURIPIDES: Enough! I shall have myself rolled out. But I have no time to come downstairs.

Euripides is rolled out from his house on the ekkuklema. He is dressed in rags and surrounded by heaps of rags and rubbish (actually tragic stage props). Euripides' Slave stands in the background.

DIKAIOPOLIS: Euripides—

EURIPIDES: Concerning what matter dost thou cry out?

DIKAIOPOLIS: —do you stay upstairs to write your poetry, when you could do it downstairs instead? *That* must be why your plays always have cripples in them![34] And how come you wear those rags right straight out of a tragedy, that "piteous clothing"? *That's* probably why you always write

---

33. Language like this is often used in prayers, but these specific words are probably borrowed from a lost Euripidean tragedy.

34. I.e., because the two floors in a house were connected with a ladder, and ladders were notoriously dangerous.

about beggars! Well, anyway, I'm here to ask you a favor, Euripides: there's a ratty piece of clothing I need from one of your old plays, because I have to make a big speech to the Chorus, and if I do a lousy job of it, I'm going to die.

EURIPIDES: Which tatters specifically? Perhaps these here *(pointing),* in which the ill-starred yet distinguished Oineus once competed?[35]

DIKAIOPOLIS: No, not Oineus; it was somebody more miserable than him.

EURIPIDES: Perhaps the tatters of blind Phoinix?

DIKAIOPOLIS: No, no, no, not Phoinix; somebody else even worse off than Phoinix.

EURIPIDES: Which rent robes could this creature be asking after? Art thou referring to those belonging to the impoverished Philoktetes?

DIKAIOPOLIS: No, it was someone who was a lot more of a beggar than he was!

EURIPIDES: Dost thou crave the squalid garb that clothed the lame Bellerophon?

DIKAIOPOLIS: Not Bellerophon! But the guy I'm thinking of *was* a crippled beggar who was full of bullshit and clever speeches.

EURIPIDES: I recognize the man—'tis Mysian Telephos![36]

DIKAIOPOLIS: Yes! That's him! Telephos! Lend me *his* clothing, please!

EURIPIDES: Slave! Offer him the rags of Telephos! They lie atop the rags of King Oineus and 'neath those of Ino.

EURIPIDES' SLAVE: *(handing Dikaiopolis the rags)* Here you go!

DIKAIOPOLIS: *(holding the rags up to the light)* O Zeus, whose eyes see through everything! *(He puts on the rags.)* Euripides, since you already did me this one favor, give me the other stuff that goes along with the rags—I mean the fancy little Mysian cap for my head! Because, you see, I have to *look* like I'm a beggar; I'm going to *be* myself, but I need to *look* different.[37] And the audience is going to know who I am, but I want the Chorus to be fooled, so I can fuck them over with my fast talking.

EURIPIDES: *(motioning to the slave)* This will I grant; for thou devisest subtle schemes within thy shrewd mind.

35. Oineus, like Phoinix, Philoktetes, Bellerophon, Telephos, and Ino (all mentioned below), was the hero of a lost Euripidean tragedy.

36. Probably a quotation from a line spoken at a key moment in Euripides' *Telephos,* when the disguised hero was finally recognized by the Greek army. See the introduction.

37. A quotation from the Euripidean Telephos' description of his plan, probably from the prologue of the play.

DIKAIOPOLIS: *(taking the hat from the Slave and putting it on)* God bless you. And I hope Telephos gets . . . exactly what he deserves![38] Hah! Excellent! I'm already full of clever phrases! Except I need a beggar's stick.

EURIPIDES: *(holding one out)* Take this and be gone from my stone-built residence!

DIKAIOPOLIS: Alas, my heart! Look how I'm being driven out of the house, and I'm still missing most of my costume! But keep it up! Don't give up begging. Euripides, I need you to give me a little basket that's got a hole burned in it.

EURIPIDES: Wretch, what need hast thou of this wickerwork?

DIKAIOPOLIS: I don't *need* it; but I want it anyway.

EURIPIDES: *(handing him a basket)* Be sure thou art a pest, and get thee from my house!

DIKAIOPOLIS: Fine! And I wish you the same sort of luck your mother had![39]

EURIPIDES: Get thee off!

DIKAIOPOLIS: No, no, just give me one more thing: a little cup with a broken rim.

EURIPIDES: *(giving him a cup)* Take it and hie thee to perdition! Know thou art irksome to my house!

DIKAIOPOLIS: By God, you don't know what a problem *you* are! But, Euripides, my very, *very* good friend, there's just one more thing I need: a tiny little cook-pot with a sponge jammed in the top.

EURIPIDES: Sir, thou wilt strip me bare of tragedy! *(handing him a pot)* Behold! Take it and go!

DIKAIOPOLIS: I'm going. But now what am I supposed to do? I still need one thing, and if I don't have it, I'm ruined. Listen, my wonderful, *wonderful* friend Euripides—if I get this, I'll go away and I'll never, *ever* come back again: give me some dried-up vegetables for my pot!

EURIPIDES: *(holding them out)* Thou wilt ruin me! Here! My dramas—gone!

DIKAIOPOLIS: That's it, that's it; I'm leaving. I *am* actually too much trouble, "though I did not think the lords would loathe me so."[40] Oh no! Aargh! I've had it! I forgot the one single thing my whole plan depends on! O my best,

---

38. Another line borrowed from the *Telephos*.

39. Aristophanes repeatedly insists that Euripides' mother was so poor she had to work as a vegetable vendor. In fact, she came from a prosperous family, and the precise point of the slander is uncertain.

40. Apparently a line borrowed from a lost tragedy, most likely the *Telephos*.

my *dearest* little friend Euripides, may I die the most horrible death imaginable if I ask you for anything else except just one thing, just this one little thing: get me some of your mother's parsley!

EURIPIDES: Insults! Impudence! *(to the Slave)* Bar the barriers of the house!

Euripides is rolled inside, and the Slave slams the door behind them.

DIKAIOPOLIS: Too bad, heart; we're going to have to do without parsley. Think what a struggle this'll be, to make a speech in defense of the Spartans! Step forward, heart! Here's the starting line! You aren't hesitating, are you? You just consumed a bunch of Euripides—so move it! That's better! Come on, heart—go over there, offer them your head, and say what you think's right. Get your courage up and move! *(as he heads to the altar)* Say—I'm impressed by my heart!

CHORUS:
What wilt thou do or wilt thou say?
A shameless, brazen man thou art,
who'll stick his head out in this way
and argue views nobody shares.
You do not shirk before such tasks;
speak, then, if that is what you want!

DIKAIOPOLIS: Gentlemen out there in the audience, I want to ask you not to get angry with me if I include a speech about our city in this comedy I'm writing, even though I'm a beggar.[41] Because comedy knows what's right, too. I'm going to say things that are awful—but true. And this time Kleon's not going to be able to slander me by claiming I defamed our city in the presence of foreigners. This time we're all alone, since this is the Lenaia festival, and that means no foreigners are here, because the representatives of the allied cities haven't come with their tribute payments.[42] Nope, we've been winnowed clean—since in my opinion, the people who live here all year round but aren't citizens aren't chaff but bran. So look— I despise the Spartans, and I wish Poseidon would send an earthquake to knock their houses down around their ears, since they've cut my vines along with everyone else's. But since we're all friends here: why do we blame the Spartans for this? The fact of the matter is that it was some of

41. Adapted from the opening of the Euripidean Telephos' speech in defense of himself and his people.

42. See the introduction.

our own people—I'm not saying anything about "the city"; don't forget
that, I'm not saying *anything* about "the city"—but some nasty individuals
mixed in with the rest of us like counterfeit coins—badly minted, worthless forgeries trying to pass themselves off as real Athenians—*they* started
denouncing cloaks made in Megara as enemy contraband. And whenever
they spotted a cucumber, or a hare, or a piglet, or a head of garlic, or some
lumps of salt anywhere, they had the stuff branded "Megarian" and auctioned off on the spot. Now you could call these minor local matters. But
then some young fellows got drunk at a party and went off to Megara and
kidnapped a whore named Simaitha. And the Megarians got all upset at this
and responded by kidnapping *two* whores who belonged to Perikles' girl-
friend Aspasia. And *that* was the cause of this huge war that broke out
among the Greeks: three professional cocksuckers! So after that Perikles
got angry and started playing Zeus, throwing thunder and lightning around,
and stirring up Greece. And he proposed a law that sounded like the old
drinking-song, since it said the Megarians couldn't remain "on the land or
in the marketplace or on the sea or in the sky."[43] And eventually the Megarians, when they started starving, asked the Spartans to get the law we
passed because of the cocksuckers annulled. And even though they asked
us over and over again, we kept saying "No," and the result was a military
showdown. "Someone will say, 'They should not have acted thus.'"[44] But
look—what *should* they have done? Just suppose some Spartan sailed off in
a ship to a flyspeck island like Seriphos, denounced a puppy-dog as contraband, and had it sold at auction; would you sit still for that? You certainly
would not! In a minute you'd drag three hundred warships down to the
sea, and the whole city would be full of the noise of soldiers, and of men
shouting to their boat's commander, and wages being paid, and ship's-
emblems being gilded. The colonnades would be full of the sound of arguments and grain being measured; there'd be wineskins, and oar-thongs, and
people buying storage jars; garlic, olives, onions in mesh bags; garlands,
fresh fish, flute-girls, black eyes right and left. The dockyard would echo
with the sound of spars being planed down, and pegs being driven, and oars
being fitted with straps, and the din of oboes, and boatswains, and whistles,

43. An allusion to Timokreon fr. 5 (Page), a denunciation of the blind god Wealth: "You
shouldn't be seen on earth or in the sea or the mainland! You ought instead to inhabit Tartaros
and Acheron, for all men's troubles are caused by you."

44. A quotation from the *Telephos*.

and pipes. I can assure you; that's exactly how *you'd* react! "And do we think Telephos would behave any differently?"[45] If we do, we're fools.

The Chorus splits into two halves.

FIRST SEMICHORUS: You filthy bastard! Can this be true? You're a beggar! How dare you say things like this about us? What business is it of yours if someone worked as an informer?

SECOND SEMICHORUS: By Poseidon, every word he's saying is true! He's not lying about a thing!

FIRST SEMICHORUS: Well, even if he's right, *he's* not the one to talk this way! *(to Dikaiopolis)* You'll be sorry for what you said!

The First Semichorus moves toward Dikaiopolis in a threatening manner.

SECOND SEMICHORUS: *(grabbing the First Semichorus)* Say! Where are you running off to? Stay right there! I've got news for you—if you hit him, you'll be hung up for a beating!

FIRST SEMICHORUS:
Lamachos whose eyes flash lightning,
you whose crest inspires terror—
lend us aid, my friend and tribesman!
Officers and Field Commanders,
Siegecraft-Masters! Give assistance!
For they've got me round the middle!

Lamachos bursts out of the door on the left. He wears a brilliant scarlet robe, body armor, and a helmet with an elaborate crest-feather; has a prominent stage-phallus; and carries a shield with a Gorgon-face painted on the front on his arm.

LAMACHOS: Whence the sound of men shouting in battle? Whither should we send reinforcements? Where should we attack? Who woke up the monster on my shield?

DIKAIOPOLIS: Lamachos, my hero! What crests! What companies!

FIRST SEMICHORUS: Lamachos, isn't this the same guy who's been saying bad things about our whole city for a long time now?

LAMACHOS: You there! Are you saying this sort of thing, even though you're a beggar?

45. Another quotation from the *Telephos*.

DIKAIOPOLIS: Oh, Lamachos, my hero, I'm so sorry if I talked a lot of nonsense, even though I'm a beggar!

LAMACHOS: What did you say about us? Let's hear it!

DIKAIOPOLIS: I'm not sure exactly; your equipment's so scary I feel dizzy. Would you mind getting rid of that horrible bogey-monster?

LAMACHOS: *(removing the shield from his arm)* There you go.

DIKAIOPOLIS: Put it right there next to you, please, upside down.

LAMACHOS: Done.

DIKAIOPOLIS: All right, now give me the feather you've got on your helmet.

LAMACHOS: Here's the plumage.

DIKAIOPOLIS: And finally, hold my head, please, so I can puke into your shield! Crests make me nauseous.

LAMACHOS: Hey, what are you doing? Are you using my plume to help you throw up? That plume came from—

DIKAIOPOLIS: What? Let me guess—a big-mouthed boaster-bird?

LAMACHOS: I'm going to kill you!

DIKAIOPOLIS: No, no, Lamachos, we're not trying to see who's the strongest! But if you're so tough, why haven't you made my dick stand at attention? You've certainly got the equipment!

LAMACHOS: You're a beggar—and you're talking this way to a general?

DIKAIOPOLIS: So I'm a beggar, am I?

LAMACHOS: Well, who are you then?

DIKAIOPOLIS: Who am I? A decent citizen, that's who! Not someone who only thinks about what prestigious appointment he can get next! And ever since the war started, *I've* been a foot-soldier. But as for *you,* ever since the war began, *you've* been getting paid to be a commander!

LAMACHOS: Yes! Because I was elected!

DIKAIOPOLIS: By three cuckoo-birds! *That's* what disgusted me so much that I made peace: I got sick of seeing old men with white hair lined up for battle, while youngsters like you were gallivanting about, some of you off to Thrace at three drachmas a day—corrupt, snotty bastards with long aristocratic names—others off to visit the Carians or maybe the Don't-Carians—another bunch of well-born big-mouths on the lookout for bribes and public honors—others heading to Sicily or Italy or Mockery!

LAMACHOS: Right! Because they were elected!

DIKAIOPOLIS: But can you tell me, please, why *you* people are always on the public payroll, but none of *them (with a gesture toward the Chorus and perhaps the audience as well)* ever is? *(to an individual member of the Chorus)* Tell me the truth, Charcoalson: you're an old man; have *you* ever been sent anywhere as an ambassador, even once? He says he hasn't; but he's perfectly level-headed and he works hard! And what about you, Timberspotter and Strongbackson and Oakwoodson? Have any of *you* ever gotten to visit Ekbatana or the Chaonians? They all say "No." But Megakles[46] and Lamachos, who just yesterday were so broke that their friends sounded like people dumping shitpots in the street in the evening—"Get out of here! Keep away from me!"—*they* go places like that all the time!

LAMACHOS: O democracy! Are we going to put up with this?

DIKAIOPOLIS: Not unless Lamachos is on the payroll!

LAMACHOS: Well, *I'm* going to wage eternal war on all Peloponnesians everywhere, and make their lives as difficult as possible by land and sea!

DIKAIOPOLIS: But *I* say to all Peloponnesians, Megarians, and Boiotians that they can trade with me—but not with Lamachos!

Lamachos and Dikaiopolis enter their houses, leaving the stage empty. The parabasis *follows, as the Chorus members step forward and address the audience directly.*

CHORUS: This fellow's arguments take the prize; he's won the people over as far as his peace treaty's concerned. Now let's strip down and start our speech!

For as long as our poet's been in charge of comic choruses, he's never once approached the audience to say how clever he is. But now that his enemies are slandering him to the Athenians—who are, of course, famous for making up their minds too fast—by claiming that he mocks our city and shows contempt for the people, he feels he has to make some response, since he knows you change your minds almost as fast as you make them up. Our poet says you really ought to be treating him very *well*, since he's put an end to your being taken in by foreigners' speeches, and being delighted when you're flattered, and running the state with a half-witted expression on your faces. It used to be that any allied ambassador who wanted to fool you would start out by calling you "violet-crowned Athenians,"[47]

46. A prominent Athenian politician from an old aristocratic family. The point of the attack is that Megakles and Lamachos have (allegedly) gotten rich overnight—presumably by means of bribes connected with their service on public embassies—so that their old friends (who had grown tired of their sponging and were trying to avoid them) are now willing to associate with them again.

47. Like "Athens, sleek with oil" (below), a reference to a famous ode by the lyric poet Pindar that celebrated Athens' role in the Persian War.

and whenever someone said that, you immediately sat up on the edge of your seats. And if they went on to mention "Athens, sleek with oil," they got whatever they wanted—by assigning you the same honor regularly accorded sardines. So our man has done you a lot of good this way, and he's also shown you what sort of "democracies" run things in the allied cities. The result is, that your subjects are going to come from the cities with their tribute payments, eager to catch a glimpse of this extraordinary poet, who has the nerve to tell the Athenians the truth. Rumors of his daring have spread so far abroad, in fact, that when the Persian king was interrogating Sparta's ambassadors recently, the first thing he asked them was which side had more warships. But then he wanted to know who this poet said nasty things about, because, he claimed, whoever's got *him* as an advisor will be immensely improved and will definitely have the edge in the war. In fact, *that's* why the Spartans are making peace proposals and trying to get Aigina back;[48] they're not interested in the *island*, it's this *poet* they want to take away from you! So don't give him up, since his comedies will tell you the truth. And he promises to teach you what's good and make you happy, not by flattering you, or offering you pay, or trying to cheat you, or pulling tricks, or sprinkling you with praise, but by teaching you what's best. So let Kleon cook up plots against me and try whatever he wants! Decency will be on my side, right will be my ally, and in all my dealings with the city, I'll never be convicted of being what he is: a coward who loves getting fucked up the ass![49]

Come fiery Muse of the district Acharnai,
vigorous, strong as a tongue of the hottest flame!
Just as an ember of charcoal from holm-oak
leaps up when fanned by the
blast of the bellows,
when fresh-caught fish are laid out ready for the pan;
one cook is mixing up lovely Thasian sauce;
others are kneading the
barley-meal into cakes.

48. Aigina is an island near Athens. Shortly after the Peloponnesian War began the Athenians expelled its inhabitants and gave the land to some of their own citizens, perhaps including Aristophanes and his family. The implication of these verses is that the Spartans had recently demanded that the pre-war status of the place be restored as part of a proposed settlement of the war.

49. A parody of a passage from Euripides, probably from the *Telephos.*

Come to me now with a vigorous countryside
song just as bold and as bustling as that, please!

We old men have got a bone to pick with the city, because you don't take
care of us the way you should, considering the naval battles we fought. Instead, you do awful things to us, getting us involved in lawsuits, even
though we're so ancient, and letting us be humiliated by young orators, despite the fact that we're weak, and mute, and all played-out, and don't have
any divine protector to save us from falling except our walking sticks. We
get up by the speakers' stand and we can't talk clearly, we're so old; and
we can't see anything, except how obscure our case is. But the youngster,
who's pulled strings to be able to serve as prosecutor, attacks his opponent
fast, clubs him with carefully chosen words, and drags him up on the witness stand and cross-examines him with tricky questions, tearing a man
Tithonos' age [50] into shreds by confusing him and mixing him up. And the
defendant's so old he mumbles, and the result is that he goes off owing a
fine, and ends up whimpering and weeping and saying to his friends, "That
money I needed to buy my coffin? I have to use it to pay my fine."

How is it fair to destroy an old graybeard
there in the courtroom, after he's fought by your
side many times, and has wiped so much manly
sweat from his brow, and has
proved he's a patriot
battling the Persian invaders at Marathon?
When we were *there* we were on the offensive;
now low-born men make us
speak for the defense,
and, even worse, we are often convicted.
What orator will deny what we're saying?

For how is it reasonable that someone like Thucydides,[51] a man so old he
couldn't even speak, was ruined when he got wrapped up in the Skythian
wilderness, by which I mean that wordy prosecutor, the son of Kephisode-

---

50. Tithonos was a mythological character who was granted immortal life but unfortunately not eternal youth by Zeus, and who grew ever older and more decrepit.

51. Thucydides son of Melesias (not to be confused with the historian) had been an important Athenian politician in the 450s and 440s B.C., but was ostracized (banished) from the
city for ten years in 443. The prosecution of him by Victor (whose name in Greek is Euathlos,
"Excellent Contender" or the like) son of Kephisodemos referred to here apparently took place

mos? *I,* at any rate, felt sorry for him, and I wiped a tear away when I saw someone as ancient as that driven to distraction by an archer.[52] When he was really Thucydides, by Demeter, he would hardly have put up with the goddess herself! No, he would've started out by wrestling ten Victors[53] to the ground, and then he would've shouted down three thousand bowmen with his bellowing, and outshot all the relatives of his opponent's father. But since you won't give your elders any rest, at least pass a law to keep the trials separate, so that old men get prosecuted by someone old and toothless, while young men face a loud-mouthed queer like Alcibiades.[54] In the future, it ought to be the rule that an old man gets driven into exile or, if he's already there, fined by an old man, and a youngster by a youngster.

The Chorus members return to their previous position. Dikaiopolis emerges from his house, carrying a handful of stones and a whip.

DIKAIOPOLIS: *(putting down the stones)* Here are the boundary-markers for my marketplace. All Peloponnesians, Megarians, and Boiotians can trade here, provided they sell their goods to me but not to Lamachos. And as for market-police, I've held a lottery and hereby appoint these three thongs from Roughville. *(to the whip)* No informer or anyone like that is allowed to enter this place! Now I'll go get the column I inscribed my treaty on, so I can set it up in my market for everyone to see.

Dikaiopolis enters his house. A ragged Megarian, carrying a large sack and trailed by two equally ragged Girls, enters from the wing. The Megarian speaks his own local dialect of Greek, which is clearly intended to sound funny to an Athenian audience and to mark him as a hick, and is represented in this translation by something approximating a rural Southern accent.

MEGARIAN: Mornin', Athenian marketplace, what us Megarians love! By thuh god of frien'ship, ah hankered for you as much as fur mah own Ma!

---

after Thucydides returned to Athens from exile, but we know little more about it than what this passage tells us.

52. The Skythians were bowmen, and Aristophanes' point is that Victor/Euathlos (whose family most likely had political connections or property in the north) is not a real Athenian but a barbarian. This is a typical form of political slander and is not to be taken seriously as historical fact.

53. Thucydides was a famous wrestler in his youth.

54. A rising Athenian politician of the younger generation; he was eventually implicated in a political and religious scandal (the "Affair of the Herms"), was banished from Athens, and gave devastatingly effective advice to Sparta in the final years of the war.

Come up here t' thuh vittles—if'n you kin find any—mah two poor daughters of a poor old man! Y'all listen now; lend me yuh . . . bellies! D'y'all wanna be sold, or d'y'all wanna starve?

GIRLS: Sell us, sell us!

MEGARIAN: Yep, tha's whut ah thinks too. But who's such a fool, what'd buy yuh, seein' as yuh ain't worth nothin'? Well, ah knows an ol' Megarian trick, so ah'll just dress yuh up an' say ah've got some pussies fur sale. [55]

The Megarian pulls a pair of crude cat-costumes out of his bag.

Put on these here pussy duds now, an' make like yuh belong t' a nice litter! 'Cause, by Hermes, if'n ah cain't sell yuh, an' ah have t' take yuh back home, ain't nothin' there 'tall fur dinner!

The Girls put on the costumes, and the Megarian pulls two "cat noses" from the bag.

Now put on these here whiskers, an' then get inside mah sack. An' make damn sure yuh purr an' mew an' make good pussy noises.

The Megarian opens up his bag and sets it on the ground. The Girls put the noses on and crawl inside.

Ah'm a-gonna holler fur Dikaiopolis. Hey now, Dikaiopolis, d'y'all wanna buy some pussies?

Dikaiopolis comes out of the house.

DIKAIOPOLIS: What's this? A Megarian?

MEGARIAN: Ah'm here tuh do some business!

DIKAIOPOLIS: So how are your people?

MEGARIAN: Well, mos'ly we jist sit by thuh fire an' wish we had a little—

DIKAIOPOLIS: Music to go with your wine, right? Sounds great! What else are the Megarians up to these days?

MEGARIAN: Whut a mess! 'Bout the time ah was a-leavin', thuh politicians was tryin' tuh figger out how we could all die thuh mos' mis'rable death possible.

DIKAIOPOLIS: So your troubles'll be over soon!

MEGARIAN: Ah reckon.

DIKAIOPOLIS: But tell me more about Megara! What's wheat cost there?

MEGARIAN: Thuh price is 'bout as high as thuh gods are up in thuh sky!

---

55. The Greek has *choiroi*, "piglets," a word that (like the English "pussies") also had the slang sense "cunts."

DIKAIOPOLIS: Did you bring me any salt?

MEGARIAN: Don' y'all control that?[56]

DIKAIOPOLIS: No salt? Well, what about garlic?

MEGARIAN: Garlic? When y'all invade, y' always dig up ever' blessed head, like a buncha damn field mice!

DIKAIOPOLIS: Well, what *have* you got, then?

MEGARIAN: Ah've got some sacred pussies![57]

DIKAIOPOLIS: Excellent! Let's have a look!

MEGARIAN: *(as the Girls crawl out of the bag)* They're beauties! Cop a feel if'n yuh wan'! Nice an' fat!

DIKAIOPOLIS: What the hell is this?

MEGARIAN: A pussy, bah Zeus!

DIKAIOPOLIS: What are you talking about? What sort of pussy is this?

MEGARIAN: Thuh Megarian kind! Are y'all denyin' that this here's a pussy?

DIKAIOPOLIS: Well . . . it doesn't look like one to *me!*

MEGARIAN: Kin yuh believe it? He don' trust no one, sayin' this ain't a pussy! C'mon now, if yuh wan', ah'll bet yuh some spiced salt that this *is* what us Greeks call a pussy.

DIKAIOPOLIS: But her father's a human being!

MEGARIAN: Tha's right, by thuh hero Diokles[58], *ah'm* her father! Who'd'ja think it was? D'ya wanna hear her talk?

DIKAIOPOLIS: Yes, by every god in heaven, I do!

MEGARIAN: All right, muh little pussy-cat, hurry up an' make some noise!

The Girl fails to react.

Yuh don' wanna? Are yuh gonna keep quiet, yuh little fool? Bah Hermes, ah'm a-gonna take yuh back home agin!

FIRST GIRL: Meow, meow!!

MEGARIAN: Ain't that a pussy?

DIKAIOPOLIS: It certainly does seem to be one *now.* But once it grows up, it'll be a cunt!

MEGARIAN: Ah guarantee yuh, give it five years an' it'll be thuh spittin' image of its Ma!

56. The joke is that Athens controlled the sea, i.e., "the salt."

57. Piglets (see note 55) were sacrificed to Demeter in preparation for the ceremonies in honor of the goddess at Eleusis (see note 10).

58. A bit of local Megarian color.

DIKAIOPOLIS: *(with a gesture toward the second Girl)* But this one here can't be sacrificed.

MEGARIAN: Why not? Wha's wrong wit' it?

DIKAIOPOLIS: It doesn't have a tail!

MEGARIAN: Tha's 'cause it's still a young'un! Once it grows up, somebody'll give it a nice, big, fat, pink one! But if'n yuh're innerested in raisin' pussies, this here's a nice one!

DIKAIOPOLIS: You know, this one's cunt looks amazingly like the other one's!

MEGARIAN: Tha's 'cause they got thuh same Ma an' Pa! But once they puts on a little weight and grows some hair, these'll be a right smart pair uh pussies tuh sacrifice tuh Aphrodite!

DIKAIOPOLIS: But pussies aren't sacrificed to Aphrodite!

MEGARIAN: Pussies aren't sacrificed to Aphrodite? Why they b'long tuh her in perticuller! An' ah'll give yuh a hint—thuh meat o' these here pussies tastes best if'n yuh stick it on your spit!

DIKAIOPOLIS: Are they old enough to eat without their mother?

MEGARIAN: Bah Poseidon, they'll eat without their Pa neither!

DIKAIOPOLIS: What's this one's favorite food?

MEGARIAN: Whutever yuh give her. Ask her yurself.

DIKAIOPOLIS: Here, kitty, kitty!

FIRST GIRL: Meow, meow!

DIKAIOPOLIS: Would you like some chickpeas?

FIRST GIRL: Meow, meow, meow!!

DIKAIOPOLIS: How about some figs?

FIRST GIRL: Meow, meow!!! [59]

DIKAIOPOLIS: *(to the other Girl)* What about you? Would you like some?

SECOND GIRL: Meow, meow, meow!!!

DIKAIOPOLIS: Well, that certainly got a response. Somebody bring some figs out for the pussies!

A servant hurries out of the house and hands Dikaiopolis a basket of figs, a few of which he tosses to the Girls before throwing the rest to the audience.

Do you think they'll eat them?

The Girls grab the figs and begin to wolf them down.

59. Given the context and the girls' extraordinarily enthusiastic response, "chickpeas" and "figs" may be sexual double entendres, in which case one might translate "Would you like a nice tube-steak to suck on? . . . How about a couple of nuts?" or the like.

Wow! By Herakles the ravenous, listen to them eat! What kind of pussy do you think they are? My guess would be Chew-shire cats!

MEGARIAN: *(holding up a single fig which has somehow escaped the Girls' notice)* But they di'n't eat *all* thuh figs! 'Cause ah grabbed this one here fur muhself!

DIKAIOPOLIS: By God, what amazing creatures! Tell me, how much do you want for the pussies?

MEGARIAN: Well, for the one o' 'em, a bunch uh garlic. An' for th' other, how 'bout a quart uh salt?

DIKAIOPOLIS: Sold! Wait right here!

MEGARIAN: Ahlright, then!

Dikaiopolis goes into the house.

Bah Hermes, god uh traders, ah jist wish ah could sell muh ol' Ma an' muh wife fur thuh same price!

An anonymous man, who quickly proves to be a professional Informer, enters from the wing.

INFORMER: You there—where are you from?

MEGARIAN: Ah'm a Megarian, here tuh sell some pussies.

INFORMER: In that case, I denounce you and this merchandise you've got with you as illegal imports from a hostile state.

MEGARIAN: Here we go agin! This is where all thuh trouble started from in thuh firs' place!

INFORMER: You'll be sorry if you keep up these stupid Megarian tricks! Give me that sack!

MEGARIAN: Dikaiopolis! Dikaiopolis! Ah'm a-bein' d'nounced!

Dikaiopolis rushes out of the house, holding a head of garlic and a bag of salt, and snatches up the whip with his free hand.

DIKAIOPOLIS: By whom? Who's denouncing you? *(to the whip)* Market-police, you're supposed to keep informers out of here! *(to the Informer)* What do you mean by *de*nouncing other people, without *an*nouncing yourself first?

INFORMER: Do you think I'm going to stop denouncing hostile aliens?

DIKAIOPOLIS: You'll be sorry, if you don't get the hell out of here and do your informing somewhere else!

The Informer beats a hasty retreat into the wing.

MEGARIAN: What uh problem y'all got with these people in Athens!

DIKAIOPOLIS: Forget about it, Megarian. Here's what you wanted for your pussies: some garlic and some salt.

The Megarian puts the garlic and the bag of salt in his sack.

And now farewell!

MEGARIAN: It's more like our style tuh fare badly!

DIKAIOPOLIS: I beg your pardon! I hope my wish comes true for me instead!

MEGARIAN: All right, muh little pussy-cats; once your ol' Pa's gone, try tuh get somebody tuh give yuh a nice, big sausage tuh go with your dinner!

The Megarian exits into the wing from which he entered. Dikaiopolis and the Girls go into his house.

CHORUS:

This fellow's really doing well! Can you see where it's heading?
He'll take his seat at his market stall and enjoy everything that's good!
And if someone like Ktesias[60]
attempts to hang around,
informers are banned, and you can be sure
he'll leave very soon with a howl!

Nobody else will be shopping there; you'll have the place all to yourself!
No Prepis[61] to smear his faggotry all over your new clothes!
No elbows from Kleonymos[62]—
just a nice little quiet stroll!
No lawsuits from Hyperbolus[63]
to put a crimp in your style!

Kratinos,[64] in this marketplace, won't swagger up to you,
his hair always cut with a single blade, like an aging adulterer,

60. Otherwise unknown.

61. A man by this name is known to have been peripherally involved in Athenian politics a few years later, but the person referred to here is otherwise unknown.

62. See note 11.

63. An Athenian politician who seems to have begun his career by prosecuting corrupt public officials.

64. Doubtless the Athenian comic poet Kratinos, who was a generation older than Aristophanes and is mocked relentlessly by him.

that dirty, nasty debauchee,
who's much too fast at writing poems,
and whose armpits have the ugly smell
of his father from Goatville!

On top of all that, that wretch Pauson[65] won't make jokes at your
                                                                    expense.
And the same is true of Lysistratos,[66] the disgrace of Cholargai,
who's deep-dyed in trouble from head to foot,
and stands about, with his teeth chattering
and starving to death a minimum
of thirty days in each month.

A Boiotian trader and his slave or assistant Ismenias enter from the wing. They carry be-
tween them a transport-stick, from which hang large numbers of animals and other goods,
some of them wrapped in bags and ropes. Behind them comes a piper, playing loudly and
out of tune. The Boiotian speaks his own local dialect of Greek, here represented by some-
thing approximating a stereotypical New York/New Jersey accent.

BOIOTIAN: By duh god Herakles, muh damn shoulduh's about tuh break!
    Ismenias! Watch it when yuh put duh mint down! 'n' you pipers what fol-
    lowed us from Thebes—stick it inna dog's ass, huh?

Dikaiopolis comes out of the house.

DIKAIOPOLIS: Goddammit, get those bumblebees away from my door!
    What a horrible sound! Where'd they fly here from?

The piper flees into the wing.

BOIOTIAN: By Iolaus,[67] buddy, yuh done me a favuh! Dey followed me duh
    whole way from Thebes wid deir huffin' 'n' puffin', 'n' dey blew duh damn
    flowuhs right offa duh mint. But if yuh wan', buy somma dese buhrdies 'n'
    wild critters what I brung.

DIKAIOPOLIS: *(noticing him for the first time)* Well hello, my roll-eating Boi-
    otian friend. What've you got with you?

65. An Athenian painter, known for his sense of humor.
66. A well-known upper-class man-about-town, often satirized in comedy. The point of
the attack is unclear, but is perhaps that Lysistratos was always trying to get an invitation to
someone's house for dinner.
67. A companion and assistant of Herakles, worshiped at Thebes.

BOIOTIAN: Whudevuh duh Boiotians got what's good: uhregano, mint, rushes, reeds, ducks, blackbuhrds, godwits, somma dem white-head coots, plovuhs, divin' burds—

DIKAIOPOLIS: This is really "fowl weather" you've brought to my market!

BOIOTIAN: I also got gooses, rabbits, foxes, moles, hedgehogs; got some nice badguhrs, couppla ferrets, ottuhs, some eels from Lake Kopais—

DIKAIOPOLIS: O thou who bringest with thee the cut of meat most prized by mortal men, if thou canst, allow me to address these eels.

The Boiotian pulls an eel out of a bag or basket hanging from the transport-stick and hands it to Dikaiopolis.

BOIOTIAN: Eldest uh fifty Kopaic maidens, come outta dere 'n' be nice tuh duh stranger!

DIKAIOPOLIS: *(addressing the eel)* O beloved and much-longed-for one, thou art come, bringing joy to comic choruses, as well as to that glutton Morychos![68] Slaves! Bring me a barbecue grill and some bellows!

Two slaves enter, carrying the items Dikaiopolis requested.

Servants, behold this eel, for whom we longed, and who has come to us now in the sixth year! Greet her, children, and I will give you charcoal for her sake. *(handing the eel to a slave)* Take her inside! *(to the eel in parting)* Not even in death shall I be sundered from thee, so long as thou art served with beet!

The slave exits into the house with the eel. Ismenias begins to unwrap and untie the Boiotian's other goods.

BOIOTIAN: But whadduh yuh gonna gimme for her?

DIKAIOPOLIS: Let's just call that your market tax. But if you want to sell any of this other stuff, let me know.

BOIOTIAN: I'm sellin' all of it!

DIKAIOPOLIS: Well, then, how much do you want? Or are you after something from here to export?

BOIOTIAN: Whudevuh yuh got in Athens what duh Boiotians don' have!

DIKAIOPOLIS: You could buy some of our local sardines to take, or maybe some pottery.

BOIOTIAN: Sardines? Pottery? We got dose! I wan' sumpin' what we *don'* got, but what youse gotta lottuv it here.

68. Elsewhere referred to as a gourmand and a tragic poet.

DIKAIOPOLIS: I know! You could export an informer! You could wrap him up like a pot!

BOIOTIAN: By duh gods, I'd make uh lotta money wid sumpin' like dat, all fulla dirty tricks like uh monkey!

DIKAIOPOLIS: And here's Nikarchos, right on schedule to denounce you!

BOIOTIAN: He ain' very big!

DIKAIOPOLIS: True; but he's one-hundred-percent bad.

Nikarchos enters from the wing.

NIKARCHOS: Whose merchandise is this?

BOIOTIAN: Dat's mine; I brung it from Thebes, by Zeus!

NIKARCHOS: In that case, I denounce these goods as enemy contraband!

BOIOTIAN: Whud's duh mattuh with dis guy, wagin' war on little buhrdies?

NIKARCHOS: And I'm denouncing *you* too!

BOIOTIAN: Whud'm I doin' wrong?

NIKARCHOS: I'll tell you, so everyone standing around understands: you're importing lampwicks from enemy territory!

DIKAIOPOLIS: You mean you're actually denouncing him because of a *lampwick?*

NIKARCHOS: Yes, because this lampwick could burn down our shipyard!

DIKAIOPOLIS: A *lampwick* could burn down the *shipyard?*

NIKARCHOS: Precisely.

DIKAIOPOLIS: How?

NIKARCHOS: Some Boiotian could put it in a tiny little beetle-boat, and light it, and then send it into the shipyard through a drain sometime when a strong north wind is blowing. And once the ships catch fire—they'll all burn up in no time!

DIKAIOPOLIS: You clown! You think the ships'll all burn up because of a little beetle and a lampwick?

Dikaiopolis grabs Nikarchos by the collar.

NIKARCHOS: I'll see you in court!

DIKAIOPOLIS: *(to a slave)* Get a hand over his mouth! And hand me some of that straw, so he won't break while they're carrying him!

Dikaiopolis and the slave wrestle Nikarchos to the ground, wrap him in some of the material originally used to pack the goods the Boiotian brought onstage, and hang him head-down from the transport-pole. Nikarchos struggles and screams ineffectively.

CHORUS:
> O best of men, now tightly tie
> this merchandise up for your friend!
> And please be sure
> he doesn't break when he is carried off!

DIKAIOPOLIS:
> I'll see to that! Already he
> is making noise he shouldn't be!
> He's cracked, I think,
> and that suggests he's hated by the gods!

CHORUS:
> What use could buyers have of him?

DIKAIOPOLIS:
> Oh, he'd be good for many things:
> a mixing bowl for stirring grief;
> a pestle fit for grinding trials;
> a lamp for shedding legal light;
> a cup for drinking misery!

CHORUS:
> But how could one with confidence
> use such a vessel in one's house?
> The sound it makes!
> I think there must be something very wrong with it!

DIKAIOPOLIS:
> Why no, my friends, it's quality!
> Why it's so strong, it wouldn't break,
> not even if
> you hung it head-down by its feet!
> *(to the Boiotian)*
> He's ready for you now, I think!

BOIOTIAN:
> Duh time is come for harvestin'!

CHORUS:
> O best of men, harvest away!
> Please take this wretch to someplace else
> and throw him anywhere you like!
> He's every inch a sycophant!

DIKAIOPOLIS: Wow! What a struggle it was to get that bastard tied up! Take your pottery and beat it, Boiotian!

BOIOTIAN: Ismenias! Get yuh shoulduh ovuh here!

DIKAIOPOLIS: Be careful when you set him down! He's completely rotten—but he's yours anyway! And if you make a profit on him . . . oddly enough, an informer will have made you happy!

The Boiotian and Ismenias exit into the wing, carrying Nikarchos. A moment later, Lamachos' Slave enters from his house.

LAMACHOS' SLAVE: Dikaiopolis!

DIKAIOPOLIS: What is it? Why're you calling me?

LAMACHOS' SLAVE: Why? *(holding up a coin)* Because Lamachos says he'll give you this drachma, if you sell him some of your thrushes for the Festival of Pitchers! And he'll pay three drachmas for a Kopaic eel!

DIKAIOPOLIS: Who's this Lamachos who wants my eel?

LAMACHOS' SLAVE: You know—the terrible one! The guy who carries a shield covered with cowhide, and waves a Gorgon around, and has three crest-feathers dangling over his head!

DIKAIOPOLIS: No eels for *him,* by God, even if he wants to trade his shield for them! He can go shake his feathers at some saltfish! And if he makes a fuss, I'll call the market-police! But as for me, I'm going to take this stuff I've bought inside to the old tune "of the wings of thrushes and blackbirds."[69]

Lamachos' Slave exits into his house. Dikaiopolis and the slave gather up the goods the Boiotian sold him and exit into their own house.

CHORUS:

Say, did you see, did you see? He's so clever, so wise, and so thoughtful!
Look at the goods he's acquired by means of his treaty with Sparta!
Some you can use in the house, and the rest you can eat hot for dinner.
Everything good comes to him of its own accord!
Never will War be a guest in my house again,
nor will he lie by my side at a party
praising old Harmodios[70] as a hard drinker.

69. Probably a fragment of or an allusion to a lost lyric poem.

70. One of the great old heroes of democratic Athens; he and his lover Aristogeiton assassinated Hipparchos, brother of the tyrant Hippias, in 514 B.C., and songs were regularly sung in their honor at Athenian drinking parties.

Since uninvited he burst in upon us and
ruined our feasting by pouring our wine out,
breaking the house up and starting a fistfight, and
then, when I offered a full bowl of friendship, he
took all the vinestakes and made a great bonfire and
used force to spill every drop from my grape clusters!

*Dikaiopolis comes out of the house, empties a basket of kitchen trimmings on the ground,
and goes back inside.*

This man is ready to fly off to dinner! He's proud and he's shown us the
way that he lives now by putting these wings in a pile by his front door!
Peace Treaty, you who were raised with the Graces and fair Aphrodite,
now I can see what a sweet, pretty face you've got!
Would that some god of desire with a garland of
roses would join us together as lovers!
Or do you think that I'm somehow too old for that?
Once you were mine, I'd approach you with three plantings:
first I would put in a long row of grape-cuttings;
then next to them fig-tree shoots, young and tender ones;
third, though I'm old, I would add cultivated vines;
and, in a circle around the whole field, olive
trees with whose oil we'd anoint ourselves monthly!

A Herald enters from the wing.

HERALD: Hear ye, hear ye! As ancestral tradition requires, everyone is to begin drinking from his pitcher the moment the trumpet sounds! Whoever
empties his pitcher first will be awarded a wineskin full of Ktesiphon.[71]

The Herald exits into the wing. Dikaiopolis comes out of his house.

DIKAIOPOLIS: Slaves! Servant-women! Didn't you hear the announcement?
What are you doing? Pay attention to the Herald! Hurry up! Start stewing
the rabbit meat and roasting it and turning it, and then pull it off the skew-

71. Apparently a notoriously fat drunk (so that "a wineskin full of Ktesiphon" means
"a skin as big as Ktesiphon and equally full of wine"), but most likely also a prominent politician, like most people mentioned by name in Aristophanes. The festival referred to here
and throughout the rest of the play is the Anthesteria, celebrated in honor of Dionysos in late
February.

ers! Weave me some garlands! And somebody bring my spits, so I can put the thrushes on them!

Servants begin to run in and out of the house, getting the cooking ready.

CHORUS:
I'm jealous of your wisdom, sir,
but much more of the food and fun
I'm watching you enjoying!
DIKAIOPOLIS: What'll you say when you see my thrushes roasting?
CHORUS: You're right about that too!
DIKAIOPOLIS: *(to one of the servants)* Stir up the fire!
CHORUS:
Just hear him talk; how like a chef!
How proudly and how festively
he's working on his dinner!

An anonymous man, eventually identified as Sharpeyes of Phyle, stumbles on from a wing. He wears a white robe.

SHARPEYES: Oh horror! misery!
DIKAIOPOLIS: Herakles! Who's this?
SHARPEYES: Somebody very unhappy!
DIKAIOPOLIS: Well, get away from here then!
SHARPEYES: My friend, you're the only one with a treaty; won't you measure me out a little peace? It could be just five years' worth.
DIKAIOPOLIS: What's your problem?
SHARPEYES: I'm ruined—I've lost my oxen.
DIKAIOPOLIS: Where'd you lose them?
SHARPEYES: The Boiotians stole them from Phyle.
DIKAIOPOLIS: If you're so miserable, why are you wearing white?
SHARPEYES: And on top of everything else, those animals nourished me with every known variety of cow manure!
DIKAIOPOLIS: So what do you want from me?
SHARPEYES: I cried so much for my oxen, I went blind. Please—if you feel any sympathy at all for Sharpeyes of Phyle, rub a little peace on my eyes right away!
DIKAIOPOLIS: You ass! What do I look like, the town doctor?
SHARPEYES: I'm begging you! Maybe I can get my oxen back!

DIKAIOPOLIS: You're not getting any peace from me. Go to Pittalos' people[72] and cry to them!

SHARPEYES: Just put one little drop of peace in this container for me!

DIKAIOPOLIS: I wouldn't give you the tiniest drop in the world! Get the hell out of here!

SHARPEYES: Oh, I'm so sad! My poor oxen!

Sharpeyes stumbles off into the wing.

CHORUS:
> The man's discovered something sweet
> in his peace treaties and, it seems,
> he'll give a share to no one!

DIKAIOPOLIS: *(to a slave)* You there—pour some honey over the sausage! Fry up the squid!

CHORUS: Did you hear what he's shouting?

DIKAIOPOLIS: And roast these eels over here!

CHORUS:
> You're killing me and all your neighbors
> with the smell of roasting meat
> and with these things you're shouting.

DIKAIOPOLIS: Roast this meat! Get it nice and brown!

A Best Man and a Bridesmaid enter from the wing. Both are richly dressed, and the Best Man carries a platter of roasted meat.

BEST MAN: Dikaiopolis!

DIKAIOPOLIS: Who's this? Who are you?

BEST MAN: A guy who's getting married today sent you this meat from the banquet.

DIKAIOPOLIS: Well, good for him, whoever he is!

BEST MAN: *(holding out a tiny jar)* And in return for the meat, so he won't have to go off to war and can stay home and have sex with his wife, he wants you to pour a tablespoon of peace into this jar for him.

DIKAIOPOLIS: Get that meat out of here! Don't even *try* to offer it to me! I'm not going to give away any of my peace! Not even for 10,000 drachmas! *(pointing to the Bridesmaid)* But who's this?

72. Presumably a physician, but otherwise unknown.

BEST MAN: The Bridesmaid wants to give you a private message from the bride.

DIKAIOPOLIS: *(putting his ear to the Bridesmaid's mouth as if to listen to her whisper)* All right, what do you have to say? *(after a brief pause)* Hah! What a funny request the bride has—and how serious she is about it! She wants the bridegroom's dick to be able to stay home! *(to a slave)* Bring the drink-offerings out here, so I can give her some, but her only; she's a woman, so she's not responsible for this war.

The slave enters the house and comes back carrying the wineskin, which he hands to Dikaiopolis.

All right, sweetheart, hold out that jar.

She does so, and he pours a bit of wine into it.

Here's what the two of you have to do: tell the bride that when the draft-lists get posted, that night she has to smear some of this on the groom's dick!

The Best Man and Bridegroom exit into the wing.

(to a slave) Take the drink-offerings back inside, and bring me a ladle so I can fill my pitcher with wine for the festival!

CHORUS: Here comes somebody in a hurry—and from the expression on his face, I'd say he's got bad news!

The Herald enters from the wing.

HERALD: O battles and lamentations and Lamachoses!

Lamachos comes out of his house without armor or weapons.

LAMACHOS: Whose voice re-echoes round about my bronze-outfitted house?
HERALD: Orders from the generals! You're supposed to take your crests and companies, march off as fast as you can, stand guard at the mountain passes, and get snowed on. Someone told them that Boiotian raiders might try to invade during the Festival of Pots and Pitchers!

The Herald exits into the wing.

LAMACHOS: Goddamn these generals! There's a lot of them, but that doesn't mean they're any good. This is awful! I don't get to enjoy the festival!

DIKAIOPOLIS: Hooray for the Lamachean expeditionary force!

LAMACHOS: And what's even worse, now *you're* making fun of me!

DIKAIOPOLIS: Do you want to fight a four-feathered Geryon?[73]

LAMACHOS: Shit! What a message that herald gave me!

DIKAIOPOLIS: Shit! What message is this fellow running up to give *me?*

A Messenger hurries on from the wing.

MESSENGER: Dikaiopolis!

DIKAIOPOLIS: What is it?

MESSENGER: Quick! Grab your food-basket and your pitcher, and head off to dinner—the Priest of Dionysos is inviting you! And hurry up—they've been waiting for you for a long time! Everything else is ready: couches, tables, pillows, blankets, wreathes for your head, perfume, desserts! There are whores there, and cakes made of nice white flour and sesame seeds and honey, plus pretty dancing-girls, the kind Harmodios loved! Get there are fast as you can!

The Messenger exits into the wing.

LAMACHOS: Oh, poor me!

DIKAIOPOLIS: Hey, you picked the Gorgon for your patron, not the other way around. *(to the slaves inside)* Lock up the house! Somebody get my dinner ready!

In the scene that follows, slaves run constantly in and out of the two houses, bringing Lamachos and Dikaiopolis the items they request.

LAMACHOS: Slave! Slave! Bring my backpack out!

DIKAIOPOLIS: Slave! Slave! Bring my food-basket out!

LAMACHOS: Bring me some spiced salt, slave, and some onions!

DIKAIOPOLIS: Bring *me* some slices of fish; I've had it with onions!

LAMACHOS: Bring me a chunk of saltfish wrapped in a fig leaf, slave! Make sure it's nice and rotten!

DIKAIOPOLIS: But *you* bring *me* a fig leaf stuffed with beef-fat and flour; I'll roast it after I get there!

LAMACHOS: Bring me the feathers that attach to my helmet!

DIKAIOPOLIS: Bring *me* my pigeons and my thrushes!

73. Geryon was a triple-bodied monster defeated by Herakles, and Dikaiopolis must be alluding somehow to Lamachos' multiplumed helmet, although his point is not clear.

LAMACHOS: How nice and white this ostrich feather is!

DIKAIOPOLIS: How nice and brown this pigeon meat is!

LAMACHOS: *(to Dikaiopolis)* Listen, buddy—stop making fun of my equipment!

DIKAIOPOLIS: *(to Lamachos)* Listen, buddy—stop looking at my thrushes!

LAMACHOS: Bring out the case my crest-feathers go in!

DIKAIOPOLIS: Bring *me* the dish my rabbit meat goes in!

LAMACHOS: Hey! It looks like some moths ate my feathers!

DIKAIOPOLIS: Hey! It looks like I'm going to eat some rabbit meat before dinner!

LAMACHOS: Look, you—I want you to stop talking to me!

DIKAIOPOLIS: It's just that me and my slave have been arguing. *(to the slave)* Do you want to put some money on it, and then let Lamachos decide which tastes better, locusts or thrushes?

LAMACHOS: Goddamn it, you're completely out of line!

DIKAIOPOLIS: *(to the slave)* I guess he likes locusts.

LAMACHOS: Hey slave! Take my spear off the wall and bring it out here to me!

DIKAIOPOLIS: Hey slave! Take my sausage off the spit and bring it out here to me!

LAMACHOS: Now I have to take my spear out of its case. Here, slave, hold on to this.

DIKAIOPOLIS: *(with a gesture toward his penis?)* And *you,* slave, hold on to *this!*

LAMACHOS: Fetch the stand for my shield, slave!

DIKAIOPOLIS: But fetch *me* some rolls for my belly!

LAMACHOS: Bring out my round shield with the Gorgon on the front!

DIKAIOPOLIS: But bring *me* my round cake with the cheese on top!

LAMACHOS: Can you deny that you're making fun of me for everyone to see?

DIKAIOPOLIS: Can *you* deny that this is a really delicious cake for everyone to see?

LAMACHOS: Pour some olive oil over my shield, slave. I see the reflection of an old man who's going to be prosecuted for cowardice.

DIKAIOPOLIS: *(holding out the cake)* You pour some honey over *this!* Over here I can clearly make out an old man telling Lamachos son of Gorgasos to go to hell!

LAMACHOS: Slave, bring out my breastplate!

DIKAIOPOLIS: Slave, bring *me* a pitcher and *not* a breastplate!

LAMACHOS: This will keep me safe when I come face-to-face with the enemy.

DIKAIOPOLIS: This will keep me drunk when I come face-to-face with the other guests.

LAMACHOS: Tie my bedroll onto my shield, slave; I'll carry my backpack by myself.

DIKAIOPOLIS: Tie my dinner onto my basket, slave; I'll put on my robe and go.

LAMACHOS: Pick up the shield, slave, and let's get going. It's snowing. Yuck! What a nasty, freezing business!

DIKAIOPOLIS: Pick up the dinner! What a lovely, drunken business!

Lamachos and Dikaiopolis, each trailed by a slave, exit into opposite wings.

CHORUS:
> Go with joy now on your missions!
> What very different roads you're taking!
> *He* will be drinking, crowned with a garland;
> *you* will shiver on guard duty,
> while he is sleeping
> with some tasty, hot, little whore and
> getting his you-know-what rubbed down!

> As for Antimachos,[74] the son of Slobber,
> a prose author who thinks he's a poet;
> to put it simply, I wish Zeus would
> blast him to pieces!
> When he produced my play last year, he was
> too cheap even to spring for a dinner!
> I'd like to see him hungry for squid, and
> one would be lying there, beached by the salt and
> sizzling, and he'd reach his
> hand out to grab it, and
> just as he did, a
> fast dog would steal it!

> That's my first curse; now comes another.
> One night when he's walking home from a horse-ride,

74. Unidentifiable.

aching and feverish, I hope a drunken
half-crazy mugger
splits his head open with a stout stick!
Then, as he's groping around in the darkness,
trying to find a stone for a weapon,
may he pick up a fresh lump of shit and,
armed thus heroically,
mount an attack and
miss his target but
hit Kratinos!

A Messenger enters from the wing into which Lamachos exited.

MESSENGER: Help! Slaves who live in Lamachos' house! Water! Water! Heat up some water in a pot! Get some strips of linen ready, and some ointment, and some unwashed wool, and a bandage for his ankle! Your master was leaping over a ditch and got wounded by a vinestake! And after that, he dislocated his ankle, and fell on a stone and cracked his head, and scared the Gorgon off his shield. And as the big boaster-bird feather fell among the rocks, he sang an extraordinary song: "O famous eye, now, as I see you for the final time, I am leaving you behind, my light! I am no more!" After he said something like that, he fell into an irrigation ditch, and then he stood up and confronted the people who were trying to run away. And meanwhile "he was attacking the raiders with his spear the whole time and driving them off."[75] But here he is himself! Open the door!

Lamachos enters from the wing, leaning on a pair of soldiers.

LAMACHOS:
Oh! Oh! Oh!
My sufferings—how cold and cruel!
I'm wounded by a hostile spear!
I only hope Dikaiopolis
won't see me lying here like this
and make fun of my misery!

Dikaiopolis enters from the opposite wing, his arms around two naked girls, one of whom carries a wineskin.

75. A line borrowed from Euripides' *Telephos*. The entire speech is a bit incoherent, doubtless intentionally.

DIKAIOPOLIS:

    Oh! Oh! Oh!

    These tits—why, they're so round and firm!

    But kiss me softly now, my sweets,

    then stick your tongues deep in my mouth!

    [I'm ready for some action, girls!][76]

    For I was first to drink my wine!

LAMACHOS:

    What terrible troubles I've got!

    What painful wounds I've got!

DIKAIOPOLIS: Why, hello, my noble Lamachos!

LAMACHOS:

    Alas, for I hurt so much!

DIKAIOPOLIS:

(to one of the girls)

                    Now why are you kissing me?

LAMACHOS:

    Alas, for I grieve so much!

DIKAIOPOLIS:

(to the other girl)

                    Now why are you biting me?

LAMACHOS:

    Alas, what a wretched charge!

DIKAIOPOLIS: Is someone trying to charge you for participating in the Festival of Pitchers?

LAMACHOS:

    O Paian, god of healing!

DIKAIOPOLIS: You must be confused; today's not the Paionia festival!

LAMACHOS:

    Alas; my leg—take hold of my leg!

    Take hold of my leg, my friends!

DIKAIOPOLIS:

    Oh joy; my dick—get hold of my dick!

    Put your hands on *that,* my friends!

76. The brackets indicate that a line is missing from the text, and the words that appear within them are an *exempli gratia* supplement; although we do not know what Aristophanes wrote, it must have been something like this.

LAMACHOS:

    I've been struck with a stone, my head's in a whirl,

    and the world is going black.

DIKAIOPOLIS:

    My pecker's hard; let's turn out the lights

    and go off to bed and fuck!

LAMACHOS:

    Please carry me off to the doctor's house;

    handle me gently, my friends!

DIKAIOPOLIS:

    But carry *me* off to the judges instead;[77]

    and hand me that wineskin there!

LAMACHOS:

    A painful spear has pierced my bone and cut into my flesh!

Lamachos is carried out.

DIKAIOPOLIS:

    Hey, look! I've drunk this whole skin dry! Tra-la-la for victory!

CHORUS:

    If that's what you say, then tra-la-la-la

    for victory, old man!

DIKAIOPOLIS:

    And add to my score a big glass of wine

    that I filled up and drank off as well!

CHORUS:

    Tra-la-la-la-la now, noble sir! Take up the wineskin and go!

DIKAIOPOLIS:

    Yes, tra-la-la-la for victory! Follow me singing, my friends!

CHORUS:

    If that's what you want,

    then tra-la-la-la!

    Your wineskin and you have won!

Dikaiopolis exits into a wing, holding the wineskin high as a token of his victory and supported by the girls. The Chorus and the piper follow him off.

77. Dikaiopolis means the judges of the drinking contest he has won, but there is also a reference to the judges of the dramatic contest, from whom Aristophanes is hoping to receive the prize.

MENANDER AND GREEK NEW COMEDY

SHAWN O'BRYHIM

INTRODUCTION

ONLY a small fraction of the thousands of literary works produced in antiquity have survived intact to the present day. In fact, the works of many authors have completely disappeared, thus leaving entire genres with only one or two representatives. Such is the case with Greek comedy. Every year, ten comedies by selected playwrights premiered in Athens. But until recently, the only specimens of this genre available to us were eleven plays by one playwright, Aristophanes, who wrote during the late fifth century B.C. The majority of his comedies revolve around fantastic situations that serve to comment upon the contemporary social and political situation in Athens: women end a war by withholding sex from their husbands, birds build a city in the clouds, a god goes to the underworld to bring back whichever dead tragedian can set the city back on a sound moral footing. But in the fourth century B.C., the outlandish plots and harsh political commentary that formed the basis of Aristophanic comedy were out of favor; comic plots now centered upon the family and the personal problems of its members. This thematic shift prompted ancient literary critics to create a new category to distinguish the plays of the fifth century, which they called "Old Comedy," from those of the late fourth century onward, which they called "New Comedy."

From Old Comedy to New Comedy

The shift from Old Comedy to New Comedy (through the little-known intermediary stage of Middle Comedy) coincided with important changes in the political and social situation in Greece; Athens lost the Peloponnesian War and its empire along with it, one Greek city would emerge as a dominant military power only to be superseded by another, the successors of Alexander the Great competed to exert influence over various parts of his empire. With these political changes came shifts in government, traditional social structures, and artistic tastes. It should come as no surprise that literary preferences changed as well.[1] While poking fun at their own governmental institutions and leaders was funny as long as the Athenians controlled them, it lost its appeal when such jibes could provoke retribution, sometimes of a violent nature. Moreover, more and more plays were being written for other cities, where the internal politics of Athens were of little or no interest.

Thus, the focus of Greek comedy changed dramatically. The move away from plots focused on contemporary political situations is apparent in Aristophanes' *Women at Assembly* (392 B.C.?) and *Ploutos* (388 B.C.), both written after Athens had lost the Peloponnesian War. Although these plays still contain a few references to politics, the *parabasis* in which the playwright traditionally voices his political concerns is severely truncated. Political references become increasingly rarer as Old Comedy gives way to Middle Comedy, which frequently dealt with mythological themes (only titles and brief fragments from this period survive).[2] With the emergence of New Comedy around 323 B.C., the *parabasis* disappears completely and political references become exceedingly scarce.[3]

Our knowledge of the transition from Old Comedy to New Comedy is based upon a few plays and many short fragments, so any generalizations are based on very slim evidence and may require revisions with the discovery of more plays. Moreover, it is important to understand that the division of Greek comedy into three separate categories does not mean that there were distinct and sudden breaks between Old, Middle, and New Comedy. Changes took place gradually as some elements favored by earlier generations of playwrights were modified or fell into disuse, while others continued to be used in all periods.[4] Therefore, the development of Greek comedy should not be seen as a

1. For an account of the changes in Greek comedy and the reasons for them, see A. W. Gomme and F. H. Sandbach, *Menander: A Commentary* (Oxford, 1973), 21–23.

2. W. G. Arnott, "From Aristophanes to Menander," *Greece and Rome* (1972): 65–80.

3. For a critical reference to Demetrios of Phaleron, see F. H. Sandbach, *The Comic Theatre of Greece and Rome* (London, 1977), 57.

4. For New Comedy's debt to earlier authors, see R. L. Hunter, *The New Comedy of Greece and Rome* (Cambridge, 1985).

series of three complete breaks with the past, but rather as a long and gradual process of development and change.

Characteristics of New Comedy

While it is difficult to speak with certainty about the nature of Greek New Comedy because so little of it survives, Menander's *Dyskolos,* the surviving fragments of several other comedies, and the Roman adaptations of lost Greek plays suggest that most of the works composed during this period shared several general characteristics: they are almost always set in Athens (Menander's *Perikeiromene* is set in Corinth); they deal with universal themes (usually family problems); they contain few references to contemporary figures or political situations; they make extensive use of stock characters such as mercenaries, cooks, and prostitutes; and some incorporated elements or themes from Euripides' tragedies.[5] The structure of these plays followed a standard pattern: they usually begin with a prologue (although it follows the first scene in Menander's *Aspis, Heros, Perikeiromene,* and *Synaristosai*), which is often delivered by a divine character (e.g., Pan, a hero, Misapprehension, Luck, Proof); these prologues reveal the general outline of the plot and sometimes even the ending, but not the exact way in which the outcome will be achieved; the action of the play is divided into five parts by four choral interludes, which usually mark the passage of dramatic time.

The stage on which New Comedy was performed measured 66 feet in length and had a skene (stage building) with three doors. The outer doors usually represented two different houses, while the middle one could represent any number of things such as the entrance to a cave, a temple, or an alleyway, or it could be hidden by a covering if not needed. The area in front of the houses may represent a city street, a country lane, or the seashore. Painted panels that depicted a city or country scene could be placed between the doors (location did not change within a play as often happened in Aristophanes). There were no indoor sets; all action took place in front of the edifices represented by the skene. When there was a compelling need to present indoor action, a wheeled platform called the *ekkuklema* was brought onto the stage through the central doorway of the skene and the audience would have to imagine that they were watching what was happening inside.

There was still a chorus, but its role in the play is uncertain. The words of the chorus do not appear in surviving manuscripts, so we do not know whether

5. For the influence of tragedy on Menander, see Hunter (above, note 4), 114–36.

its members sang and danced as in Aristophanes' day, although this seems likely. All that remains is an indication of its entrances, which occurred four times during the play. The disappearance of the chorus from the action of the play may account for the lack of metrical variety that had been common in Old Comedy; the meters of Greek New Comedy are primarily confined to iambic ($\smile$-) trimeter, iambic trimeter catalectic, and trochaic (-$\smile$) tetrameter.[6] The costumes of the actors underwent a change as well. Gone were the huge leather phalluses (penises) and the exaggerated padding of Old Comedy; New Comedy replaced them with natural clothing, which is more consonant with its realistic plots. All of the roles, both male and female, were still played by men as in Old Comedy, but it appears (although it is not certain) that New Comedy allowed only three actors with speaking parts on stage at one time (there could be any number of additional mute actors). As in Old Comedy, the use of masks enabled the actors to play multiple parts and even to share the same role if necessary. Some masks represented stock characters, which allowed the audience to intuit the probable behavior of many characters immediately upon seeing their masks (e.g., the stern father, the prostitute, the young lover). Since the expression on the mask was static and many spectators sat far from the stage, actors were forced to exaggerate their gestures and vary their intonation in order to indicate who was speaking and to convey emotion.

Menander's Life

Little is known about most playwrights of New Comedy beyond their names, a few anecdotes, and the titles of some of their plays. The most successful authors wrote between 320 and 280 B.C. and came from throughout the Greek world: Menander (from Athens), Diphilos (from Sinope on the Black Sea), and Philemon (probably from Syracuse on Sicily). According to the *Suda,* a Byzantine compendium of classical knowledge, Menander was "the son of Diopeithes and Hegestrate, about whom much has been written by all, a comic poet of New Comedy, cross-eyed but sharp-witted, and crazy for women; he wrote one hundred and eight comedies, *Letters to King Ptolemy,* and a large number of other prose works." Fortunately, several other details can be gleaned from many sources. Menander was born about 342 B.C. and lived until around 290 B.C., when he is said to have died while swimming off Peiraeus, the main port of Athens. Tradition holds that he learned to write comedy from Alexis, one of

---

6. Fragments of other plays may have anapests ($\smile\smile$-) and dactyls (-$\smile\smile$), but these may have been special cases.

the great figures of Middle Comedy, and that he was the student of the philosopher Theophrastus, whose descriptions of character types are thought by some scholars to have influenced the depiction of stock characters in New Comedy (although both Theophrastus and the playwrights of New Comedy may have drawn independently upon Old and Middle Comedy for their material).[7]

Menander wrote over one hundred plays (ninety-seven titles survive) and won first prize at Athenian festivals only eight times (the Roman author Quintilian says that he was not judged fairly during his lifetime). This information presents a problem, because only two Athenian festivals included the presentation of comedies every year: the Dionysia and the Lenaia. It would have been impossible for all of Menander's plays to have been performed in Athens during his lifetime, so many of them were probably written for other cities (e.g., Epidaurus) and for local festivals in Attica.

Even though Menander (like other writers of New Comedy) avoided references to politics in his plays, he still suffered because of political turmoil. When Athens surrendered in 322 B.C. to the Macedonians, its conquerors installed a garrison in Peiraeus and imposed a property qualification for many civic activities. Athenian autonomy was further restricted when Demetrios of Phaleron became the pro-Macedonian governor of Athens in 317 B.C. When he was expelled in 307 B.C., his supporters and associates were driven out along with him. Among these was Menander, who was restored through the intercession of one of the relatives of Demetrios Poliorcetes, who had come to power in Athens.

Menander's Reputation

Throughout antiquity Menander was reputed to be the greatest writer of Greek New Comedy. The Hellenistic scholar Aristophanes of Byzantium ranked him second only to Homer among all Greek poets; the Greek biographer Plutarch asked, "Why should an educated man go to the theater except to see Menander?" The Romans appreciated his talent as well. Plautus and Terence created several Latin adaptations of his plays: Plautus' *Bacchides* is based on Menander's *Dis Exapaton, Cistellaria* on *Synaristosai,* and *Stichus* on *Adelphoi,* while Terence's *Adelphoe, Andria, Eunuchus,* and *Heautontimoroumenos* are all based on unidentified Menandrian originals (they may have had the same titles as Terence's Latin adaptations). Although many of these Latin adaptations were very popular, the Romans still appreciated Menander's Greek originals. Julius Caesar praises Me-

7. Hunter (above, note 4), 147–51.

nander at the expense of Terence when he calls the latter a "half-pint Menander," while Quintilian recommends his plays highly for the training of orators. In spite of his popularity, all of Menander's plays had been lost by the ninth century A.D., probably because they were not part of the school curriculum and were not copied by Byzantine scholars as were the plays of Aristophanes, who was considered an excellent writer of Attic Greek. Therefore, his works survived only in fragments and, indirectly, in the adaptations of Plautus and Terence.

This situation has begun to change fairly recently, thanks to the discovery of several important papyri in Egypt. In 1898 came the publication of about eighty lines of *Georgos* (almost one complete scene) followed by fifty lines of *Perikeiromene*. Then came the publication in 1907 of parts of five plays (*Heros, Epitrepontes, Perikeiromene, Samia,* and an unidentified play) found at Aphroditopolis near Egyptian Thebes, which were part of a codex that had been reused as covering for documents belonging to a sixth-century lawyer named Flavius Dioscuros from Kome Aphrodite in Egypt. The Bodmer Codex (third century A.D.) from Egypt, which contained the entire *Dyskolos* and fragments of *Samia* and *Aspis* (*Dyskolos* was published in 1959, *Samia* and *Aspis* in 1969), gave us our first complete sample of Greek New Comedy. Afterwards large parts of *Sikyonios* (recovered from material reused as mummy wrappings) and *Misoumenos* appeared. In addition to this, the discovery of a fragment of Menander's *Dis Exapaton,* the source for Plautus' *Bacchides,* enabled scholars to gain some insight into the way in which Plautus modified his Greek originals.[8]

Not only do these finds provide a much larger sample of Menander's comedies for analysis, they also help us to understand why the ancients admired his work: his plots were carefully constructed; his use of traditional stock characters was often innovative; he incorporates elements of tragedy and philosophy to make his plays more meaningful; and his characters are accessible to people of different cultures and different times. All of these aspects are present in our only complete extant example of Greek New Comedy, Menander's *Dyskolos.*

The Plot of *Dyskolos*

Dyskolos, perhaps best translated as *The Grouch,* derives its title from one of the play's main characters: the misanthrope Knemon, whose contempt for the be-

---

8. E. Handley, *Menander and Plautus: A Study in Comparison* (London, 1968). See also Aulus Gellius 2.23.5, comparing a section of one of Caecilius' Latin plays with his Menandrian original.

havior of his fellow man drove him to isolate his family on a farm of moderate size in Phyle, a rural area outside Athens, where he had once lived with his wife, their daughter, a stepson named Gorgias, and a decrepit old female slave named Simiche. Eventually, his intolerable behavior drove his wife to divorce him and move to a small plot next door with Gorgias and his male slave, Daos. This left Knemon with Simiche and his daughter, who works alongside him in his field. The two households are thus mirror images of each other: father, daughter, and female slave in one house and mother, son, and male slave in the other.[9] Between the farms of Knemon and Gorgias lies a cave inhabited by the nymphs and the rustic god Pan. In the prologue, Pan explains to the audience that he intends to reward Knemon's daughter because she is a pious girl who never fails to leave some small sacrifice at the cave and offer a prayer to its resident deities. Even though this is the god's only appearance in the entire play, his presence is continually felt as he directs the action toward his ultimate goal: rewarding Knemon's daughter by finding a suitable husband for her.

The play opens with the entrance of two characters who are earnestly engaged in conversation. Sostratos, the son of a wealthy farmer, tells his companion Chaireas that he has fallen in love at first sight with a country girl he recently observed crowning the statues of the nymphs with flowers. While they discuss the best way for Sostratos to make this girl his wife, a slave runs onstage in a panic. He had approached the girl's father at Sostratos' urging, only to be pelted with rocks, clods of dirt, and pears for daring to trespass on his farm. Chaireas, fearing lest he suffer the same abuse, remarks that all poor farmers are excessively bad-tempered, then beats a hasty retreat followed in short order by the frightened slave.

This leaves Sostratos alone to confront the petulant farmer, who turns out to be none other than the girl's father, Knemon. The prospect of facing the angry misanthrope weakens his resolve, so he decides that it would be better to seek the help of Getas, his father's crafty slave, rather than approach Knemon on his own. But just as he is about to leave, he is stopped dead in his tracks by the sudden entrance of his beloved, who is extremely agitated over a mishap that just occurred inside the house. She explains that Knemon told her to draw him a bath, so she sent Simiche outside to fetch a pail of water. But just as she was drawing the water out of the well, the bucket fell to the bottom and she was unable to retrieve it. In order to save the old woman from a beating,

9. N. J. Lowe, "Tragic Space and Comic Timing in Menander's *Dyskolos,*" *Bulletin of the Institute of Classical Studies* 34 (1987): 129.

Knemon's daughter has come to borrow some water from a spring owned by
the nymphs inside the cave. Sostratos overhears her story, remarks on how
well-mannered the girl is for someone from the country, then approaches her
and offers to help fetch the water. In spite of her fear that she will be beaten by
her father if he catches her outside, she agrees.

At this point Gorgias' slave, Daos, comes out of the house and is about to
pass the cave of Pan on his way to the fields. But he stops suddenly when he sees
his master's half-sister with this strange man. Daos suspects that Sostratos is
trying to seduce this naive young girl, who has lived her entire life on the farm
in virtual isolation from society, so he speeds off to tell Gorgias of this potential danger to his half-sister, hoping that he will protect her from disgrace and
the family from scandal. [10] When Gorgias sees Sostratos walking down the country road dressed in expensive clothing, he is sure that Sostratos' intentions toward his half-sister must be sinister. This conclusion is based solely on Sostratos'
rich attire, which identifies him as a member of the upper class and, in the eyes
of a poor farmer like Gorgias, as an arrogant social superior who has no concern
for the sensitivities of the poor. Gorgias warns Sostratos off, but in a respect-
ful manner appropriate for a member of a lower social class. Sostratos counters
by declaring his love for Gorgias' half-sister and his sincere wish to marry her.
This heartfelt declaration of love is proof enough for Gorgias of Sostratos' good
intentions, so he agrees to speak to Knemon about the marriage. Nevertheless,
he advises Sostratos to abandon all hope of marrying the girl because Knemon
is determined to give her only to a man who is exactly like himself. If this were
not bad enough, Gorgias informs Sostratos that Knemon hates the rich and
would easily recognize him as a member of the upper class by the costly clothing he wears. But Sostratos' love is so strong that he is willing to do anything
to marry the girl, so he readily agrees to a malicious suggestion offered by Daos,
who still mistrusts Sostratos because of his wealth. Knowing full-well that this
rich young man is not accustomed to manual labor, he suggests that Sostratos
take off his expensive cloak and join them in doing field work so that Knemon
will see him when he passes by and think that he is a hard-working farmer who
would be a suitable mate for his daughter.

What follows their departure for the field provides both comic relief and a
clear indication of Pan's control over the action of the play. A cook named Sikon

---

10. Even though Gorgias is under no obligation to do so, he takes it upon himself to play
the role of father that Knemon appears to have abdicated when he allowed his daughter to wan-
der about unprotected. See Lowe (above, note 9), 130.

enters in the company of Getas, the slave who belongs to the family of Sostratos. The two are struggling with the accoutrements of a sacrifice, most notably a plethora of pots and pans and a recalcitrant sheep. These are destined for a propitiatory offering at the cave of Pan that has been arranged by Sostratos' overly superstitious mother. In a recent dream, she saw Pan place her son in chains, hand him workman's clothes and a mattock, and make him dig in a field near the cave. She believes that the dream portends that something terrible will befall Sostratos, so she has come to Pan's sanctuary to ask the god to avert this evil omen. But the audience knows what the dream really means: Pan has enslaved Sostratos to Knemon's daughter with chains of love and was ultimately responsible for his plan to work in Gorgias' field. Knemon, who has been watching this commotion from the front of his house, flies into an uncontrollable rage when Getas approaches him to borrow a pot. In no mood to tangle with this "gray-haired old viper," Getas returns empty-handed to the cave and tells Sikon the cook about his misadventure. Sikon accuses him of being rude to the old man and decides to try a smooth-tongued approach. But before he can utter a word, Knemon threatens to beat him with a leather strap. Sikon retreats to the security of the cave without the pot and wisely decides to make a casserole instead.

At this point, Sostratos returns to the cave after hours of hard work in the fields, sunburned and suffering from an aching back. He meets Getas outside the cave, informs him that he intends to invite two more guests to the feast, then sets out to find Gorgias and Daos. Suddenly, Knemon's old slave-woman, Simiche, rushes onstage shrieking in mock-tragic misery as she recounts her latest mishap. In an ill-conceived attempt to retrieve the bucket she had lost, she tied Knemon's mattock to a length of rotten rope and lowered it into the well. But the rope snapped and she lost both the bucket and the mattock. To make matters worse, Knemon wants to use the mattock to move some manure and is looking all over his property for it, shouting at the top of his lungs. He enters in a rage and threatens to lower Simiche down into the well with the same rotten rope that had snapped under the weight of the mattock. But he suddenly reverses himself and brusquely orders her inside the house, having decided to climb down the rope himself to retrieve the lost items. Getas offers to provide Knemon with a strong rope for the job, but he is roundly abused for his kindness. Instead of the expected curse, this elicits a sympathetic response from Getas, who remarks that the life of an Attic farmer is constant misery, a continual war against rocky and unproductive soil that produces no profit, just weeds.

The climax of the play comes when Simiche runs out of the house a second time, even more hysterical than before, and reports that Knemon has fallen into the well and cannot get out. It may have seemed to the audience that Knemon had finally realized his fondest wish: to be left completely alone.[11] His daughter and slave-woman, whom he had treated as no more than talking tools as they labored in the fields or at the well, are replaced by the mattock and the bucket, their inanimate and non-vocal counterparts. Now Sostratos, Gorgias, and Daos rush to the rescue. Soon afterward, the old misanthrope is carried onstage with a few injuries and a somewhat different outlook on life. He explains that his brush with death has finally made him realize that no one can live without help from others. He had lived a solitary life up to this point because he was certain that true friendship could not exist, for men were concerned with nothing but their own profit. But Gorgias' willingness to rescue him proved him wrong. As a reward for his kindness, Knemon adopts Gorgias and puts all of his property under his control. In addition, he makes Gorgias guardian of his daughter and asks him to find her a husband, since he now realizes that no man could ever satisfy his requirements. Half of his property is to go to her as a dowry, the other half will provide for Knemon and his wife, who will rejoin his household. Before Knemon is taken back into his house to recover from his wounds, Gorgias introduces Sostratos to him as his choice to marry his daughter. Knemon sees the sunburn that Sostratos had gotten while working in the field, assumes that he is a farmer, and does not oppose the marriage. Gorgias then betroths his half-sister to Sostratos, who has given ample proof that he does not despise the poor and is even willing to treat them as equals. Sostratos' father Kallippides, a wealthy farmer, now arrives at the cave to share in the sacrificial meal. Sostratos goes inside with his father to discuss his marriage plans, while Gorgias goes back to his house to await the outcome.

In the final act, Kallippides generously agrees to allow his son to marry Knemon's daughter without a dowry, but he draws the line at letting Gorgias marry Sostratos' sister; one pauper in the family is more than enough, he insists. Thereupon, Sostratos lectures his father on the changeability of fortune and the profits that accrue from an act of generosity. Kallippides relents and gives permission for the double wedding, but Gorgias is not as easy to persuade. He is worried that his low social status will make it seem that he is behaving presumptuously by marrying into a wealthy family and accepting a large

---

11. Note that Pan describes Knemon as living μόνος, "alone," even though he lived with his daughter and Simiche (lines 30–31).

dowry. Kallippides persuades him to agree to the match and all three go into the cave to join the party. Knemon's family is invited as well; Simiche and Knemon's wife come, but Knemon refuses. All except Knemon exit into the cave for the wedding celebration.

Thus, the scheme that Pan had put in motion at the beginning of the play has come to fruition: Knemon's daughter has been rewarded for her piety with a rich and loving husband. This would seem an appropriate place to end the play, but Menander is not finished yet. While everyone is occupied with the wedding celebration, Getas comes out of the cave to take vengeance for the abuse that Knemon had heaped upon him when he asked to borrow a pot. He is aided by Sikon, who had also been one of Knemon's victims. But their motive goes beyond pure vengeance: now that Knemon is part of the extended family, they want to change his irascible and solitary behavior (lines 904–5):

> Now it's completely up to us
> to see that he gets civilized.
> He's our relation, one of us.
> If he's like this forever, then
> we'll have our work cut out for us.
> And you know that as well as I.

Getas and Sikon gently carry the sleeping invalid from inside his house onto the stage, then bang incessantly on his door, asking to borrow luxury items that they know the miserly farmer does not own. Knemon calls for Simiche to bring him a strap, forgetting that he had ordered her to go to the wedding feast with everyone else. There is no one at home to help him, so he must endure all the tortures that his tormenters inflict upon him. They begin by forcing him to listen to a detailed description of everything that is happening at the celebration in the cave, with special emphasis on the drinking and communal dancing. Then they make Knemon suffer a terrible indignity: they force the injured man to stand and dance with them. When Knemon realizes that he is at their mercy, he agrees to enter the cave and join in the celebration. Getas and Sikon claim victory over the grouch and lead him inside as the play comes to an end.

DANCE, OLD MAN, DANCE!

THE TORTURE OF KNEMON IN MENANDER'S *DYSKOLOS*

I N 1959 the sands of Egypt surrendered a papyrus book that contained large portions of three plays by Menander, whose works had been lost since late antiquity. This find produced great excitement among scholars of ancient literature because it provided the first substantial sample of Greek New Comedy, which had been known only through scattered fragments and the Latin adaptations of Roman comic playwrights. The praise that Menander had garnered in the later Hellenistic and early Roman periods heightened the anticipation that preceded the publication of the papyrus.[1] Most scholars were certain that this find would at long last confirm the judgment of Aristophanes of Byzantium, a renowned Hellenistic philologist and head of the library of ancient Alexandria: that among Greek poets, Menander took second place only to Homer (testimonium 61c Körte). When the plays were finally published, many proclaimed them works of genius. Some, however, were gravely disappointed. One critic even went so far as to call them "second-rate hackwork."[2] The greatest dispute has focused on *Dyskolos,* the only one of Menander's plays that has survived in its entirety (only a few lines have been lost). Even though this play earned Menander first prize from the Athenians in 316 B.C., it has brought criticism from some modern scholars primarily because of its seemingly unneces-

---

1. For Greek and Roman assessments of Menander's talent, see testimonia 32–61 (A. Körte, *Menander quae supersunt* [Leipzig, 1951]).

2. P. Green, *Alexander to Actium: The Hellenistic Age* (London, 1990), 71–79, provides a critical assessment of Menander's talent. For an account of ancient and modern views of Menandrian comedy, see E. W. Handley, *The Dyskolos of Menander* (Cambridge, 1965), 12–17.

sary farcical ending. While each reader must reach his own conclusion about the literary merits of the play as a whole, a better understanding of its ending may remove some of the tarnish from Menander's reputation.

N. J. Lowe expresses the puzzlement that many readers feel about the ending of *Dyskolos:* "[it] suffers from a puzzling finale in which the plot has to be awkwardly cranked back into life after what appears a perfectly satisfactory resolution in the fourth act. Cnemon has delivered the definitive recantation speech that is so much a pattern in Menander, and the lovers have permission to marry with all financial obstacles removed. Why this apparent anticlimax, at a point when the play is apparently over? What, in fact, is the purpose of the final scenes?"[3] Many scholars dismiss the humiliation of Knemon as little more than Menander's attempt to pander to the lowest common denominator in his audience by loading the final scene with base humor. Others point to New Comedy's tendency to devote the ending of the play to the reformation of the character (often called the "blocking character") who has attempted to impede the successful resolution of the problem at the heart of the play; he must be humiliated and then reintegrated into the group from which he has become alienated.[4]

Knemon certainly fits this description: his misanthropic behavior threatens to frustrate Pan's scheme to marry Knemon's pious daughter to Sostratos. It might be argued that these problems were resolved after Knemon's rescue from the well, when he abandons his belief that he can live without the help of others and gives Gorgias complete authority to oversee his affairs, which includes the betrothal of his daughter to Sostratos. But the resolution of the family's problems is only partial: even though his daughter is free to marry, Knemon himself is not completely reformed. Far from integrating himself into society, Knemon's grant of power of attorney to Gorgias enables him to cut himself off from all contact with the outside world.[5] His desire to be left completely alone is so strong that it prompts him to send both his wife and his slave away to attend the wedding of his daughter despite his recent injuries, which he himself describes as potentially life-threatening (line 730). But the consequences of

3. N. J. Lowe, "Tragic Space and Comic Timing in Menander's *Dyskolos*," *Bulletin of the Institute of Classical Studies* 34 (1987): 129.

4. E.g., K. Reckford, "The *Dyskolos* of Menander," *Studies in Philology* 58 (1961): 19.

5. B. van Groningen, "The Delineation of Character in Menander's *Dyscolus*," *Recherches de papyrologie* 1 (1961) 111; W. G. Arnott, *Menander, Plautus, Terence* (Greece and Rome: New Surveys in the Classics 9; Oxford, 1975), 20; and S. Goldberg, *The Making of Menander's Comedy* (Berkeley, 1980), 86.

Knemon's continuing misanthropy do not fall upon him alone; his behavior threatens to tear apart his nuclear family. The insufferable disposition that had once led Knemon's wife to divorce him has not improved, so it is doubtful that her reconciliation with the unreformed misanthrope could last for long. Even old Simiche, who had been absolutely terrified of her master up to this point, shows signs of rebellion when she leaves for the wedding and says "I'm leaving too, by Artemis! You'll lie there all alone. It's too bad for you that you're like that. By the god, they wanted to take you, but you refused. There's something terrible in store for you, by the goddesses, much worse than what's happened now" (lines 876–78). Furthermore, the double marriage bond between the families of Knemon and Kallippides means that the consequences of Knemon's aberrant behavior will affect his extended family as well. For his own good and for the good of his nuclear and extended families, Knemon must be forced to reform himself completely.

Lowe is undoubtedly right when he says that Knemon is "made to pass voluntarily through that door, and inside the shrine to be voluntarily reintegrated into the social world and the newly extended family from which he can no longer withhold."[6] But whereas the need to reintegrate Knemon into society explains the purpose of the final scene of *Dyskolos,* it does not explain why Menander chose to accomplish this by making Knemon perform a humiliating dance with two servants. The answer lies in Menander's use of stock characters. Though usually associated with the comic theater of Rome, ancient authors indicate that stock characters were an integral part of Menandrian comedy as well. Ovid (*Ars Amatoria* 1.15.17–18) implies that stock characters formed the very heart of Menander's plays when he says that "as long as the tricky slave, the stern father, the shameless madame, and the charming courtesan live, Menander will live." Manilius (*Astronomica* 5.471–72) adds to Ovid's list "boys in love, girls carried off in the name of love, old men who have been deceived, and slaves who can accomplish anything."[7] Most of the minor characters in

6. Lowe (above, note 3), 133–34. See also W. T. MacCary, "Menander's Characters: Their Names, Roles, and Masks," *Transactions of the American Philological Association* 101 (1970): 283 and "Menander's Old Men," *Transactions of the American Philological Association* 102 (1971): 306. Van Groningen (above, note 5), 112, argues that the abuse of Knemon is justified because he must receive his just deserts for his behavior.

7. In a series of articles, MacCary suggested that personal names were associated with certain characters. See W. T. MacCary, "Menander's Slaves: Their Names, Roles, and Masks," *Transactions of the American Philological Association* 100 (1969): 277–94, (1970): 277–90, (1971): 303–25; and "Menander's Soldiers: Their Names, Roles, and Masks," *American Journal*

Dyskolos exhibit the behavior associated with stock characters. Pyrrhias, the slave who runs onstage at the beginning of the play to warn Sostratos and Chaireas of Knemon's imminent arrival, is a stock character known as the *servus currens,* "the running slave," whose primary purpose is to run onto the stage and deliver a message.[8] Simiche is one of the many slave-women in New Comedy who enter in a state of mock-tragic agitation to report on events that have occurred offstage.[9] Sostratos' father, Kallippides, who permits his son to marry a girl without a dowry and then allows himself to be talked into betrothing his own daughter to a poor farmer, plays the part of the indulgent father. Sostratos' mother is a type known as the *deisidaimon,* the overly superstitious woman.[10] Sikon, like other cooks who appear in New Comedy, is overly proud of his craft, talks constantly, and can always be counted on for comic relief.[11]

While these characters diverge little from well-established conventions, Menander will occasionally break tradition by using a technique called "cross-characterization," that is, he will transfer the characteristics associated with one stock character to another.[12] Menander appears to have employed this strategy in his depiction of Chaireas and Getas. At the beginning of the play, Sostratos is too frightened to confront Knemon on his own, so he decides to seek the aid of his father's slave Getas: "Maybe I'll go to Getas, my father's slave. Yes, by the gods, that's what I'll do! He's a spirited sort with experience in all kinds of things. He'll purge the bile out of him, I know it" (183–84). On the basis of this description, Menander's audience would have expected Getas to play the part of a stock character called the *servus callidus,* the tricky slave who

---

of Philology 93 (1972): 279–98. Against this view, see P. Brown, "Masks, Names, and Characters in New Comedy," *Hermes* 115 (1987): 181–202. Van Groningen (above, note 5), 95–112, demonstrated that minor characters in the *Dyskolos* can be identified with traditional comic stereotypes. See also MacCary (1969), 291, and E. Ramage, "City and Country in Menander's 'Dyskolos'," *Philologus* 110 (1966): 202–4.

8. E. Csapo, "Plautine Elements in the Running-Slave Entrance Monologues?," *Classical Quarterly* 39 (1989): 148–63; and MacCary (above, note 7, 1969), 291.

9. Goldberg (above, note 5), 83.

10. Theophrastus, *Characters* 16; and G. Arnott, "The Confrontation of Sostratos and Gorgias," *Phoenix* 18 (1964): 112.

11. H. Dohm, *Mageiros* (Munich, 1964).

12. G. Arnott, "Time, Plot, and Character in Menander," *Papers of the Liverpool Latin Seminar* 2 (1979): 353–55. See also Goldberg (above, note 5), 82–84, noting that Sikon has some of the characteristics of another stock character, the parasite, which the manuscript attributes to Chaireas.

helps his young master win the object of his desire.[13] But Getas proves to be a complete failure in this role; he cannot even manage to get a stewpot from Knemon, much less his daughter.[14] Menander seems to have transferred the role of the tricky slave from Getas to Chaireas, Sostratos' friend who boasts that he is expert in devising methods for obtaining lovers for his friends (57–68):

> In such matters, Sostratos, this is what I do. One of my friends who's in love with a call-girl asks for my assistance. Straight off I snatch her and carry her away—get drunk, burn down the door—I'm completely deaf to reason. You've got to get her first and ask questions later. "In sloth grows love's raging fire, but quickness leads to quenched desire." Someone mentions marriage and a free girl—I'm a different person then. I look into her family, her assets, her character. That way I've left my friend an eternal monument to my handling of his affair.

But in spite of his claims, Chaireas is no more successful in this role than is Getas—at the first sight of Knemon he hurries away and never returns. Thus, Menander has twice foiled his audience's expectation that a typical tricky slave will appear in this play, and for good reason. The subterfuge employed by the tricky slave to obtain his master's lover would be counterproductive in this play because it would confirm Gorgias' erroneous suspicions about Sostratos' character—that he is a spoiled rich boy who will use any means necessary to get what he wants from those who are poor and powerless. Instead of using trickery, Sostratos must earn the girl by persuading Gorgias that his intentions toward his half-sister are honorable. Moreover, the action of the play is being managed by Pan, who manipulates events in such a way that Sostratos will end up with Knemon's daughter. So, much to the delight of the audience, the god himself appropriates the role of the tricky slave, which is traditionally reserved for the lowest of mortals.

Just as the audience expects a certain type of behavior from stock characters, many of the characters in the play judge each other on the basis of social stereotypes. For example, the poor farmers of New Comedy are frequently depicted as bitter and misanthropic human beings, so the urban characters in *Dyskolos* attribute Knemon's behavior to the stereotypical behavior of the irascible subsistence farmer.[15] When Pyrrhias runs on stage at the beginning of the

---

13. P. Harsh, "The Intriguing Slave in Greek Comedy," *Transactions of the American Philological Association* 86 (1955): 135–42.

14. Arnott (above, note 10), 111.

15. Goldberg (above, note 5), 72–73.

play and reports that Knemon is approaching with harmful intent, Chaireas offers an instant analysis of his angry behavior based upon a stereotype: "a poor farmer is a caustic type . . . not just this one, almost all of them" (129–31). Sostratos' slave Getas resorts to the same stereotype near the end of the play to explain Knemon's irascible behavior: "What a miserable soul this man is. What a life he lives. That's an Attic farmer through and through. He makes war on rocks that produce thyme and sage and wins torment for himself. Nothing good comes of it" (603–6). Clearly, these urban characters believe that poverty has made all subsistence farmers ill-tempered. And since Menander's audience had already seen the poor farmer in countless plays, they could reasonably expect that not only Knemon but also Gorgias and Daos would conform to this stereotype.

Poor farmers stereotype wealthy urbanites as well.[16] Gorgias, who barely ekes out a living on a small farm, has a distinct bias against the rich. In his opinion, they are dissolute, corrupt, and eager to trample on those weaker than themselves without provocation.[17] Therefore, he feels confident that he can divine Sostratos' character and his intentions toward his half-sister before they exchange a single word. His critical assessment of Sostratos' character is based solely upon his outward appearance. Sostratos wears an article of clothing called the *chlanis* (χλανίς), an expensive cloak worn by rich men and women (line 257). This was clearly out of place in the country, where everyone wears work clothes. In Gorgias' eyes, such ostentatious attire marks Sostratos as rich and possibly effeminate as well.[18] This, along with the sinister look he claims to detect in Sostratos' eyes, is all that Gorgias needs to label him an evildoer (line 258). So even before they speak, Gorgias believes that he knows all he needs to know about Sostratos' character and his motives. While this appraisal is based partly upon Gorgias' misinterpretation of Sostratos' intentions toward his half-sister, it is heavily influenced by the fact that Sostratos is, in Gorgias' opinion, just another of the idle rich who care nothing about the dignity of the poor.[19]

Gorgias' bias against the rich is apparent in his speech to Sostratos (lines

---

16. Ramage (above, note 7), 194–211; and D. Del Corno, "Il problema dell'urbanismo in Menandro," *Dionisio* 43 (1969): 85–94.

17. Lowe (above, note 3), 137.

18. A. Gomme and F. Sandbach, *Menander: A Commentary* (Oxford, 1973), 177; and Handley (above, note 2), 180–81 and 193–95.

19. Arnott (above, note 10), 115–17.

271–87), which focuses on the connection between wealth and good behavior. Riches, he says, can lead one to commit crimes that bring about a decline in fortune, but a poor man will become prosperous if he keeps clear of evil. Although his argument is couched in general terms so as not to offend his social superior, its relevance to the matter at hand is clear. Gorgias thinks that this rich young man intends to violate his half-sister, so he tries to dissuade Sostratos from committing this act by appealing to what he thinks is of the utmost importance to this young man—and thereby betrays his low opinion of the rich. He does not mention Sostratos' sense of fair play or even the possible harm that this crime may do to his reputation, for he believes that these factors are of no concern to the upper class when they are intent upon doing harm to their social inferiors. Instead, he appeals to the one thing that he thinks will avert Sostratos from his evil plan: the inevitable loss of wealth that accompanies wrongdoing.[20] If this were not enough, Gorgias ends his lecture on morality with a threat: "Well, it isn't right for your leisure to cause trouble for those of us who are leisureless. Mark my words: when a poor man's been wronged, he's the bitterest man of all. First he's pitiful, then he takes all that he has suffered not as an injustice, but as a personal insult!" (lines 293–96).

In his speech, Gorgias allows that it is possible for a rich man to remain prosperous if he avoids injustice. Thus, he admits that the retention of wealth depends upon character. This concession is extremely important for the development of the play because it makes character the mediator between riches and poverty. Gorgias assumes that Sostratos is a miscreant just because he is wealthy, but Sostratos proves him wrong in a speech that not only demonstrates the depth of his love for Gorgias' half-sister, but also reveals his good character (lines 301–14):

> You're speaking before you know the whole story. I saw a girl here. I love her. If you call this an injustice, maybe I'm unjust. What's left to say except that I haven't come here to meet her—I want to see her father. I'm freeborn, wealthy enough, ready to marry her without a dowry and to swear an oath to love her forever. If I've come here for some evil purpose or intend to accomplish some evil plan behind your backs, young man, may this Pan and the nymphs strike me down now, right here by the house. Mark my words, I'm upset . . . very upset . . . if I appear to you to be that kind of person.

20. See also Arnott (above, note 10), 116.

When Gorgias puts aside his prejudices and listens to Sostratos' words, he finally realizes that riches and arrogance do not necessarily go hand in hand; apparently some of the rich do care about the feelings of the poor. Gorgias' reevaluation of Sostratos' character is validated by Sostratos' willingness to work in the fields, which prompts him to tell Knemon later in the play that Sostratos is "not the pampered kind. He's not a shiftless gadabout who strolls around all day" (lines 754–55). Gorgias gives full expression to his change of heart when he betroths his half-sister to Sostratos (lines 764–69):

> When you began this task
> you didn't hide your character; you opened up to us
> and thought this marriage worth whatever it was going to take.
> You lived in luxury, but took a mattock, dug, and worked.
> A rich man, when he acts like he's no better than the poor,
> he shows his worth and bears the twists of fate with self-control.
> You've given ample proof of this. I hope you never change.[21]

Just as Gorgias changed his mind about the rich by speaking with Sostratos, Sostratos gives up some of the stereotypes that he held concerning poor farmers when he gets to know Gorgias. Getas' expression of surprise when he sees Sostratos with Gorgias and Daos indicates that his master had up to this point little contact with those of lower social standing: "But here comes my master with his guests in tow. They're some workers from the neighborhood. Weird. Why is *he* bringing *them* here? Where did he get to know them?" (lines 607–11). Sostratos himself reveals his own preconceptions about the backwardness of country folk after he speaks to Knemon's daughter for the first time: "She's so refined for a country girl" (lines 201–2). But Sostratos' encounter with Gorgias forces him to recognize that the stereotypes associated with poor farmers are not valid. As a result, he is willing to invite Gorgias and Daos to the sacrificial feast in the cave of Pan, to marry Gorgias' half-sister without a dowry, and to persuade his father to allow Gorgias to marry into the family.

Most of the characters in this play attempt to force each other into one of two categories: the malevolent rich or the acerbic poor. However, Gorgias and Sostratos quickly discover that these stereotypes are based on superficial criteria such as clothing styles, economic status, and the location of their homes. By

21. Note that Sostratos' father turns out to have gained wealth through farming (lines 774–75).

speaking with each other, they come to realize that internal qualities determine character and that these qualities can be assessed only through social discourse. This, according to Reckford, is the chief concern of this play: "as discourse and action strip away the prejudices about character . . . true individuality shines forth and nobody is left typical."[22]

Nobody, that is, except Knemon.[23] While Gorgias and Sostratos have come to realize that the prejudices they had held of each other are not valid, Knemon stubbornly retains his biases and continues to judge others by their external appearances (lines 355–57; 753–55). His surly behavior conforms to that of the embittered subsistence farmer, a stereotype delineated by Chaireas and Gorgias. Moreover, he fits the description of another stereotype called the "grouchy man," a stock character described in a monograph on stereotypical human behavior by Theophrastus (*Characters* 15), a philosopher and contemporary of Menander:

> Grouchiness is verbal hostility in social contacts. The grouch is the sort who, when asked "Where is so-and-so?" responds "Don't bother me." If someone speaks to him he doesn't answer. . . . If people honor him by sending him some of the food on a festival day, he tells them not to expect anything in return. . . . He isn't likely to wait very long for anyone. He won't sing or recite a speech or dance. He is apt to ask for nothing—even from the gods.[24]

Pan describes Knemon in the same way in the prologue (lines 5–13):

> On the farm to my right lives Knemon, a man-shunning man indeed and grouchy to everyone. He doesn't greet the crowd of people . . . "crowd," did I say? This man's lived a fairly long time and hasn't spoken willingly to anyone, hasn't uttered the first word to anyone except me, Pan, his next-door neighbor. He only does this because he's obligated and he regrets it immediately, I'm sure.

Elsewhere in the play we see that Knemon hates to be delayed by others (lines 442–47), suspects the motives of his fellow man (lines 447–53; 718–22), and refuses to dance at the cave of Pan during his daughter's wedding. While Gorgias and Sostratos—two of the three main characters in the play—have come to realize (along with Menander's audience) that the prejudices they held about

---

22. Reckford (above, note 4), 8.

23. For Knemon as a stereotype, see W. Schmid, "Menanders Dyskolos und die Timonlegende," *Rheinisches Museum* 102 (1959): 157–82; W. Görler, "Knemon," *Hermes* 91 (1963): 268–87; and Ramage (above, note 7), 195.

24. Translated by J. Rusten in the Loeb volume.

each other are not valid, Knemon's words and behavior correspond to the patterns exhibited by a stock character. Moreover, he stubbornly retains his biases and continues to judge the other characters by their external appearances.

Knemon plays the role of the embittered subsistence farmer to the hilt, so it comes as a complete surprise when Gorgias says that Knemon is not what he seems (lines 327–37):

> His farm is worth a good deal of money. He works it all by himself without a single man to help him—not a family slave, not a hired man from the neighborhood, not a neighbor—he does it all by himself. His greatest pleasure is to see no one at all. Usually he works with his daughter at his side. He talks to her alone; he'd find it difficult to do that with anyone else. He says that he'll marry her off when he finds a groom with a personality identical to his own.

Clearly, Knemon's hard work is self-inflicted.[25] His farm is a large one, at least thirty-five acres, so he could afford to hire laborers to reduce his workload. In fact, he has more in common with Kallippides, the rich father of Sostratos whose farm is worth many talents (lines 39–41), than with a poor subsistence farmer.[26] Thus, Knemon is playing the role of a stock character and social stereotype to which he has no claim.

To make matters worse, his aberrant behavior is forcing those around him to abrogate their proper roles in society. Knemon keeps his daughter isolated from everyone by making her work in the fields like a slave and refuses to allow her to marry until he finds a husband for her with the same misanthropic disposition. As Sostratos remarks, there is little chance of him finding such a man (lines 337–38). Thus, he prohibits his daughter from playing her proper role in Athenian society: that of wife and mother. This, in turn, frustrates Pan's scheme to reward Knemon's daughter for her piety by finding her an appropriate husband. Even after Knemon allows his daughter to marry, his refusal to change his misanthropic ways bodes ill for the future harmony of the extended family (lines 902–5). For the good of everyone involved, he must be compelled to play his proper role. Menander chooses to accomplish this through dance.

In his book on Greek dance, Lounsdale noted that the ritual components of a marriage, especially the wedding dance, unite the entire community through group participation.[27] So when Knemon is forced to take part in a dance out-

---

25. Lowe (above, note 3), 131.

26. For the value of Knemon's farm, see Handley (above, note 2), 278–79, and Gomme and Sandbach (above, note 18), 187.

27. S. Lounsdale, *Dance and Ritual Play in Greek Religion* (Baltimore, 1993), 207.

side the cave where the wedding is taking place, he is compelled to participate in a communal activity that eases his transition into the extended family and effects his reintegration into society. But Knemon's dance also forces him to stop playing the inappropriate role that he has chosen for himself, a role to which he has no claim whatsoever: that of an angry subsistence farmer. The way in which Menander accomplishes this becomes clear through a careful examination of the final scene.

Getas and Sikon emerge from the cave and, after a brief exchange, agree that Knemon must be made to alter his misanthropic personality for the good of the family. But first they take turns wreaking vengeance on him for his previous abuse by making outlandish requests to borrow luxury goods that they know he does not possess: stewpots, basins, seven tripods, twelve tables, nine rugs, an imported curtain one hundred feet long, and a large bronze mixing bowl for wine. When they have had their fill of revenge, Sikon berates Knemon for his behavior (lines 931–35):

> Sit down and stop your grumbling.
> You flee the crowd, you hate the girls,
> you don't allow yourself to go
> inside when there's a sacrifice.
> You'll have to take what we dish out.
> You'll get no help. Just bite your lip
> and hear [what happened in the cave.]

Sikon proceeds to describe in great detail the wedding celebration that is taking place in the cave: the entrance of the women, the embraces, the greetings, the toasts from both sexes—in short, social activity. He saves his description of the most social event of all for last (lines 950–53):

> And then a girl,
> her face hid by the shade of her hair,
> got tipsy from the wine and stepped
> into the rhythm modestly—
> now hesitating, trembling.
> Another took her hand and danced.

To avoid boring the audience with a long descriptive speech, it is likely that Sikon's account of the activity in the cave was accompanied by miming, probably with the assistance of Getas, who would otherwise be standing around during Sikon's speech with nothing to do. The two of them may have acted out the embraces, the handshakes, the preparations for the banquet, the drinking, and finally the dance that Sikon describes in such detail.

The type of dance that Sikon and Getas perform can be discerned through two remarks that Getas makes about Sikon in the final scenes. Immediately after Sikon comes out of the cave, Getas asks him (loosely translated) τιμωρίαν βούλει λαβεῖν ὧν ἀρτίως ἔπασχες: "You want to get revenge for when he shoved you out behind?" (line 891). Thereupon, Sikon angrily retorts ἐγὼ δ' ἔπασχον ἀρτίως; οὐ λαικάσει φλυαρῶν; "For what he shoved in my behind? You lie! It's you who'd suck a cock, not me!" (line 892). These lines are confusing in English because they depend upon Sikon's misinterpretation of Getas' use of the verb πάσχειν, which has more than one meaning in Greek. When Getas asks "You want to get revenge for when he shoved you out behind," he is referring to the abuse that Sikon "suffered" or "took" back at the house of Knemon. Sikon, however, takes the verb πάσχειν in its obscene sense, "to play the passive role in a homosexual encounter," and thinks that Getas is accusing him of allowing himself to be used sexually by the men in the cave.[28] This is why Sikon replies by accusing Getas of engaging in a type of sexual behavior that the Greeks usually associated with women.[29] Getas again accuses Sikon of exhibiting feminine behavior while Sikon is describing the wedding celebration. In the midst of Sikon's account, Getas calls him μαλακὸς ἀνήρ, "a sissy" (line 945).[30] This is the first time that these characters have questioned each other's masculinity, even though they had ample opportunity to do so in previous scenes of comic relief. Therefore, these imputations of feminine behavior and their timing must be significant: they prepared the audience for the type of dance that these two characters are about to perform.

At Greek weddings, the male guests performed individual free-form acrobatic dances. The women, however, were more restricted. They performed a chain dance in which each girl grasped the wrist or hand of the dancer in front of her, thus forming a line. The success of this type of dance depends on the cooperation of each participant in carrying out standardized movements in a set sequence.[31] Any divergence from the norm would ruin the dance. Since Sikon and Getas begin their dance immediately after Sikon's description of the women's dance, it is unlikely that they performed the individual acrobatic

28. J. Henderson, *The Maculate Muse: Obscene Language in Attic Comedy* (Oxford, 1991), 153.

29. H. Jocelyn, "A Greek Indecency and Its Students: LAIKAZEIN," *Proceedings of the Cambridge Philological Seminar* 206 (1980): 12–66.

30. Handley (above, note 2), 299.

31. Handley (above, note 2), 210–18.

dances of the men. Surely they performed the chain dance of the women. When they have completed a few steps (no doubt in the most effeminate and humorous way possible), they turn to Knemon and order him to get up and dance with them. They succeed in pulling him up off his bed and force him to dance as they hold his wrists in a burlesque of the chain dance. Knemon protests, then Getas offers him the choice of staying outside the cave and receiving more abuse or going inside to the celebration. When Knemon waivers, Getas threatens to begin the dance again. Finally, Knemon decides that it would be better to go inside than to suffer this humiliation any longer, so he joins the celebration in the cave and Getas proclaims victory.

The significance of this scene to the play as a whole lies in the roles that Getas, Sikon, and Knemon play in it. At the beginning of the play, Pan deprived Getas of his role as the tricky slave, a stock character in New Comedy who abuses the character who threatens to block the successful resolution of the play. At the end of the play, Getas is allowed to resume this role because Pan has accomplished his goal: the marriage of Knemon's daughter. Sikon reminds the audience that he is the stereotypical cook of New Comedy when, in the midst of a detailed description of the preparations for the feast, he exclaims "Remember, I happen to be a cook!" (line 945). Thus, these two stock characters are entrusted with the job of overcoming Knemon, who has chosen to behave like another stock character (the poor subsistence farmer) and to judge others on the basis of stereotypes instead of joining Sostratos and Gorgias, who have given up their stereotypical views and behavior.[32] When Getas and Sikon perform the women's wedding dance, they temporarily take on another role that is not rightfully theirs. This is a common occurrence in New Comedy, where the tricky slave and his allies often take on different identities in order to defeat the blocking character. Thus, Getas and Sikon are adhering to the behavior expected of their characters when they act like women to overcome Knemon. But unlike Getas and Sikon, Knemon is a complete failure at the women's dance. They have given him the opportunity to join them in playing the part of a lower-class stock character, but he has failed.

Just as he is ill-suited for this role, he is equally ill-suited for the role of the poor farmer, another lower-class stock character to which he has no claim because he owns a fairly substantial farm. As a result, he must become more like Gorgias and Sostratos, who have broken with their stereotypes and have come to see society from a broader perspective. He must also give up his belief,

32. Goldberg (above, note 5), 84.

which he continued to hold even after his rescue from the well, that his way of life should be adopted by everyone: "If all the men on earth would simply take me as their guide, there'd be no courts, no jail time, no going off to war" (lines 742–45). While this may be Knemon's conception of an ideal world, it is also a prescription for the destruction of society. For if everyone were like Knemon, there would be no social interaction; everyone would live apart, never cooperating or even speaking with each other. This view is antithetical to the action of the play, which centers on the breaking down of social barriers and the widening of family connections. For the good of all, Knemon must be forced to give up his aberrant views and integrate himself into a family and a society that are ready to accept him.

SELECT BIBLIOGRAPHY

Menander and New Comedy:

Arnott, W. G. "From Aristophanes to Menander." *Greece and Rome* (1972): 65–80.

———. *Menander, Plautus, Terence* (Greece and Rome: New Surveys in the Classics 9). Oxford, 1975.

Brown, P. "Masks, Names, and Characters in New Comedy." *Hermes* 115 (1987): 181–202.

Goldberg, S. *The Making of Menander's Comedy.* London, 1980.

Gomme, A., and F. Sandbach. *Menander: A Commentary.* Oxford, 1973.

Handley, E. *Menander and Plautus: A Study in Comparison.* London, 1968.

Handley, E., and A. Hurst, eds. *Relire Ménandre.* Geneva, 1990.

Harsh, P. "The Intriguing Slave in Greek Comedy." *Transactions of the American Philological Association* 86 (1955): 135–42.

Hunter, R. L. *The New Comedy of Greece and Rome.* Cambridge, 1985.

MacCary, W. T. "Menander's Slaves." *Transactions of the American Philological Association* 100 (1969): 277–94.

———. "Menander's Characters." *Transactions of the American Philological Association* 101 (1970): 277–90.

———. "Menander's Old Men." *Transactions of the American Philological Association* 102 (1971): 303–25.

———. "Menander's Soldiers." *American Journal of Philology* 93 (1972): 279–98.

Sandbach, F. H. *The Comic Theatre of Greece and Rome.* London, 1977.

Turner, E., ed. *Ménandre.* Geneva, 1970.

Webster, T. B. L. *Studies in Menander,* 2d ed. Manchester, 1960.

———. *Studies in Later Greek Comedy,* 2d ed. Manchester, 1970.

———. *Introduction to Menander.* Manchester, 1974.

Wiles, D. *Masks of Menander: Sign and Meaning in Greek and Roman Performances.* Cambridge, 1991.

Dyskolos:

Anderson, Michael. "Knemon's *Hamartia.*" *Greece and Rome* 17 (1970): 199–217.

Arnott, W. G. "The Confrontation of Sostratos and Gorgias." *Phoenix* 18 (1964): 112.

———. "Time, Plot, and Character in Menander." *Papers of the Liverpool Latin Seminar* 2 (1979): 343–60.

del Corno, Dario. "Il problema dell'urbanismo in Menandro." *Dionisio* 43 (1969): 85–94.

Goldberg, S. "The Style and Function of Menander's *Dyskolos* Prologue." *Symbolae Osloenses* 53 (1978): 57–68.

van Groningen, B. "The Delineation of Character in Menander's *Dyscolus.*" *Recherches de Papyrologie* 1 (1961): 95–112.

Handley, E. *The* Dyskolos *of Menander.* Cambridge, 1965.

Ireland, S. *Menander: The Bad-Tempered Man.* Warminster, 1995.

Post, L. A. "Virtue Promoted in Menander's *Dyscolus.*" *Transactions of the American Philological Association* 91 (1960): 152–61.

Ramage, E. "City and Country in Menander's 'Dyskolos'." *Philologus* 110 (1966): 202–4.

Reckford, K. "The *Dyskolos* of Menander." *Studies in Philology* 58 (1961): 1–24.

Schäfer, A. *Menanders Dyskolos.* Meisenheim, 1965.

DYSKOLOS; OR, THE GROUCH

PAN, *a rustic god*

KNEMON, *the grouch*

KNEMON'S DAUGHTER

SIMICHE, *Knemon's old slave-woman*

GORGIAS, *Knemon's stepson*

MYRRHINE, *Gorgias' estranged wife*

DAOS, *Gorgias' slave*

SOSTRATOS, *Kallippides' son*

KALLIPPIDES, *Sostratos' father*

SOSTRATOS' MOTHER

PLANGON, *Sostratos' sister? (mute part)*

GETAS, *Sostratos' family slave*

PYRRHIAS, *Sostratos' family slave*

CHAIREAS, *Sostratos' friend*

DONAX, *a slave (mute part)*

PARTHENIS, *a flute player (mute part)*

SIKON, *a cook*

SYROS, *a slave (mute part)*

CHORUS, *a band of drunken Pan worshipers*

SCENE: *Phyle, in the countryside west of Athens. A lane runs across the stage. The exit at stage left is a public road that leads to Cholargos; at stage right are the fields. There are two buildings: at stage left stands the poor, run down home of Gorgias; at stage right the modest but well kept home of Knemon. Between these houses is the cave of Pan and the nymphs.*

Enter Pan from the cave.

PAN: Imagine this place is Phyle, part of Attica, and that I came out of the shrine of the nymphs. It belongs to the people of Phyle and to those who are able to till the stones here. It's a very famous holy place. On the farm to my right lives Knemon, a man-shunning man indeed and grouchy to everyone. He doesn't greet the crowd of people . . . "crowd," did I say? This man's lived a fairly long time and hasn't spoken willingly to anyone, hasn't uttered the first word to anyone except me, Pan, his next-door neighbor. He only does this because he's obligated and he regrets it immediately, I'm sure. But in spite of his temperament, he married a widow, whose former husband had recently died and left behind a son, who was a little boy at the time. Arguing with her not only during the day but most of the night as well made his life miserable. A daughter was born—even worse. When it got so bad that there was no hope for improvement and life became painful and bitter, the woman went back again to the son she'd had earlier. He owns a small piece of land here in the neighborhood that now barely supports his mother, himself, and one faithful family slave. Now he's a fine boy with wisdom beyond his years; experience makes you grow up fast. The old man lives alone with his daughter and an old slave woman carrying wood, digging, always working. From the neighbors and his wife over here all the way to the town of Cholargos down there—he hates everyone without exception. But the girl mirrors her upbringing: there's not a mean bone in her body. Her utmost concern is to be gracious to the nymphs who live with me and to revere them, and so she's inspired in us some concern for her. There's a young man with a very rich father, who farms a plot of land here that's worth a great deal of money. The boy spends his time in the city, but he came out to hunt with a certain sportsman friend. When he chanced upon this place, I took control of him and made him fall in love. That's the long and the short of it. As for the rest, you'll see it if you want. I hope you do. In fact, I think I see that young lover coming here with his sportsman friend, sharing something with each other about this situation.

Exit Pan into the cave.

Enter Sostratos and Chaireas stage right.

CHAIREAS: What are you saying? You saw a freeborn girl from here crowning the nymphs next door, Sostratos, and you fell in love at first sight?

SOSTRATOS: At first sight.

CHAIREAS: That was quick. Or had you planned on falling in love with someone when you left home?

SOSTRATOS: You're making fun of me. Chaireas, I feel terrible.

CHAIREAS: Oh, I don't doubt it.

SOSTRATOS: That's why I've come and brought you in on this business; I thought you were both a friend and, most important, a man who can deal with any situation.

CHAIREAS: In such matters, Sostratos, this is what I do. One of my friends who's in love with a call-girl asks for my assistance. Straight off I snatch her and carry her away—get drunk, burn down the door—I'm completely deaf to reason. You've got to get her first and ask questions later. "In sloth grows love's raging fire, but quickness leads to quenched desire." Someone mentions marriage and a free girl—I'm a different person then. I look into her family, her assets, her character. That way I've left my friend an eternal monument to my handling of his affair.

SOSTRATOS: Very good! *(aside)* But I don't like it at all.

CHAIREAS: And in this situation we have to hear the facts first.

SOSTRATOS: At dawn I sent Pyrrhias, my hunting companion, from home . . .

CHAIREAS: To whom?

SOSTRATOS: To meet the girl's father himself or the head of the family, whoever he is.

CHAIREAS: Herakles! What are you saying?!

SOSTRATOS: I made a mistake. Maybe it wasn't a job for a slave. But it isn't easy to know what's best when you're in love. I wonder what's taking Pyrrhias so long. I told him to come home right after he got the information for me.

Enter Pyrrhias stage left.

PYRRHIAS: Gangway! Watch out! Everybody get out of the way! He's crazy . . . the man who's chasing me . . . he's crazy!

SOSTRATOS: What's going on, boy?

PYRRHIAS: Run for your lives!

SOSTRATOS: What is it?

PYRRHIAS: I'm getting hit with dirt-clods . . . with rocks! I'm done for!

SOSTRATOS: You're getting hit? Where are you going, you maniac?

PYRRHIAS: Maybe he's not chasing me anymore.

SOSTRATOS: No, by Zeus.

PYRRHIAS: But I thought he was.

SOSTRATOS: What are you talking about?

PYRRHIAS: Let's get out of here. I'm begging you!

SOSTRATOS: And go where?

PYRRHIAS: As far away from that door as possible! You sent me to the son of Pain or somebody possessed by demons or a lunatic who lives in that house. Oh, this is big trouble! I've stubbed and broken almost every one of my toes!

SOSTRATOS: Oh, Herakles! What's he done, coming here and pulling some drunken trick?

CHAIREAS: He's out of his mind. Anybody can see that.

PYRRHIAS: By Zeus, Sostratos, I'd rather be utterly exterminated! Keep a lookout just the same. . . . But I can't talk. . . . I can't catch my breath. . . . I knocked on the door of his house and said I was looking for the master. Some old woman answered the door, stood as far from me as you are now, and pointed him out up on the hill there, going around his damn pears or gathering up a back-breaking heap of gallows wood.

CHAIREAS: Such anger! What's wrong, my good man?

PYRRHIAS: I stepped onto his land and walked toward him. When I was still some distance from him—I wanted to be friendly and tactful—I spoke to him: "I've come about something, sir," I say, "to see you about something, to promote some business that's to your benefit." But he shoots back, "You heathen, you're on my land! What's the idea?" He picks up a dirt-clod and heaves it right into my face!

CHAIREAS: Go to hell!

PYRRHIAS: While I shut my eyes and said, "Poseidon damn you," he picks up a stake again. He kept beating me with it while he said, "What's your business with me? Don't you know where the public road is?" He was shouting at the top of his lungs.

CHAIREAS: You're talking as though this farmer's a perfect madman!

PYRRHIAS: Here's how it ended. I ran and he chased me maybe two miles— first around the hill then right down into this woods, all the while throwing dirt-clods, rocks, even pears when he ran out of everything else. A savage piece of work, an absolute heathen, that farmer. I'm begging you, get out of here!

SOSTRATOS: You're talking like a coward.

PYRRHIAS: You don't understand the trouble we're in. He'll eat us alive!

CHAIREAS: Perhaps he was upset about something just now. That's why I think we should put off seeing him, Sostratos. You know perfectly well that proper timing is most efficacious in every matter.

PYRRHIAS: Think about it.

CHAIREAS: A poor farmer is a caustic type . . . not just this one, almost all of them. But tomorrow morning I'll go to him alone, since I know where he lives. Now you go home too and wait. It'll be alright.

PYRRHIAS: Let's do that.

Exit Chaireas stage right.

SOSTRATOS: He's happy to have found an excuse. It was clear from the beginning that he wasn't overjoyed to come with me and didn't think much
of my plan to marry. *(to Pyrrhias)* As for you, may all the gods destroy you,
you fool!

PYRRHIAS: What did I do wrong, Sostratos?

SOSTRATOS: It's obvious that you tore up his land or stole something.

PYRRHIAS: I stole something?

SOSTRATOS: You mean to tell me that someone lashed out at you when you
did nothing wrong?

PYRRHIAS: Yes, and here he is! *(to Knemon)* I'm leaving, sir. *(to Sostratos)* You
talk to him!

Exit Pyrrhias stage right.

Enter Knemon stage left.

SOSTRATOS: I couldn't. I never get anywhere when I start talking. How
would you describe a man like that? He doesn't look to me like a very char-
itable sort, by Zeus. He's definitely got his mind on something. I'll move
away from his door a little. That's better. He's walking by himself, but he's
yelling. Looks to me like he's out of his mind. By Apollo and the gods, he
scares me! Why shouldn't I be honest?

KNEMON: *(to the audience)* Well, wasn't Perseus lucky, and for two reasons at
that: because he had wings so he didn't meet up with any of those pedes-
trians on the ground and because he had something that turned everybody
who pestered him into stone! I wish I had one now. Then there'd be no
shortage of statues anywhere! But now life's unbearable, by Asclepius.
They come onto my land . . . and talk! Oh sure, I'm in the habit, by Zeus,
of wasting my time on the side of this road. I don't even work this piece of
land! I've abandoned it because of all the traffic! Now they're chasing me
up to the hilltops. The immeasurably immense crowd! *(sees Sostratos)* Oh,
no, not again! Somebody's at our door!

SOSTRATOS: *(aside)* Is he going to hit me?

KNEMON: A man can't be alone anywhere, even if he's of a mind to hang
himself!

SOSTRATOS: *(aside)* Is it me he's angry with? *(to Knemon)* Sir, I'm waiting here
for somebody. I made an appointment.

KNEMON: Didn't I tell you? Do you people think this is a thoroughfare or a public park? If you want to see somebody, arrange to meet him in my doorway. Better yet, build a bench, if you like. No, no . . . a town hall! *(to himself)* Ah, me! Malicious interference . . . that's the problem in my opinion!

Exit Knemon into his house.

SOSTRATOS: It seems that this is going to take more effort than you'd think. No doubt about it. Maybe I'll go to Getas, my father's slave. Yes, by the gods, that's what I'll do! He's a spirited sort with experience in all kinds of things. He'll purge the bile out of him, I know it. I've made up my mind not to waste any time in this matter. A lot can happen in one day. Someone's opening the door!

Enter Knemon's daughter from Knemon's house.

KNEMON'S DAUGHTER: Oh, no. I'm in trouble now. What'll I do? While the nurse was hauling up the bucket, she dropped it in the well!

SOSTRATOS: *(aside)* Father Zeus and Phoebus the Healer and beloved Dioscuroi, what irresistible beauty!

KNEMON'S DAUGHTER: When Daddy came inside, he told me to heat up some water.

SOSTRATOS: *(aside)* Audience, she's a vision!

KNEMON'S DAUGHTER: If he finds out about this, he'll beat her to within an inch of her life! I don't have time to stand around babbling. Dearest nymphs, I'll have to get the water from you. I'd be ashamed to barge in if there's a sacrifice going on in there.

SOSTRATOS: If you give me the water jar, I'll dip it in and bring it right back to you.

KNEMON'S DAUGHTER: By the gods, yes! But hurry!

SOSTRATOS: *(aside)* She's so refined for a country girl. Honored gods, which of you could save me?

Exit Sostratos into the cave.

KNEMON'S DAUGHTER: Oh, no! I'm done for! Who made that noise? Is Daddy coming? I'll get a spanking if he catches me outside!

Exit Knemon's daughter into the cave.

Enter Daos from Gorgias' house.

DAOS: *(shouting back to Gorgias' mother in the house)* I've wasted plenty of time serving you here while he's been digging all alone. I have to go to him. O Poverty, the most destructive goddess of all, why are we so poor? Why have you squatted in our house for such a long time without a break?

Enter Sostratos and Knemon's daughter from the cave.

SOSTRATOS: Take it.
KNEMON'S DAUGHTER: Bring it over here.
DAOS: *(aside)* What does that guy want?
SOSTRATOS: Goodbye. And take care of your father.

Exit Knemon's daughter into Knemon's house.

Oh, I'm miserable! Stop whining, Sostratos. It'll all work out.
DAOS: *(aside)* What will work out?
SOSTRATOS: Don't panic. Do what you were going to do just now. Get Getas, bring him back, and explain the whole thing to him clearly.

Exit Sostratos stage right.

DAOS: Something bad is happening . . . what is it? I don't like this at all. A young man is serving a girl. Nothing good can come of that. As for you, Knemon, you bastard . . . may all the gods blast you! You let an innocent girl go out alone in an isolated place without giving her the proper protection. Maybe this man found out about it and sneaked up here, thinking it was his lucky day. No doubt about it; I have to tell her brother as quickly as I can so we can keep an eye on the girl. I'd better go and do it now. I see some people coming this way—some Pan worshipers—and they're a little drunk. I don't think this is a good time to get in their way.

Exit Daos stage left.

The Chorus of Pan worshipers enters for a musical interlude.
After the Chorus exits, Gorgias and Daos enter stage left in midconversation on the way to Knemon's house.

GORGIAS: But tell me, did you really treat this matter indifferently and trivially?
DAOS: What do you mean?
GORGIAS: By Zeus, you should have seen the man who approached the girl, Daos, whoever he was, right away and told him that, from now on, no one will see him doing that again. But instead you stayed out of it as if it were none of your business. In my opinion, you can't escape family ties, Daos.

My sister is my responsibility. Her father doesn't want anything to do with us. We shouldn't copy his sour attitude. If she's disgraced, so am I. Outsiders don't know who is to blame; they just know what happened. Let's knock.

DAOS: But sir . . . Gorgias, I'm afraid of the old man. If he catches me coming up to his door, he'll hang me on the spot!

GORGIAS: Yes. If you struggle with him, he won't budge. There's no way that anyone will force him to improve or change his ways by giving him advice [like a friend].[1] Against force he has the law, against persuasion . . . his disposition.

Enter Sostratos stage right.

DAOS: Wait a minute. We didn't come here for nothing. Didn't I tell you? He's coming back again.

GORGIAS: The one with the expensive cloak? He's the one you're talking about?

DAOS: He's the one.

GORGIAS: He's up to no good. You can tell straight off by the look in his eyes.

SOSTRATOS: I found out that Getas wasn't in the house and that my mother was going to sacrifice to some god; I don't know which one. She does this every day—goes around the whole town sacrificing. She sent Getas out to hire some cook from around here. I said "so long" to that sacrifice and came back here again. I think the best plan is to stop this wandering around and speak for myself. I'll knock on the door. That will put an end to this constant waffling.

GORGIAS: Young man, would you be willing to listen to some rather serious advice from me?

SOSTRATOS: Yes, gladly. Go ahead.

GORGIAS: There exists, I believe, for all human beings—both the successes and the ones having a difficult time—a limit and a change to their lot in life. For the fortunate man, his prosperous life continues to flourish only so long as he can accept his good fortune without doing anything unjust. But when his wealth induces him to do wrong, then there is a change for the worse. But for those who are needy, if they do nothing evil while they are in dire straits and bear their fate bravely, then in time they gain credit and expect their lot to improve. So what am I saying? If you are very rich,

---

1. Brackets indicate that part of the papyrus is lost and that a conjectural restoration has been made by the translator.

don't rely on it and don't look down your nose at those of us stricken by poverty. Show the public that you deserve your good luck to continue.

SOSTRATOS: Do you think I'm doing something now that's out of place?

GORGIAS: You seem to me to have set your mind on a disgraceful act. You intend to persuade a freeborn girl to make a terrible mistake, or you're looking for a chance to accomplish something worthy of death many times over.

SOSTRATOS: Apollo!

GORGIAS: Well, it isn't right for your leisure to cause trouble for those of us who are leisureless. Mark my words: when a poor man's been wronged, he's the bitterest man of all. First he's pitiful, then he takes all that he's suffered not as an injustice, but as a personal insult!

SOSTRATOS: Young man, please, listen to me for a minute.

DAOS: Well said, master. Bless you!

SOSTRATOS: You're speaking before you know the whole story. I saw a girl here. I love her. If you call this an injustice, maybe I'm unjust. What's left to say except that I haven't come here to meet her—I want to see her father. I'm freeborn, wealthy enough, ready to marry her without a dowry and to swear an oath to love her forever. If I've come here for some evil purpose or intend to accomplish some evil plan behind your backs, young man, may this Pan and the nymphs strike me down now, right here by the house. Mark my words, I'm upset . . . very upset . . . if I appear to you to be that kind of person.

GORGIAS: Well, if I spoke more forcefully than necessary, don't let it bother you any longer. You've changed my mind about this and you have me on your side, too. I'm telling you this, my friend, not as an impartial observer, but as the girl's half-brother.

SOSTRATOS: By Zeus, you'll be useful to me with what comes next!

GORGIAS: What do you mean by "useful"?

SOSTRATOS: I see that you're a man of good character . . .

GORGIAS: I don't want to send you off with some lame excuse but to make it perfectly clear how things stand. Her father is like no man, dead or alive.

SOSTRATOS: He's difficult. I know that well enough.

GORGIAS: He's the epitome of trouble! His farm is worth a good deal of money. He works it all by himself without a single man to help him—not a family slave, not a hired man from the neighborhood, not a neighbor— he does it all by himself. His greatest pleasure is to see no one at all. Usually he works with his daughter at his side. He talks to her alone. He'd find it difficult to do that with anyone else. He says that he'll marry her off when he finds a groom with a personality identical to his own.

SOSTRATOS: That'll be never!

GORGIAS: Don't cause trouble for yourself, friend, because you'll be wasting your time. Let those of us who are his relatives bear this burden. It's our fate.

SOSTRATOS: By the gods, young man, haven't you ever been in love?

GORGIAS: That's not an option for me, friend.

SOSTRATOS: Why? Who's stopping you?

GORGIAS: Keeping track of my problems leaves no time at all for diversions.

SOSTRATOS: It's obvious to me that you haven't been in love. Even the way you talk about it is so naive. You urge me to give up. That's no longer in my hands, but in the hands of the god.

GORGIAS: So then you're not wronging us, just torturing yourself pointlessly.

SOSTRATOS: Not if I get the girl!

GORGIAS: You won't get her. [I'll prove it to you.] Follow me. Her father works in the valley near us.

SOSTRATOS: How will you prove it?

GORGIAS: I'll mention something about the marriage of his daughter. Personally, I'd be happy to see such a thing happen. Straight off he'll attack everybody, finding fault with the lives they lead. If he sees you pampered and living a life of leisure, he'll refuse even to look at you.

SOSTRATOS: Is he there now?

GORGIAS: No, by Zeus, but a little later he'll come out on his usual route.

SOSTRATOS: My good friend, are you saying he'll bring the girl with him?

GORGIAS: Maybe, maybe not.

SOSTRATOS: I'm ready to go wherever you say. But I'm begging you—help me out.

GORGIAS: How?

SOSTRATOS: How? Let's go to the field.

DAOS: What? You're going to stand next to us in that expensive cloak while we work?

SOSTRATOS: Why not?

DAOS: Straight off he'll throw those clods of his at you and call you a lazy pest. No, you have to dig with us. If he happens to see this, he might put up with a little conversation—even with you—because he thinks you live the life of a poor farmer.

SOSTRATOS: *(Removes his cloak)* I'm ready to put myself completely under your command. Lead on.

GORGIAS: Why are you forcing yourself to suffer?

DAOS: *(aside)* I want us to work as much as possible today and for him to break his back at the same time. Then he'll stop annoying us and coming around here.

SOSTRATOS: Bring out a mattock.

DAOS: Take mine and go. In the meantime, I'll rebuild the fence. That has to be done, too.

SOSTRATOS: Give it to me. *(to Gorgias)* You've saved my life!

DAOS: I'm going, master. You two follow me there.

Exit Daos stage left.

SOSTRATOS: This is how things stand with me: I must die now in the attempt or get the girl and live.

GORGIAS: If you mean what you say, good luck!

Exit Gorgias stage left.

SOSTRATOS: O much honored gods! Those arguments that you used just now to change my mind—or so you thought—have made me twice as eager to act! If the girl hasn't been brought up around women, doesn't know about life's vices and hasn't been terrified by an aunt or grandmother, but was raised nobly with a rustic, vice-hating father, how is it not a blessing to win her?

But this mattock weighs a ton! It'll kill me! Nevertheless, I must not weaken once I've begun to wear myself out at this.

Exit Sostratos stage left.

Enter Sikon stage right.

SIKON: This sheep's no ordinary beauty . . . damn it to hell! If I pick it up and carry it in the air, it chomps on the olive shoots, eats the leaves on the fig branches, and wrenches itself out of my hands. But if you let it down on the ground, it won't walk. Talk about role reversals: I'm the cook, but I'm being cut to pieces by this sheep while I tug it down the road like a barge. What luck! Here's the cave of the nymphs where we'll sacrifice. Hello, Pan!

Hey, slave! Getas! Why are you so far behind?

Enter Getas stage right.

GETAS: Those damn women tied up a four-donkey load for me to carry!

SIKON: It looks like a big crowd's coming. The number of rugs you're carrying is unbelievable!

GETAS: What [do I do now?]

SIKON: Lean them over here.

GETAS: *(puts down the rugs)* There. If she had a dream about that cave of Pan
twenty miles from here, I know we'd head straight over there to sacrifice.

SIKON: Who had a dream?

GETAS: Please, don't bother me.

SIKON: Tell me anyway, Getas. Who had it?

GETAS: My mistress.

SIKON: By the gods, what was it?

GETAS: You're killing me! It seemed that Pan . . .

SIKON: Are you talking about this one?

GETAS: This one.

SIKON: What was he doing?

GETAS: My master, Sostratos . . .

SIKON: A fine young man, indeed!

GETAS: He was putting leg irons on him.

SIKON: Apollo!

GETAS: Then he gave him work clothes and a mattock and ordered him to dig
on his neighbor's property.

SIKON: Weird!

GETAS: And that's why we're sacrificing, to make this bad dream have a happy
ending.

SIKON: I understand. Pick all this stuff up again and carry it inside. Let's prepare the couches in there and get everything else ready. Nothing must stand
in the way of the sacrifice when they get here. I hope everything turns out
alright. And stop making faces, you poor put-upon man. I'll give you a
proper feeding today.

GETAS: I'm a fan of you and your profession—always have been . . . *(aside)*
but I don't believe you for a minute.

Exit Getas and Sikon into the cave.

The Chorus enters for a musical interlude.
Enter Knemon from his house, shouting back to Simiche.

KNEMON: Old woman! Shut the door and don't open it for anyone until I
come back here again. That'll be when it's pitch black, I think.

Enter Sostratos' mother, Plangon, and Parthenis stage right.

SOSTRATOS' MOTHER: Plangon, come quickly! We should have finished the
    sacrifice by now.
KNEMON: What's the meaning of this mischief? A crowd! Damn them to hell!
SOSTRATOS' MOTHER: Parthenis, play the hymn of Pan. They say you
    shouldn't approach this god in silence.

Enter Getas from the cave.

GETAS: By Zeus, you've arrived safely.
KNEMON: Herakles, how annoying!
GETAS: We've been sitting around waiting for such a long time.
SOSTRATOS' MOTHER: Is everything ready for us?
GETAS: Yes, by Zeus. The sheep is, anyway.
SOSTRATOS' MOTHER: Poor thing, it's almost dead. It can't wait for you to
    get started. Come inside. Bring the baskets and the holy water. Prepare the
    sacrificial cakes.

Exit Sostratos' mother, Plangon, and Parthenis into the cave.

GETAS: *(to Knemon)* What are you gawking at, you idiot?

Exit Getas into the cave.

KNEMON: *(to the group as they enter the cave)* To hell with you bastards!
    At the very least, they're making me lounge around here. There's no
    way I could leave my house unattended. As far as I'm concerned, nymphs
    are always problem neighbors. It's gotten so bad I think I'll have to tear
    down my house and move away from here.
    Look at those thieves sacrifice. They're carrying food baskets and wine
    jars—it's not for the gods, but for themselves. Incense and sacrificial cakes
    are holy; the god gets it all when it's put on the fire. But the tail and the
    spleen go to the gods because they're inedible . . . and they eat the rest!
    Old woman, hurry up and open the door. It looks to me like we have
    to work inside.

Exit Knemon into his house.

Enter Getas from the cave, shouting back inside.

GETAS: You're telling me you forgot the stewpot? You all act like you're sleep-

ing off a hangover! So what'll we do now? We have to go bother the god's
neighbors, it seems.

Getas knocks on Knemon's door.

SLAVE!
    By the gods, there aren't more worthless slavegirls anywhere, in my
opinion.
    SLAVES!
    The only thing they know how to do is get screwed.
    GOOD SLAVES!
    And to lie about it if somebody finds out.
    SLAVE!
    What the hell is going on here?
    SLAVES!
    Not a single person is inside. Huh? Seems that someone's running to-
ward the door.

Enter Knemon from his house.

KNEMON: Why are you beating on the door, you bastard? Speak up, man!
GETAS: Don't bite me!
KNEMON: By Zeus, I'll eat you alive!
GETAS: No, by the gods!
KNEMON: Do we have business with each other, you heathen?
GETAS: No business. I haven't come here to recover a debt or with witnesses
    to serve a summons, but to ask for a stewpot.
KNEMON: A stewpot?!
GETAS: A stewpot.
KNEMON: You scum! Do you think I sacrifice cattle and do all those things
    that you all do?
GETAS: I don't think you'd even sacrifice a snail! Well, goodbye, sir. The
    women ordered me to knock on your door and ask you. I did it. You don't
    have one. I'll go and report back to them. *(aside)* Much honored gods, that
    man's a gray-haired old viper!

Exit Getas into the cave.

KNEMON: Homicidal beasts! They come right up and knock on my door as
    though I were a friend. If I catch one of them coming toward my door and

don't make an example of him for everyone around here, consider me a no-body! That man doesn't know how lucky he was . . . whoever he was.

Exit Knemon into his house.

Enter Sikon from the cave, shouting back at Getas.

SIKON: Damn you to hell! He yelled at you? Maybe you asked in a demand-ing tone of voice, you shit-eater. Some people don't know how to go about such things. I've discovered the proper technique. I serve thousands in the city. I bother their neighbors and get equipment from everybody. You have to kiss ass when you need something. Some older fellow answers the knock at the door. Straight off I call him "father" and "dad." An old woman: "mother." If it's a middle-aged woman, I call her "priestess." If a slave, I call him "sir." You all can go hang yourselves. Oh, the stupidity! You all shout for a slave. But I say, "Come out, Daddy, I want you!"

Enter Knemon from his house.

KNEMON: You again?!
SIKON: Oh, boy! What's this?
KNEMON: You're provoking me on purpose. Didn't I tell you to stay away from my door? Give me a strap, old woman!

Knemon grabs Sikon.

SIKON: No way! Let go!
KNEMON: Let go?
SIKON: Yes sir, by the gods!
KNEMON: Come back!

Knemon hits Sikon.

SIKON: May Poseidon . . .
KNEMON: Are you still blabbering?
SIKON: I came to ask you for a pot.
KNEMON: I don't have a pot or an ax or salt or vinegar or anything else. I al-ready told everybody in the neighborhood to stay away from me!
SIKON: You didn't tell me.
KNEMON: Well, I'm telling you now.
SIKON: *(aside)* Yes, and you're going to be sorry! *(to Knemon)* Tell me, couldn't you say where a person could go and get one?

KNEMON: Didn't I tell you? Are you still blabbering to me?

SIKON: A hearty farewell!

KNEMON: I don't want a "farewell" from any of you.

SIKON: Fare badly, then.

KNEMON: Oh, the incurable evils!

Exit Knemon into his house.

SIKON: He really plowed into me! It *is* possible to ask skillfully. It does make a difference, by Zeus. Should I go to somebody else's door? But if they're so ready for boxing practice in this place, it'll be painful. Is it best for me to roast all the meat? It looks like it. I've got a fish pan! Go to hell, people of Phyle—that's what I say. I'll use what I've got.

Exit Sikon into the cave.

Enter Sostratos stage left.

SOSTRATOS: Whoever's free of trouble should come hunting in Phyle. I'm a total wreck: my tailbone, my back, my neck . . . my whole body when you come right down to it!

I threw myself into it straight off with the vigor of a young man. I swung the mattock up with gusto and, just like a workman, I slammed it down deep into the dirt. I pressed on with my mind on the work, but not too long. Then I'd turn around a little to see when the old man would come with the girl. And then, by Zeus, I'd rub my lower back—secretly at first. But when the work went on and on with no end in sight, my spine started to bow. Little by little I became as stiff as a board. No one was coming. The sun was beating down on me. Gorgias looked over and saw my whole body swaying back and forth like a tree in a windstorm. "It doesn't look like he's coming, young man," he said. "So what should we do," I replied, "look for him tomorrow and give up for now?" Daos arrived to take over the digging. Such was our first attempt. So I've come here . . . why, I can't say, by the gods. But this situation I'm in seems to draw me back here on its own.

Enter Getas from the cave, shouting back into it.

GETAS: What the hell? Do you think I've got sixty hands? I fire up the charcoal, I take the guts from you, I carry them off, I clean them, I cut them up. I knead the dough, I get the pots ready. I've been completely blinded by smoke. A fine holiday this is!

SOSTRATOS: Getas!

GETAS: Who's calling me?

SOSTRATOS: I am.

GETAS: And who are you?

SOSTRATOS: Don't you see me?

GETAS: I see. It's my master.

SOSTRATOS: What are you doing here? Tell me.

GETAS: What am I doing? We've just sacrificed and we're getting lunch ready
for all of you.

SOSTRATOS: Is mother here?

GETAS: For a long time.

SOSTRATOS: And father?

GETAS: We're expecting him. But come on inside.

SOSTRATOS: After I've run an errand. In a way, the sacrifice in there hasn't
come at a bad time. I'll invite that young man right away and his servant,
too. After they've shared the offerings, they'll be more useful allies later
on for the marriage.

GETAS: What are you saying? You're going to go and invite somebody to
lunch? Make it three thousand as far as I'm concerned! I've known for a
long time that I'm not going to get so much as a taste. How could I? Bring
them all here. You've sacrificed a beautiful animal, a fine thing to see. But
these females . . . oh, sure, they're polite, but would they give me anything? By Demeter, they wouldn't even give me a pinch of bitter salt!

SOSTRATOS: All will go well today, Getas. I predict it myself, Pan. I always
pray to you as I go by . . . and I'll be kind to my fellow man.

Exit Sostratos stage left.

Enter Simiche from Knemon's house.

SIMICHE: Oh, no! Oh, no! Oh, no!

GETAS: Oh, hell. The old man's woman has come outside.

SIMICHE: What will happen to me? I wanted to haul the bucket out of the
well myself, if I could do it somehow without the master knowing about
it. I tied the mattock to a weak, rotten piece of rope and it broke on me
straight away. Poor me, I've let the mattock drop right into the well along
with the bucket.

GETAS: There's one thing left to do: throw yourself in.

SIMICHE: And just my luck, he wants to move some dung piled up inside.

He's been running around for a long time looking for it and shouting
and—I hear the door!

GETAS: Run, you pitiful woman, run! He'll kill you, old woman! Better yet,
fight him off!

Enter Knemon from his house, holding a rotten piece of rope.

KNEMON: Where's that thieving woman?

SIMICHE: I dropped it in, master, but it was an accident!

KNEMON: Get inside!

SIMICHE: What are you going to do? Tell me!

KNEMON: What am I going to do? I'm going to tie you up and send you down
on a rope.

SIMICHE: No, don't! Oh, poor me.

KNEMON: And with this very rope, by the gods!

GETAS: An excellent idea . . . that is, if the rope is completely rotten.

SIMICHE: Shall I call Daos from next door?

KNEMON: You'll call Daos after you've done me in, you heathen? Didn't I tell
you? Get inside . . . fast!

Exit Simiche into Knemon's house.

I'm done for, done for, all because of the solitary life I'm now [living].
There's not a single person [to help me]. I'll go down into the well. What
else can I do?

GETAS: We'll provide a hook and a rope.

KNEMON: May the gods doubly destroy you if you blabber anything to me.

GETAS: And I'd deserve it, too.

Exit Knemon into his house.

He burst inside again. What a miserable soul this man is. What a life he
lives. That's an Attic farmer through and through. He makes war on rocks
that produce thyme and sage and wins torment for himself. Nothing good
comes of it.

Enter Sostratos, Gorgias, and Daos stage left with their mattocks.

But here comes master with his guests in tow. They're some workers from
the neighborhood. Weird. Why is *he* bringing *them* here? Where did he get
to know them?

Exit Getas into the cave.

SOSTRATOS: I wouldn't let you do otherwise. We have everything we need. Herakles, who in the world rejects a lunch invitation out of hand from a friend who's made a sacrifice? Have no doubt that I was your friend long before you realized it.

Daos, take these things and put them inside your house, then come on over.

GORGIAS: Don't leave mother home alone. See to whatever she needs. I'll be back soon.

Exit Daos into the house of Gorgias.

Exit Sostratos and Gorgias into the cave.

The Chorus enters for a musical interlude.

Enter Simiche from Knemon's house.

SIMICHE: Somebody help! Oh, poor me. Somebody help!

Enter Sikon from the cave.

SIKON: Lord Herakles! By the gods and spirits, let us make our offerings! You abuse us, you beat us, you . . . go to hell! What a weird house.

SIMICHE: The master is in the well.

SIKON: How?

SIMICHE: How? He was climbing down to drag out the mattock and the bucket, then he slipped on the way down, and now he's fallen.

SIKON: Not that old monster? Well done, by Heaven. Dearest old woman, now it's up to you.

SIMICHE: How?

SIKON: Take a mortar or a rock or some such thing and throw it down the well!

SIMICHE: Dearest man, climb down the well.

SIKON: Poseidon! You want me to fight with that dog in the well? I know how that story ends. No way!

SIMICHE: Gorgias, where in the world are you?

Enter Gorgias from the cave.

GORGIAS: Where in the world am *I*? What is it, Simiche?

SIMICHE: What is it? I'll say it again: the master is in the well.

GORGIAS: Sostratos, come here!

Enter Sostratos from the cave.

> *(to Simiche)* Lead the way. Go inside. Hurry!

Exit Simiche, Sostratos, and Gorgias into the house of Knemon.

SIKON: The gods do exist, by Dionysos! You didn't give a stewpot to the sacrificers, you sacrilegious bastard. No, you refused. You fell into the well, now drink it dry so you won't have water to give to anybody. Now the nymphs have taken vengeance on him for me, and rightly so. Nobody hurts a cook and gets away with it. Our trade is somehow sacred. But as far as waiters go, do whatever you want with them . . .

Surely he hasn't died? Some woman is moaning, crying for daddy dearest. [No, wait! They're cries of joy. Now it's all] clear. [He hasn't died after all. They must be] hauling him up [with a new piece of rope. I can just see it now—] oh, the sight of him! By the gods, can you imagine what a drenched, shivering, [pathetic fool he'll be]? Fabulous! *(speaking to the audience while pointing to a small representation of Apollo in the area)* I'd like to see that, audience, I swear by this Apollo here! *(shouting into the cave)* You, women! Pour an offering on behalf of the rescuers. Pray that the old man's salvation be . . . denied, that he be maimed and lame! Then he'll be the least objectionable neighbor to the god and to those who are always sacrificing here. That's important to me, in case anyone ever hires me.

Exit Sikon into the cave.

Enter Sostratos from Knemon's house.

SOSTRATOS: Oh audience! By Demeter! By Asclepius! By the gods! Never in my life have I seen a man almost get himself drowned at a more convenient time! What a delightful diversion! The minute we got inside, Gorgias jumped straight into the well. But the girl and I stayed up above and did . . . nothing! What did you expect us to do? Well, she tore out her hair, cried, beat her breast ferociously. But I, precious idiot that I was, stood there next to her, by the gods, like some kind of a nanny. I begged her not to do this, I pleaded with her, fixing my eyes on that extraordinary work of art. I couldn't have cared less about that injured man down there, except for constantly having to haul him up! That was really tedious. By Zeus, I almost finished him off on my own! While I was staring at the girl, I let go of the rope . . . maybe three times! But Gorgias wasn't your ordinary At-

las. He held on and finally managed to get him up to the top. As the old
man emerged, I came out here. I couldn't hold myself back any longer. I almost went up to the girl and gave her a kiss! That's how madly in love I am.
I'm getting ready to—the door is opening! Zeus the Savior, what a weird
sight!

*Enter Gorgias, Knemon, and Knemon's daughter from Knemon's house; Knemon may have
been carried on a stretcherlike bed.*

GORGIAS: What do you want, Knemon? Tell me.
KNEMON: What's there to say? I feel terrible.
GORGIAS: Cheer up.
KNEMON: I *have* cheered up. Knemon will no longer be a bother to you in the
     future.
GORGIAS: Do you see what trouble isolation brings? You came within a hair's
     breadth of dying just now. At your age, you ought to live out your life with
     someone to watch over you.
KNEMON: I know I'm in bad shape. But call your mother, Gorgias. It's urgent.

Exit Gorgias into his house.

     Only disasters can teach us, it seems. Little daughter, would you hold me
     and help me stand up?
SOSTRATOS: Lucky man!
KNEMON: Why are you standing over there, you low-life scum?

Enter Gorgias and Myrrhine.

     [I think it's time to tell you all about the plan I've made,
     about the way I've led my life and how it's going to change.
     I used to farm my land alone all day from dawn to dusk.
     My fields gave me solitude, a refuge from the crowds.
     But now that I'm a broken man, I'm forced to give this up.]
     Not one of you could change my mind. You have to let me be.

     I made just one mistake: I thought that I could live alone,
     that I'm the only man on earth who needed no one else.
     But now I know the end of life is swift and unforeseen.
     I've come to realize that I was wrong as I could be.
     You've got to have someone nearby to lend a helping hand.

Hephaistos! When I watched the way they act, it threw me off.
When profit's all that's on his mind, who'd help his fellow man?
Now that's the thing that held me back. But one man proved me wrong:
that's Gorgias, whose deed revealed innate nobility.
For even though I always kept him far from my front door,
and never helped in any way with matters great or small,
and even though I never spoke a single word to him,
he went ahead and saved my life in spite of all of this.
Now any other man would say (and he'd be right, I'm sure):
"You want to be alone and that's exactly what you'll get.
You've been no help to me, so now I'll be no help to you."

But what's the matter, my young man? For if I die right now
(my present state makes me believe I'll die most miserably)
or if I live, you're my adopted son and legal heir.
So I entrust this girl to you. Her wedding's your concern.
For even if I did get well, she'd never have a mate.
There's not a man alive who'd ever be all I'd require.
But if I live, then let me live the way I want to live.
So you're in charge of everything. The gods gave you good sense.
Your sister's under your control, that's only natural.
Divide my property in two; the dowry should take half,
your mom and I will live off of the other half that's left.

Now, daughter, lay me on the bed. I've made my point. Enough.
But boy, know this—I want to tell you why I am this way.
If all the men on earth would simply take me as their guide,
there'd be no courts, no jail time, no going off to war.
It's moderation, that's the key to happiness for all.
But maybe how things are today is more to modern tastes.
Do what you want. Here's one old cranky grouch out of the way.

GORGIAS:

Well, I accept all that. But now we have to find a groom
as quickly as we can for her. If it's alright with you . . .

KNEMON:

Now look, I told you what I thought. Don't bother me, by god!

GORGIAS:

But someone wants to talk to you . . .

KNEMON:

No chance of that, by god!

GORGIAS:

. . . about the marriage of your girl.

KNEMON:

That's no concern of mine.

GORGIAS:

He helped to save you.

KNEMON:

Who?

GORGIAS:

This man. Come over here.

KNEMON:

He's burned.

A farmer?

GORGIAS:

Father, yes he is. But not the pampered kind.
He's not a shiftless gadabout who strolls around all day.
[What do you think?]

KNEMON:

[It's up to you.] Now wheel me to the house!

Exit Knemon, Myrrhine, and Knemon's daughter into Knemon's house.

GORGIAS:

(to the women as they leave)
Take care of him.

SOSTRATOS:

One thing remains: betroth the girl to me.

GORGIAS:

You're sure your father will approve?

SOSTRATOS:

My father won't say no.

GORGIAS:

Well, in that case, I give her in betrothal before the gods.
Sostratos, she's your just reward. When you began this task,
you didn't hide your character; you opened up to us
and thought this marriage worth whatever it was going to take.
You lived in luxury, but took a mattock, dug, and worked.

A rich man, when he acts like he's no better than the poor,
he shows his worth and bears the twists of fate with self-control.
You've given ample proof of this. I hope you never change.
SOSTRATOS:

That's just the start for me! But bragging's such an awful bore.

Enter Kallippides stage right.

I see my father coming here. What luck!
GORGIAS:

Kallippides?

That man's your father?
SOSTRATOS:

Yes indeed!
GORGIAS:

By Zeus, he's very rich.
And rightly so, since he's a farmer without equal here.
KALLIPPIDES:

Perhaps I've missed the lunch. By now they've eaten up the sheep
and gone back to the farm.
GORGIAS:

Poseidon, he looks like he's starved!
Well, should we tell him right away?
SOSTRATOS:

First let him have his lunch.

Then he'll be easier to manage.
KALLIPPIDES:

Hey, what's all of this?
Sostratos, have you eaten lunch?
SOSTRATOS:

But some is left for you.
So go ahead inside.
KALLIPPIDES:

Well, that's exactly what I'll do.
GORGIAS:

Now you go in and talk to him alone, if that's your plan.
SOSTRATOS:

And you'll wait in the house, won't you?

GORGIAS:

I won't set foot outside.

SOSTRATOS:

In just a little while I'll call for you to come out here.

Exit Sostratos into the cave and Gorgias into his house.

The Chorus enters for a musical interlude.

Enter Sostratos and Kallippides from the cave.

SOSTRATOS: You aren't doing everything as I wanted, Father, nor as I expected from you.

KALLIPPIDES: What? Didn't I give my consent? I want you to have the girl you love and I say that you must.

SOSTRATOS: That's not how it seems to me.

KALLIPPIDES: Yes it is, by the gods. I know that a young man's marriage is sound if he's persuaded to enter into it out of love.

SOSTRATOS: Then I'll marry the young man's sister, knowing that he's worthy of us. But how can you go on to say that you won't give my sister to him in return?

KALLIPPIDES: Are you saying that this is something shameful? I don't want to get an indigent bride and bridegroom all at the same time. One of the two is enough for me.

SOSTRATOS: You're talking about money, something that's not secure. If you know that it'll stay with you forever, guard it, don't share what you have with anyone. But you don't have control over it. Everything you have isn't yours; it belongs to Chance. Don't begrudge any of it to someone else, Father. For luck may take everything away from you again and give it to another man, maybe someone who doesn't deserve it. So I say that as long as you have control over it, you must use it nobly, Father, that you must help everyone, that you must make as many as possible rich by your efforts. This is a thing that remains forever. And if you happen to stumble in the future, it will bring the same treatment back to you again. "A visible friend revealed is much better than hidden wealth you keep buried in the ground."

KALLIPPIDES: You know what kind of a man I am, Sostratos. I won't bury in my grave what I've accumulated. How could I? It's yours. You want to keep a good friend whose worth you've tested. Go ahead, and good luck to you. Why are you quoting proverbs to me? Off with you! Give it, share it. You've persuaded me completely.

SOSTRATOS: You agree?

KALLIPPIDES: I agree, rest assured. Don't let it worry you.

SOSTRATOS: Then I'll call Gorgias.

Enter Gorgias from Knemon's house.

GORGIAS: I heard your entire conversation as I was coming outside. Well, now. I admit that you, Sostratos, are an excellent friend and I'm extremely fond of you, but I don't want any part in something above my station nor, by Zeus, would I be able to handle it if I did want it.

SOSTRATOS: I don't understand what you're saying.

GORGIAS: I give you my sister as your wife, but to take your sister—no thank you.

SOSTRATOS: No thank you?

GORGIAS: It leaves a bad taste in my mouth to live in luxury off other people's work. I make my own way.

SOSTRATOS: You're talking nonsense, Gorgias. Do you think that you're not worthy of this marriage?

GORGIAS: I've decided that I'm worthy of the girl, but not worthy of receiving so much when I have so little.

KALLIPPIDES: By Zeus the Greatest, you act nobly but you're [being unreasonable].

GORGIAS: How?

KALLIPPIDES: You're poor, but don't wish to seem so. Since you've seen me convinced, [you should give in, too.]

GORGIAS: That's convinced me. I'd be doubly deficient—both in money and in intelligence—[if I were to refuse the man who] can help me out of my troubles.

SOSTRATOS: [Excellent!] All that's left is the engagement.

KALLIPPIDES: Well, I now betroth to you my daughter, young man, for the purpose of sowing legitimate children, and I give to you a dowry of three talents for her.

GORGIAS: And I have one talent for the dowry of the other girl.

KALLIPPIDES: You have? Don't give too much.

GORGIAS: But I have the land.

KALLIPPIDES: You keep all of it, Gorgias. Now bring your mother and your sister out to be with our ladies.

GORGIAS: I'll do that.

SOSTRATOS: We'll all stay [at the cave of Pan] tonight [and tomorrow] we'll have the wedding. And you all bring the old man here, Gorgias. Maybe he'll get better treatment here with us.

GORGIAS: He won't want to come, Sostratos.

SOSTRATOS: Persuade him.

GORGIAS: If I can.

Exit Gorgias into Knemon's house.

SOSTRATOS: We have to have a good drinking party now, Dad, and the women have to stay up all night.

KALLIPPIDES: The other way around, I'm sure. They'll do the drinking and we'll be kept up all night! I'll go now and make some of the preparations for you.

SOSTRATOS: You do that.

Exit Kallippides into the cave.

The man who thinks clearly should never despair completely about any undertaking. All things are attainable through concentration and effort. I now offer myself as an example of this. In one day I've achieved a marriage that no one in the world would have thought at all possible.

Enter Gorgias from Knemon's house.

GORGIAS: *(calling to his mother and Knemon's daughter inside the house)* Come on now. Quickly!

SOSTRATOS: Right this way. *(leads them to the cave and calls inside)* Mother, take charge of these ladies. *(to Gorgias)* Knemon isn't here yet?

GORGIAS: Why, he begged me to bring the old woman out too so that he'd finally be all alone.

SOSTRATOS: He just won't give an inch.

GORGIAS: That's how he is.

SOSTRATOS: Oh well, so long to him! Let's go.

GORGIAS: Sostratos, I'm embarrassed to be with women in the same . . .

SOSTRATOS: What is this nonsense? Why don't you go on in? You have to think of all of them as part of the family now.

Exit Sostratos and Gorgias into the cave.

Enter Simiche from Knemon's house.

SIMICHE: *(to Knemon inside the house)* I'm leaving too, by Artemis! You'll lie there all alone. It's too bad for you that you're like that. By god, they wanted to take you, but you refused. There's something terrible in store for you, by the goddesses, much worse than what's happened now. *(praying)* [I hope everything goes] well!

Enter Getas from the cave.

GETAS: *(calling into the cave)* I'll come out here and see how he's doing.

The manuscript indicates that a flute player begins playing.

> Why blow that flute at me, you bum?
> I've got no time for such things now.
> They've sent me to the cripple. Stop!

SIMICHE:
(calling into the cave)
> And one of you can go inside
> and sit yourself down next to him.
> I want to chat with mistress now,
> to send her off, to say goodbye,
> to give her one last warm embrace.

GETAS:
> A good idea. Now you go in
> and I will see to him myself.

Exit Simiche into the cave.

> [Well, I've been looking] for a chance
> like this for quite a while now,
> but [I've been working like a slave].
> [So I'll just peep inside the door
> and see that he's in bed. That's great!
> I'd just begun to fear that I'd
> be robbed of my revenge. But no!
> I think I need some help.] Hey cook!
> Come over here, Sikon. Be quick!
> Poseidon, what a chance for fun!

Enter Sikon from the cave.

SIKON:

  You're calling me?

GETAS:

                        That's right. I am.

  You want to get revenge for when

  he shoved you out behind . . .

SIKON:

                                For what

  he shoved in my behind? You lie!

  It's you who'd suck a cock, not me!

GETAS:

  The grouchy geezer sleeps alone.

SIKON:

  And how's he doing?

GETAS:

                        Not dead yet.

SIKON:

  He couldn't stand and swing at us?

GETAS:

  He can't stand up, I'm pretty sure.

SIKON:

  How sweet it is! And now I'll go

  inside and ask him for some things

  and he'll go absolutely nuts!

GETAS:

  Heh, you know what? Let's roll him out.

  We'll put him here and beat the door,

  then ask for things and watch him burn.

  Oh, what a pleasure that will be!

SIKON:

  But I'm afraid that Gorgias

  might catch us. Then he'd tan our hides.

GETAS:

  It's loud and they're all drinking wine.

  No one will hear, I'm sure of that.

  Now it's completely up to us

  to see that he gets civilized.

  He's our relation, one of us.

If he's like this forever, then
we'll have our work cut out for us.
And you know that as well as I.

SIKON:

Well just be careful no one sees
you when you bring him out in front.

GETAS:

Go on.

SIKON:

Now just a minute, please!
Make sure you don't run off and leave
me here.

GETAS:

Don't make a sound, by god!

SIKON:

But I'm not making noise, by Earth!

*Enter Getas and Sikon into Knemon's house, then they return to the stage carrying the
sleeping Knemon, probably on a bed.*

GETAS:

To the right!

SIKON:

There!

GETAS:

Put him here. It's time!

SIKON:

Alright.
(to the flute player)
I'll start, you keep the rhythm.
(beating on the door in rhythm)
Oh slave! Little slave! My dear, good slaves!
Slave! Little slave!

KNEMON:

I'm done for! Oh, no!

SIKON:

(knocking in rhythm)
Oh slave! Little slave! My dear, good slaves!
Slave! Little slave!

KNEMON:

I'm done for! Oh, no!

SIKON:

And who is this? Are you from here?

KNEMON:

That's obvious. What do you want?

SIKON:

I want a kettle and a pot.

KNEMON:

Will someone get me on my feet?!

SIKON:

You've got them. Yes, you do. It's true!
And tripods—seven; tables—twelve.
Well, slaves, go tell the staff inside.
Come on! I'm in a hurry now.

KNEMON:

But I've got none!

SIKON:

But you've got none?

KNEMON:

You've heard it said a thousand times!

SIKON:

Then I'll be on my way again.

Sikon moves to the background.

KNEMON:

Poor me! How did I get outside?
Who put me out in front?

Getas approaches Knemon.

Away!

GETAS:

And now . . .
(beating on the door)
O slave! Little slave! O women!
O men! O doorman!

KNEMON:

You're insane!
You'll beat my door to pieces, man!

GETAS:

Please [lend] us nine rugs—fancy ones.

KNEMON:

Impossible!

GETAS:

And [could you lend]
an oriental tapestry,
about a hundred feet in length?

KNEMON:

I wish I had a [strap] right now.
Old woman! Where's that woman now?

GETAS:

Should I go to another door?

KNEMON:

Away!
Old woman! Simiche!
May all the gods destroy you, scum!

Getas moves to the background as Sikon approaches Knemon.

What do you want?

SIKON:

I'd like to get
a big bronze mixing bowl for wine.

KNEMON:

Could someone get me on my feet?!

Getas joins Sikon.

GETAS:

You've got them. Yes, you do. It's true!
The tapestry, Dad . . . Daddy.

KNEMON:

No!
[Look, I don't have a rug, by Zeus],
and I don't have a mixing bowl.
I'll kill that Simiche, I will!

SIKON:

Sit down and stop your grumbling.
You flee the crowd, you hate the girls,

you don't allow yourself to go
inside when there's a sacrifice.
You'll have to take what we dish out.
You'll get no help. Just bite your lip
and hear [what happened in the cave.]

Kallippides came in and said
we'd have two weddings, not just one.
Then everyone was filled with joy.
And then] your daughter and your wife
were met with hugs—and kisses, too.
A pleasant time was had by all.
And I was not too far away
preparing for the men's soirée.
The men. . . . Hey, listen! Don't you sleep!

GETAS:
No, don't you dare!

KNEMON:
My god!

SIKON:
[What's wrong?]
But don't you want to be with them?
Now listen to the rest of it.

We hurried to prepare the feast.
I spread the rug out on the ground,
I put the food out on the tables—
well, that's my job. You listening?
Remember, I'm a cook.

GETAS:
A fag!

SIKON:
Then with his hands one man poured out
some old gray Bacchus in a jar,
and mixed it with the Naiads' spring.
He toasted all the men and then
a toast went to the women folk.
That's pouring water on the sand.

Know what I mean? And then a girl,
her face hid by the shade of her hair,
got tipsy from the wine and stepped
into the rhythm modestly—
now hesitating, trembling.
Another took her hand and danced.

GETAS:

You've suffered much.

                              Get on your feet!
Come, dance with us! We'll help you out.

KNEMON:

What do you want, you low-life scum?

GETAS:

Come on and try. Get on your feet!
We'll help you out.

Knemon attempts to dance.

                              You're such a hick!

KNEMON:

By all the gods, don't do that! Please!

GETAS:

Well, should we take you in the cave?

KNEMON:

Now what am I to do?

GETAS:

                              You'll dance!

KNEMON:

Then help me in the cave. Perhaps
What's going on in there's no worse.

GETAS:

A wise decision, too.

(to Sikon)

                              We've won!
A glorious triumph! Slave! Donax!

Enter Donax from the cave.

You too, Sikon. Pick him up and carry him inside. *(to Knemon)* You watch
out. If we catch you causing trouble again, you can be sure that you won't

get off so easily next time. *(calling into the cave)* Hey! Somebody bring out garlands for us and a torch. *(giving them to Knemon)* Take this.

Exit Knemon, Sikon, and Donax into the cave.

Well, if you've enjoyed our victory over this troublesome old man, give us your kind applause—youths, boys, and men. May that daughter of a noble father, the laughter-loving virgin goddess Nike, be well disposed to us forever.

Exit Getas into the cave.

PLAUTUS
AND ROMAN
NEW COMEDY

GEORGE FREDRIC FRANKO

INTRODUCTION

The Author

"PLAUTUS, with the name that barks," quips the speaker of the prologue to *Casina*. An ancient commentator explains the joke by pointing out that "Plautus," which literally means "flat," here specifically alludes to the flat ears of a hound. The name Plautus may also give us a clue to the author's origin, for the word appears to be a Latinized form of an Umbrian word, and ancient sources claim that his home was Sarsina (an Umbrian town to the northeast of Rome). While we have no way of proving that Sarsina was in fact Plautus' home, it is a reasonable assumption that he, like the overwhelming majority of Rome's earliest Latin authors, was not a native Roman.

Writers since Plautus' time have usually referred to him simply as Plautus, though several bits of evidence suggest that his full name was Titus Maccius Plautus. This may, in fact, be a pen name. While "Titus" is a common enough first name, "Maccius" is very suspicious, for it clearly derives from "Maccus," the clown, a stock character of ancient Italian farce. Now if our author was not a native Roman, then he should not have had three names like a Roman patrician; this suggests that at least part of his name was a pen name. With our suspicions raised, we note that "Plautus" can also mean "flat-footed" and thus could refer to shoeless actors in mimes, and "Titus" might carry the obscene connotation of "penis." In short, while our author may have been blessed with a name happily appropriate to his profession (like the English poet Wordsworth), it is more likely that he adopted a significant, silly name for himself, one meaning something like "Dick MacClown the Mime-Guy."[1]

---

1. For further detail on the name, see A. S. Gratwick, "Titus Maccius Plautus," *Classical Quarterly* 23 (1973): 78–84.

Aside from a possible Umbrian origin, we know virtually nothing about Plautus' life. The scant information about him preserved in other ancient sources is of doubtful veracity, and it is dangerous to use information contained within the scripts to reconstruct the poet's personal history. We can only speculate that his involvement with the theater included acting or production of plays.

Plautus and Early Roman Literature

Plautus' plays were evidently popular with his contemporaries, and Romans continued to perform and read his scripts even after his death. Indeed, such was the popularity of Plautus that by the middle of the second century A.D. approximately one hundred thirty scripts were circulating under his name. Not all were genuine, which suggests that producers or writers sought to increase the marketability of their own works by attaching to them Plautus' name. The scripts of twenty-one plays have survived; these are almost certainly the twenty-one scripts identified in the first century B.C. by the Roman scholar Varro as the unquestionably genuine works of Plautus. No doubt other scripts of disputed authenticity were genuine, but they have not survived.

The traditional dates for Plautus' period of activity (ca. 210–184 B.C.) rest upon a variety of evidence, including the production notices preserved in our manuscripts that date his plays *Stichus* to 200 and *Pseudolus* to 192/1. Lines 11–19 (in the Latin text) of *Casina* reveal that the prologue as we have it is not from the original production but from a repeat performance of roughly a generation later and that Plautus and his peers, the cream of Rome's poetic crop, were already dead. While the speaker of the prologue may exaggerate the qualitative difference between living and deceased authors, it is worth emphasizing that Plautus did indeed belong to a generation of talented and pioneering poets who shaped the course of Latin literature. Unfortunately, the works of those other innovators—Livius Andronicus, Gnaeus Naevius, Quintus Ennius, Caecilius Statius—are almost wholly lost, surviving only in fragmentary quotations preserved by later Roman authors.[2] Thus the importance of Plautus: he is our earliest extant Roman author, whose work is barely a generation removed from the birth of Latin literature.

2. Andronicus (dates uncertain, but spanned 240–207 B.C.) wrote tragedies, comedies, and a translation of Homer's *Odyssey;* Naevius (died ca. 200 B.C.) wrote an epic on the First Punic War, comedies, tragedies, and plays on Roman History; Ennius (239–169 B.C.) wrote an epic on Roman history, tragedies, comedies, and numerous minor works; Caecilius (died 168 B.C.) wrote comedies. Plautus appears to have been the first to specialize in one genre.

We can speak of the "birth" of Latin literature because of the striking fact that Rome, whose political history began in the eighth century B.C., had no literary history until the second half of the third century. According to tradition, Latin literature began in 240 B.C. when Livius Andronicus staged a translation of a Greek play. Two things stand out in this scrap of information. First, the earliest piece of Latin literature identified as such by the Romans themselves was a play and not, as in other European cultures, an anonymous epic poem. Compare this to the earliest specimens of other European literatures such as Greek (*Iliad*), Spanish (*Poema del Mio Cid*), French (*Chanson de Roland*), or English (*Beowulf*). Though an ephemeral production on stage, Andronicus' play was given pride of place in the Romans' construction of their literary history.

Second, a translation of a Greek play marks the genesis of Latin literature. The Romans thereby qualified literary translation as a form of art. Nonetheless, great Roman poets such as those mentioned above did not merely seek to render faithful replicas of the Greek originals; instead, they adapted, reshaped, and renovated Greek works in a process they called "turning" (*vortere*), the root of our English word "version." Roman playwrights appropriated Greek models and made them their own in ways discussed below. While the phenomenon may have begun with Greek drama, it soon spread to other genres, such as epic and history, as well as to the visual arts. The birth of Latin literature signals the birth of the Roman state as a cosmopolitan Mediterranean power; it is probably more than coincidence that Andronicus' play is dated to 240 B.C., the year following Rome's victory over Carthage in the First Punic War. In this context, the plays of Plautus bear witness to the infancy of an authentically national literature generated by a burst of creative, nationalist spirit.

The Occasion

The prologue to *Casina* reveals that the play was staged during a holiday celebration. During such holidays (*ludi*), normal business was suspended: we read in the prologue to *Casina* that the bankers are not collecting and that the forum—Rome's social, political, religious, and commercial center—is quiet. The festivals could be quite lavish affairs lasting several days. The *ludi Romani*, for example, opened with a large, noisy procession that included images of the gods, chariots, dancers, athletes, and other groups decked out in various outfits and accompanied by musicians. Entertainment subsequent to the procession included athletic contests, sacrifices, and plays. Plays were part of a larger celebratory atmosphere rather than the main event of the celebration. The number of plays staged in one day is not known, and it is doubtful that plays were presented in a judged competition, although some competition may be implied in the claim that *Casina* "topped them all." Admission was free.

The *ludi* were religious celebrations in honor of various deities. Thus, plays at Rome, as at Athens, were staged as part of a religious ritual. But if it is difficult to discern connections between Athenian drama and the worship of Dionysus, it is nearly impossible to perceive the religious sense of Roman drama. There is no trace of religious influence on the plays themselves, nor is it possible to claim a relationship between the verses of Roman drama and hymns or prayers to the gods. It would be more accurate to say that plays were part of festivals that celebrated Roman political power, of which the gods were the protectors and extenders. Besides, our notion of separating religion and state would have seemed incredible to the ancients: the religious was political, and vice versa. Politics did loom in the background of the *ludi*. The state provided some of the funding, but individual magistrates had to come up with the rest, and no doubt some saw the potential for gaining positive publicity through their patronage of lavish public display. The extent to which political forces directly influenced the content of the plays themselves is hard to gauge, and was probably minimal. While a passage from one of Terence's prologues tells us that the sponsoring magistrates previewed the scripts, we cannot conclude that they meddled in the actual staging of the plays. A comparison with the works of Aristophanes shows that the works of Plautus, because of either the apolitical nature of New Comedy or a fear of official reprisals, contain only few and veiled political references. In short, the religious and political setting of the festivals does not impinge upon the content of the plays in any significant degree.[3]

Actors, Staging, and the Theater

The troop of actors involved in the staging of *Casina* included at least five speaking actors (the minimum necessary for the final scene), plus some mute char-

3. Two cautions are in order. First, the Roman *ludi* were not a form of medieval carnival, a raucous final fling before the strictures of Lent, and therefore parallels between the two are deceptive. Second, the *ludi* should not be assimilated to Roman Saturnalia. The so-called Saturnalian spirit of the plays—a celebration of topsy-turvydom modeled on carnival—is a modern imposition that can obscure as much as it enlightens. Indeed, the plays were not staged during Saturnalia, and Saturnalia itself at that time was apparently a quiet rustic festival, quite unlike the popular modern portrayal of it. This is not to say Roman *ludi* were not fun; no doubt a good time was had by all, but one must avoid a reductionist view that derives the humor of the plays solely from a Saturnalian sense of psychological release. For an approach to Plautus that emphasizes the Saturnalian spirit, see E. Segal, *Roman Laughter: The Comedy of Plautus,* 2d ed. (Oxford, 1987).

acters. The actors were all males, even for the female roles.[4] By the time of Plautus, it seems that one could make a living in the theater: regular *ludi* offered perhaps a dozen days for dramatic presentations, and other opportunities for staging plays did exist.[5] Those involved in the theater may have been jacks of many trades, such as, for example, one Lucius Ambivius Turpio, who produced and acted for both Terence and Caecilius Statius.

Without providing the names of any characters, the prologue to *Casina* presents an old man, a wife, a son, a foundling girl, a foreman of the farm, and a squire. How would the audience tell the old man from the squire? It is virtually certain that actors in the time of Plautus wore masks whose stereotyped features (mouth, hair color, etc.) served to identify the character. While this mode of presentation did have the disadvantage of precluding facial expressions—expressions lost on more distant members of the audience anyway—it offered one great advantage. Masks allowed the instant identification of character types and their attendant traits; that is, particular masks not only denoted an old man, clever slave, soldier, slave dealer, and so forth, but also connoted a stereotyped personality. For example, the audience would expect soldiers to be loud, boastful, and slow-witted and slave dealers to be sleazy, greedy, and cowardly. Plautus was never obliged to spend time on the exposition of character because one glance at the masks conveyed the stereotype and expectation. Whether Plautus would choose to uphold or subvert that stereotype is another question. Masks may also have allowed one actor to play multiple roles and conversely multiple actors to play one role. There are eight speaking parts in *Casina,* yet five speaking actors can stage it. Plautus also employed mute characters (e.g., cooks), but we cannot know to what extent he exploited their potential for slapstick or mime to enhance the dialogue of the speakers. We can only imagine the potential for pandemonium produced by the entrance of a company of cooks clanging pots and pans.[6]

4. This gives an additional twist to *Casina,* with its transvestite wedding. It also spices up the prologue's joke in lines 84–86: pay some money and the actor who plays the girl Casina will be yours.

5. Such occasional opportunities for staging plays included triumphs and funeral games; see L. R. Taylor, "The Opportunities for Dramatic Performance in the Time of Plautus and Terence," *Transactions of the American Philological Association* 68 (1937): 284–304.

6. In general, props were few and often tied to characterization. *Casina* requires a cane for the old man, pots and pans for the cooks, wool-working equipment for the women, a wedding torch, a wallet, an urn, and lots. Plautus could exploit the symbolic value contained in these props: witness how Lysidamus' loss of his staff near the end of the play makes tangible his loss of dignity and status.

The setting for the plays almost invariably consisted of a street, usually identified as one in Athens, with a backdrop of two or three houses. The scenery required for *Casina* is typically simple: two facades of houses with working doorways and a nook or alley of some sort between them, suitable for an eavesdropper to hide in. Exits on the wings of the stage were understood as leading to the forum (stage left) and to the port or countryside (stage right). The action takes place in the street in front of the houses, which is appropriate and natural for an outdoor theater. While an outdoor setting may occasionally strain realism in some plays, the movement of characters in *Casina* seems quite natural. Moreover, Plautus skillfully exploits the convention of not showing what transpires inside the houses with Pardalisca's suspenseful parody of a tragic messenger speech, as well as the humorous accounts of Olympio and Lysidamus of their attempts to woo "Casina." Smartly done, the report of events may provoke more laughter than the actual portrayal of events.

There was no permanent stone theater in Rome until 55 B.C.; prior to this time temporary, prefabricated wooden stages were assembled for the occasion. Seats apparently were also set up, and after a law of 194 B.C. the best seats were reserved for senators. Comparative evidence from southern Italy, wall paintings, and clues from the plays themselves lead us to believe that the stage was raised, with a painted scene behind, and wings. There was no orchestra (logically enough, since there was no chorus). Unlike modern theater, the Roman stage had no lights or other such technical equipment. A curtain could be raised from the stage floor to mark the opening and closing of the play but did not mark acts and intermissions; consequently, the action was continuous and rapid, especially without choral interludes to show the passage of time or division into acts.[7]

The Audience

Prologues to the plays of Plautus indicate that men, women, and children, of all ages and social classes, were in the audience. The prologue to *Casina* closes with an exhortation to soldiers, and the play's liberal use of military imagery is significant. Rome in Plautus' era was continually at war with its neighbors, and, since Roman armies were comprised of conscripted citizens rather than volunteer professional soldiers, the audience must have been full of men who served

7. For more on staging, see W. Beare, *The Roman Stage,* 3d ed. (London, 1964), and R. C. Beacham, *The Roman Theatre and Its Audience* (Cambridge, Mass., 1991).

in the legions. Whether the Roman spectators of this era should be seen as unsophisticated rubes is a matter of opinion. Many of the typically Plautine traits discussed below can (and have) been seen as a dumbing-down of Greek New Comedy to meet the boorish tastes of Roman audiences. Yet some of those traits can also be understood as self-conscious mockery of naturalistic conventions in Greek New Comedy. Most likely Plautus aimed his humor both low (e.g., farce and slapstick) and high (e.g., metatheater). At the very least his audience knew and had appreciated for over a generation Roman adaptations of Greek New Comedy.

The audience is not presumed by Plautus to be a passive viewer. It serves as the confidant for eavesdroppers, as the target for asides, and as the sharer of joyful monologues or conspiracies. There is in Plautus' work a self-conscious theatricality, unlike what we find in Menander or Terence. Plautine characters seem aware that the audience knows that they are really just actors engaged in role-playing.

Plautus and His Greek Models

The prologue to *Casina* makes a very important admission to the audience: Plautus did not compose this play from whole cloth; rather, he reworked a play from a Greek author named Diphilus (a contemporary of Menander in the late fourth century B.C.). As mentioned above, the appropriation of Greek models is typical of early Latin literature. *Casina* belongs to a genre known as the *palliata,* comedies based on Greek plays and performed in Greek attire (the *pallium,* a Greek cloak). The process of adapting Greek models is not mere translation, still less plagiarism, but a thorough reworking of material into a new, original work of art.[8] When studying works of Latin literature in the light of their Greek originals, as with Roman art, it is often more fruitful to place emphasis on the differences rather than on the similarities. We should concentrate not only on the retention of the Greek tradition, but also on the transformation of that tradition, the ways in which Roman authors renovated Greek material in order to articulate their own national character, preoccupations, and tastes.

Not a single quotation from Diphilus' script has survived to allow direct comparison with Plautus' *Casina.* How, then, can we know to what degree Plau-

---

8. To get some sense of how a playwright can successfully adapt material from another culture, one might compare Shakespeare's *Comedy of Errors* with its Plautine original, *Menaechmi.* Certainly no one would accuse Shakespeare of being a hack copier for having reworked a Plautine play; likewise, we should not view Plautus as the hack copier of Diphilus or Menander.

tus modified the original?[9] Investigation of Plautus' methods of adaptation has long dominated scholarship on Plautus, and with good reason, for his modifications reveal his creativity as an artist and indicate the tastes of the audience to which he catered. Given our current lack of any complete Greek script for which there is an extant Roman adaptation, we rely primarily upon four sources to appreciate how Plautus renovated his models: fragments from a Greek original of a Plautine play; a passage from a Roman scholar comparing Greek and Roman comedy; clues within Plautus' own plays; and pervasive Plautine traits that are rare or absent from Menander and his more faithful translator, Terence.

The publication in 1968 of papyrus fragments containing roughly fifty legible lines from Menander's *Dis Exapaton,* the original for Plautus' *Bacchides,* allowed scholars for the first time to compare a Plautine adaptation with its original and thereby concretely illustrate several alterations that readers had long suspected. First, Plautus changed realistic but trite names of characters into highly individualized creations based on Greek words. For example, Plautus renames the character Moschos (a common name in Greek life and drama) as Pistoclerus ("Trusting in Fortune"), a name unattested elsewhere but one that befits the character. Second, Plautus changed the meter of the dialogue from prosaic iambs to more excited, musically enhanced trochees (on meter, see below). Plautus' widespread introduction of musically enhanced verses has a profound impact on the pace, emotive effect, and verisimilitude of a play.

Third, Roman comedy, unlike Greek, did not have choral interludes to divide the play into acts or represent the passage of time required for offstage action.[10] Responding to dramatic necessity, Plautus had to create bridges between these act divisions. His solution (or lack thereof) for this passage in *Bacchides* is striking: a character exits to transact some business and returns five lines later claiming that he has done it. Dramatic time is divorced from real time, and the audience is often required to imagine that, say, fifteen minutes have elapsed.[11] This leads to a fourth point, the self-conscious theatricality of Plautus. While Menander succeeds in portraying characters and situations with

9. For useful speculation on Plautus' alterations to Diphilus' script, see W. S. Anderson, *Barbarian Play: Plautus' Roman Comedy* (Toronto, 1993), 30–59; S. O'Bryhim, "The Originality of Plautus' *Casina,*" *American Journal of Philology* 110 (1989): 81–103.

10. Act divisions in our texts of Plautus were created by Renaissance editors who sought to divide the plays into five acts. Note in the synopsis of *Casina* how the empty stage in four places does readily divide the play into five parts.

11. In *Casina,* observe how Lysidamus goes to the forum at line 531 and returns at line 563, claiming to have wasted the entire day.

naturalism, Plautus often seeks to draw our attention to the fact that we are watching theater. Characters relay their thoughts to the audience aloud and conveniently pause for other characters to speak in the interval. Observe how Plautus milks the tension in an imminent confrontation between two friends:

> PISTOCLERUS: Is that my friend there?
> MNESILOCHUS: Is that my enemy I see?
> PISTOCLERUS: Yup, it is.
> MNESILOCHUS: It is. I'll approach him and confront him.
> PISTOCLERUS: Greetings, Mnesilochus!
> MNESILOCHUS: Hello.

In Menander's script, that same encounter is much more natural, if less spectacular:

> MOSCHOS: If he's heard I'm here, where on earth is he? Oh! Greetings, Sostratos.
> SOSTRATOS: Greetings.

While other changes in staging and characterization emerge from further analysis of the two passages,[12] those that we have considered with respect to meter, act divisions, and self-conscious theatricality are most significant because they create a different rhythm in the performance of the plays.

Our second source for evaluating Plautine originality suggests that Plautus altered not only the rhythm of the plays, but also their tone. Roman adaptation substantially modified the diction and content of Greek dialogue. Despite its brevity, a passage from the Roman scholar Aulus Gellius (*Attic Nights* 2.23), in which he compares three short excerpts from a script of Menander with their adaptations by Caecilius Statius, is remarkably instructive. This analysis helps us understand how Plautus reworked his originals because the surviving fragments of Caecilius reveal pervasive stylistic affinities with the extant scripts of Plautus.[13] Consider the following excerpts. First Menander:

> HUSBAND: My wife, the heiress, is a shrew. Haven't I told you that? I haven't? She's
> in charge of my household and lands and everything. By Apollo, I've the hard-

12. For the texts and translations, see J. Barsby, *Plautus: Bacchides* (Warminster, 1986). For analysis, one can begin with E. W. Handley, *Menander and Plautus: A Study in Comparison* (London, 1968) and Anderson (above, note 9), 3–29.

13. See J. Wright, *Dancing in Chains: The Stylistic Unity of the Comoedia Palliata* (Rome, 1974). Significantly, Wright indicates that Terence stood somewhat outside the tradition.

est of hard things: she doesn't just nag me, but also my son and especially my
daughter.

FRIEND: You can't fight it.

HUSBAND: I know it well.

Now Caecilius:

FRIEND: But tell me, is your wife a pain?

HUSBAND: You have to ask?

FRIEND: How so?

HUSBAND: I hate to talk about it. As soon as I come home and sit down, she immediately gives me a stinky kiss.

FRIEND: No doubt about it: she wants you to puke up what you've been out
drinking.

Caecilius renders Menander's smooth, natural monologue as a choppy, salty
exchange. The serious complaint about a wife's control of property becomes a
vaudeville routine equivalent to "take my wife . . . please." In his critical assessment Gellius laments that Caecilius chooses to play the fool rather than portray
the characters with realism. He also criticizes the Latin author for "dragging in
farcical stuff" and "sewing together mangled excerpts of Menander with bits of
tragic bombast." The tone is different because Roman playwrights willingly
forgo consistency and naturalism in order to portray their characters as comedians. Such alterations presumably were intended to satisfy the tastes of a live
Roman audience.

Although Gellius' entire discussion repays further study for the way it
vividly demonstrates the freedoms and priorities with which Roman authors
reworked a Greek original, it badly misses the point from the outset. Gellius
says he often has read the scripts with his friends; he did not see the plays; thus,
his analysis of the plays is as limited as a discussion of two films based solely
upon their screenplays.

The third source of evidence for Plautine renovation—clues within the
plays themselves—is the most tricky. For example, several items from the
prologue of *Casina* suggest that Plautus may have altered drastically the plot of
Diphilus' play. A typical story pattern for New Comedy included the revelation that a foundling girl was actually a freeborn citizen, thus eligible for marriage, and a marriage or betrothal would ensue. The Romans would repeatedly
have seen this pattern, even in other comedies of Plautus. Yet *Casina*'s prologue
tells us not to expect the young male lover onstage because *Plautus* broke the

bridge on his route home. This implies that Plautus excised the youth's arrival from Diphilus' play. If the young lover never does arrive, the expected betrothal or wedding cannot be celebrated. Furthermore, the prologue promises that Casina will be revealed as a chaste, freeborn Athenian citizen. An audience expecting to witness this revelation will be disappointed, for it does not happen in Plautus' play and only two lines in the epilogue tell us that this will happen eventually. The epilogue also proclaims that the young couple will marry in due time. No recognition scene, no wedding. These are significant alterations. Did Plautus really chop out such large portions of his originals? Terence claims that he did. In the prologue to his play *The Brothers,* Terence accuses Plautus of leaving out an entire scene from his adaptation of another play by Diphilus, the *Synapothneskontes.* By omitting an entire scene, Plautus either drastically reduced the length of a piece or used the space created by a deletion to allow time for more silly antics.

The fourth method of diagnosing Plautine alterations—identifying his pervasive stylistic traits—is addressed below.

Native Italian Influences

Little can be said with certainty about the influence of native Italian comedy on Plautus because no scripts have survived. One Italian genre that may have had a profound influence on the development of early Roman comedy is the so-called *fabula Atellana* ("Atellan Farce"), which originated among the neighboring Oscan people and gained a lasting popularity with the Romans.[14] These dramas were evidently simple rustic comedies in verse, with a liberal dose of improvisation and obscenity. They employed a limited cast of masked, stock characters such as Bucco the boastful glutton, Dossennus the clever trickster, Pappus the duped old man, or Maccus the clown. There is a superficial similarity to some of these character types in Plautus, which raises the possibility that some of what we find distinctively Plautine may ultimately derive from a native Italian tradition. Other bits of information about the *fabula Atellana* suggest that they emphasized farce and trickery. This too leads us to posit that farcical elements in Plautus—elements largely absent from Menander and Terence—may derive from a native Italian element. The lack of evidence limits the fruitfulness of such speculation. Since we have neither a script for an Atellan Farce nor a complete script for any Greek New Comic author other than Menander,

14. On Atellan Farce and other Italian genres, see G. E. Duckworth, *The Nature of Roman Comedy* (Princeton, 1952), 3–17; and Beare (above, note 7), 128–58.

we cannot know whether the ribald, farcical scenes in *Casina* reflect the zest of Diphilus' original, or of native Italian comedy, or of Plautus' own genius.

A Baker's Dozen of Plautine Traits

Linguistic Features

In general, Plautine Latin is lively yet artificial, colloquial yet surreal. It is "swift-moving, yet copious to the point of verbosity."[15] The Romans extolled the exuberance of Plautus' Latin; the scholar Aelius Stilo went so far as to claim that if the Muses wished to speak Latin, they would have spoken like the verses of Plautus.

Puns and wordplay. Line 24 of *Casina* is fairly representative: *ludi sunt, ludus datus est argentiis,* meaning roughly, "it's the *ludi,* the bankers are e-luded" (*ludum dare* means "to deceive"). Such wordplay must be experienced in the original Latin since, as in the present example, most puns are impossible to translate neatly.

Alliteration. Plautus shares with most archaic Latin poets a fondness for alliteration. Assonance is also common and, when combined with alliteration and wordplay, lends a bouncy, jingling quality to the Latin. One need not know Latin to appreciate the alliteration and assonance of the opening lyrics in Pardalisca's parody of a tragic messenger speech (lines 621–26):

> *nulla sum, nulla sum; tota, tota occidi.*
> *cor metu mortuomst, membra miserae tremunt.*
> *nescio unde auxili, praesidi, perfugi,*
> *mi aut opum copiam comparem aut expetam.*
> *tantu factu modo mira miris modis*
> *intus vidi, novam atque integram audaciam.*

Varied linguistic register. On the one hand, Plautine characters are often chatty and their speeches are peppered with colloquial expressions and oaths (such as "by Hercules," "by Pollux," or "by Castor"); on the other hand, those same characters are made to speak with elegant vocabulary and convoluted syntax. The same character can slip back and forth between lofty and colloquial language because role-playing to fit the mood of a particular scene overrides a demand for consistency and naturalism.

---

15. Thus Duckworth (above, note 14), 331.

Neologisms (newly coined words). Two examples from the final scene of *Casina* are typical: *lumbifragium* ("dickwreck," line 968) and *dismaritus* ("bigamist," line 974, from the Greek *dis,* "twice," and the Latin *maritus,* "married").

Quick jokes and gags. Plautus, like Caecilius in the passage quoted above, cannot resist turning his actors into comedians. One verbal formation seems especially dear to Plautus: the riddling identification, such as at *Casina* lines 720–21: Olympio: "Cover your thorns!" Cook: "What do you mean? Why are they thorns?" Olympio: "'Cause they snag in a jiffy whatever they touch; and they rip you to shreds if you try to escape!"

Mythological hyperbole. Plautine characters often scurrilously compare themselves with gods. Typical mythological hyperbole is apparent in *Casina* when Lysidamus fancies himself to be Jupiter and Cleostrata naturally is compared to Juno. The very name Olympio, with its overtones of Mount Olympus, is hyperbolic for a farm overseer.

Military imagery. Scheming slaves in Plautus frequently boast of their exploits in military metaphors. The presence of many citizen-soldiers in the audience may explain Plautus' predilection for military imagery. Its pervasiveness in *Casina* is noted in the next chapter.[16]

Nonlinguistic Features

Romanization. While Terence works hard to maintain the Athenian facade, Plautus delights in puncturing it with Roman allusions. Although the plays are set in Greece and the characters are dressed as Greeks, characters often refer to things Roman. *Casina* contains scattered allusions to such Roman realities as legions, the forum, the senate, and Roman deities.

Broad topicality. Although Plautus never names any living or deceased Roman leaders in his plays, we can detect oblique references to such general concerns of his day as military triumphs, lawmakers, sumptuary laws, and usury sprinkled throughout the scripts. For example, we find in *Casina* references to the Bacchae and the discontinuation of their celebrations (lines 978–81).[17]

---

16. The fundamental study of Plautine imagery and diction remains E. Fraenkel's *Elementi Plautini in Plauto* (Florence, 1960; originally published in German in 1922). Unfortunately, there is as yet no English translation.

17. The Bacchae, female devotees to the god Dionysus, purportedly engaged in wild, orgiastic rites. The stereotype of their frenzied behavior, such as their destruction of Pentheus in Greek myth, was disseminated by artists and dramatists, and Plautus himself mentions them in

Plautus mentions them, but without the overt social or moral criticism so prominent in Aristophanes.

Disregard for dramatic illusion. Eavesdropping, confiding in, and appealing to the audience are self-consciously theatrical activities that occur throughout *Casina*. Characters even invite the active participation of the audience, as Olympio does at line 879.

Physical humor. We can only speculate about the amount of slapstick and other types of nonverbal humor in the plays. The scripts do not provide stage directions, and verbal clues are scarce (e.g., *Casina* line 406: "Who gave you the right to strike him?"). Actors cannot have stood delivering lines with arms folded, and one suspects a great deal of posturing and gesturing; one's enjoyment of the script is enhanced by pausing to imagine the physical comedy implicit in scenes such as the opening confrontation between Olympio and Chalinus.[18]

Predominance of the clever slave. Plautus manifestly enjoyed one character above all others: the cunning slave. In many of Plautus' finest plays this character claims to be the author and director of the plot, thereby effectively making the play his own production; indeed, several comedies are named after their dominant and charismatic slave (e.g., *Pseudolus*). At first glance, *Casina* appears to lack this trait; when we examine the issue more closely, we find that several characters are vying for the role of clever slave.

Metrical variety. See the following section.

Meter and Its Effects

One hallmark of Plautus' Latin—a hallmark emphasized in this translation—is metrical variety. The purportedly autobiographical epitaph of Plautus makes the point well: "Since Plautus has died, Comedy mourns, the stage is deserted, then Laughter, Sport, Wit, and *Numeri Innumeri* all wept together." *Numeri Innumeri* means, roughly, "the infinite variety of meters." There is nothing comparable to his extensive use of polymetric lyric verses in Greek New Comedy, nor in Terence.

---

several plays. In 186 B.C. the Roman senate authorized measures to suppress this cult. On Plautine topicality, see E. S. Gruen, *Studies in Greek Culture and Roman Policy* (New York, 1991), 124–57.

18. See the fourth chapter of Beacham's work (above, note 7, pp. 86–116), which is a commentary on his staging of *Casina*.

Some explanation of meter is in order, but necessarily a brief one since we are not analyzing the Latin text in this anthology. Latin versification depends on the interplay of stress accent and syllabic quantity. By "quantity" we mean that Latin syllables may be termed either "heavy" or "light." Heavy syllables, denoted with a -, contain a long vowel, a diphthong, or a short vowel under certain conditions; light syllables, denoted with a ˅, always contain a short vowel. These syllables are arranged in discrete units called "feet." For example, an "iambic" foot contains a light syllable followed by a heavy syllable (˅-), while a "trochaic" foot contains a heavy syllable followed by a light syllable (-˅). Each line of poetry contains a fixed number of feet. For instance, iambic senarii consist of, ideally, six iambs per line while trochaic septenarii consist of, ideally, seven and a half trochees per line.

Much of Plautus' verse is in *iambic senarii,* the verse form most resembling daily speech. These lines were spoken without musical accompaniment and thus represent a lower level of dramatic intensity. In this translation they have been rendered as prose.

Passages of heightened dramatic intensity are in other longer meters, most often *trochaic septenarii* (in fact, the most common meter in Plautus). These verses were delivered with the accompaniment of the *tibia,* a reed instrument that looks like two recorders joined at the mouthpiece and probably sounded like an oboe. In this translation, trochaic septenarii have been rendered as eight-beat trochaic verse, as in Longfellow's *A Psalm of Life:*

Art is long and Time is fleeting, / And our hearts, though stout and brave,
Still, like muffled drums, are beating / Funeral marches to the grave.

Keep in mind that this is at best a rough equivalent because in English the verse form depends upon an alternation of stressed and unstressed syllables rather than the interplay of stressed syllables with syllabic quantity.

Finally, passages of the greatest emotional intensity are in *lyric* verse. These verses, also accompanied by the *tibia,* display extraordinary metrical variety and complexity.[19] *Casina* contains more lyric verses and more metrical variety

19. As an example of this variety: in the initial confrontation between Cleostrata and Lysidamus the meter changes eight times in twenty-three lines. Such metrical effects are difficult to reproduce in English, and since the result does not sound at all like verse, this translation sticks to a given meter within a lyric passage. For a general overview of ancient meter, see J. Halporn, M. Ostwald, and T. Rosenmeyer, *The Meters of Greek and Latin Poetry* (Indianapolis, 1963).

than any other extant Latin play: over one-third of the script is in lyric meters.[20] The present translation attempts to make the lyric verses stand out by
using shorter lines and varied syllable-stressed meters to convey a sense of ra-
pidity, excitement, and fun. Although Plautus often used bacchiacs ($\smile$--) and
cretics (-$\smile$-), English prosody does not smoothly accommodate such meters.
Therefore, this translation frequently employs anapests ($\smile\smile$-) and dactyls (-$\smile\smile$),
which, with their relatively greater proportion of unstressed syllables, give the
English verses a frisky, festive feeling appropriate to Plautine comedy.[21]

    Plautus uses meter to convey meaning; it is not mere window-dressing.[22]
For examples from *Casina*, consider two entering monologues of Lysidamus.
At line 217 he is upbeat, waxing poetic on the power of love, and bursts onto
the stage with a flourish of anapests; at line 563 he returns from the forum depressed and irritated, and appropriately speaks in unadorned iambs. Changes
in meter generally mark entrances and exits and establish a pattern of tension
and release: Lysidamus and Olympio plot strategy for the lottery in iambs
(lines 309–52), the exciting lottery scene itself is in trochees (lines 353–423),
after which a crestfallen Chalinus reflects on his defeat in iambs (lines 426ff.).
Information necessary for understanding the plot is generally presented in
unaccompanied iambs. Lyric passages are reserved for attractive, sympathetic
characters while unsympathetic types such as bankers and soldiers are generally denied lyrics. It is a striking feature of *Casina* that nearly everyone delivers
lyrics; only Alcesimus does not, though Chalinus, a man of martial occupation,
has only two lyric verses.

    We cannot claim to know how the actors delivered lyric and trochaic

---

20. The success of this play in translation depends upon a vivacious rendering of Plautus'
lyrics. Indeed, "it should be the obligation of every honest translation of Plautus to shape Plautine lyric passages into a metrical form which stands out as different from the sections of
[iambic and trochaic verses] so that the special rhythmical lilt and the verbiage which supports
it can have an appropriate effect." Anderson (above, note 9), 126.

21. Two further points. First, Plautine verse is usually end-stopped, that is, a line of verse
corresponds with a unit of sense; this translation attempts to retain this feature. Second, the
prosody of this translation is excessively regular. Good, serious English poetry will vary its
rhythms by substituting, for example, trochees into a line of iambic pentameter. Continual ad-
herence to a given meter produces an unnatural, singsong quality undesirable in serious poetry;
I believe, however, that a histrionic, singsong "lilt" is a positive feature for representing Plautus' melodramatic, metatheatrical language.

22. On some uses of meter to enhance dramatic meaning, see T. Moore, "Music and
Structure in Roman Comedy," *American Journal of Philology* 119 (1998): 245–73.

verses, and several features make an analogy difficult. Although the meters are certainly different, there may have been no difference in delivery between trochaic and lyric verse because both are termed *cantica* by the ancients. Perhaps trochaic verses were delivered in recitative while lyric verses were "sung," but there is no direct evidence for such a distinction. Furthermore, it is probably misleading to think of lyric verses as "songs" in the modern sense; Plautus' lyric passages are not confined to what might be considered "show tunes" or "arias" but are employed for dialogue as well. We may do best to understand the verb *canere* ("to sing," whence *cantica*) as "to speak with attention to pitch and rhythm."[23] Such an approach might lead us to a comparison with recitative in opera or some of the more accomplished rap artists. In short, notwithstanding the catchiness of songs in *A Funny Thing Happened on the Way to the Forum,* our ignorance should make us hesitate to embrace the initially attractive analogy of Plautine comedy to modern musicals.

Music was important enough to include the name of the musician in the production notice of Plautus' *Stichus,* something not done in Greek production notices. The loss of the musical scores to these plays is exasperating; imagine reading the script to Mozart's *Magic Flute* without an inkling of the accompaniment. In a play such as *Casina,* which is roughly one-third lyric, musical accompaniment is crucial to the full effect of the performance. My own experiences directing Plautine plays over several summers have driven this point home: the best performances were those augmented by a talented band providing catchy tunes behind the actors' lyrics.

The Characters and a Synopsis of *Casina*

New Comedy's tendency to omit names from prologues indicates that the audience was, at least initially, to pay more attention to stock character types than to individual personalities. Likewise, when Menander and Terence reuse the same trite names, they allow an audience to identify characters as representatives of a stock type rather than as individuals. Plautus, on the other hand, exploits the semiotic potential of names by giving his characters highly individualized, fantastic, and significant names. Sometimes these names reveal the personality or profession of a character (for example, the soldier Pyrgopolynices is literally "Conqueror of Many Citadels"), and other times they encapsulate the recurrent themes of a play. In *Casina* the names of characters underscore

---

23. F. H. Sandbach, *The Comic Theatre of Greece and Rome* (London, 1977), 120.

the importance of three dominant motifs: fragrances, animals, and warfare.[24] The names Casina and Myrrhina have olfactory significance. "Casina" is derived from *casia,* the oil or essence of a cinnamonlike spice. She is an aromatic treat, so exotic that she herself never appears in the play. Whether "Myrrhina" is derived from "myrtle" (*myrtus*) or "myrrh" (*myrrha*), either sweet-smelling plant aligns her with Casina (who, the epilogue reveals, is her daughter).

The play's two big winners bear names that tout their military excellence. "Cleostrata," perhaps best translated as "Glory of the Army," is the master tactician who wins the domestic war over her husband. The son who does not appear in the play is aptly named "Euthynicus" ("Victorious") because he ultimately defeats his father and gains Casina. Cleostrata's two main helpers have names suggesting animal imagery. "Chalinus," Greek for "bridle," not only is appropriate for a squire but also is appropriate for his dramatic function: he reins in Lysidamus' animalistic lust. The maid "Pardalisca" ("Little Panther") behaves as a sly predator of Lysidamus. The old man's helpers bear ironic names that underscore their impotence: Olympio the foreman hardly wields Olympian power and Alcesimus ("Helper") seems helpless. The cook is unnamed in the text, as is the old man commonly known as Lysidamus. The name "Lysidamus" is taken from the scene headings of a manuscript penned roughly five centuries after the death of Plautus and scholars use that name out of convenience; it is more likely that Plautus left him unnamed.[25]

After an expository prologue introduces these characters and provides some essential background, an irritated Olympio enters, hounded by Chalinus. The two slaves argue directly and naturally in iambs, without musical accompaniment. Olympio has come from the farm to marry Casina, but Chalinus wants her as well. Threats of violence abound, making clear that this play will be a comic war for a slave girl. The two depart, leaving the stage empty.

Cleostrata enters and addresses the audience in agitated lyrics. She is enraged partly at her husband's infatuation with the maid Casina and partly at

---

24. These three pervasive metaphors, along with culinary metaphors, define sexual hierarchies within the households. For example, Lysidamus and Olympio are reduced to defeated, hungry, and stinking beasts. See G. F. Franko, "Imagery and Names in Plautus' *Casina,*" *Classical Journal* 95 (1999): 1–17.

25. Several of our manuscripts call him simply *senex* ("the Old Man"). Unnamed characters are fairly common in Plautus: see G. E. Duckworth, "The Unnamed Characters in the Plays of Plautus," *Classical Philology* 33 (1938): 267–82. Duckworth points out that of approximately 220 characters, 30 are unnamed, plus 9 or 10 unnamed except in the scene headings, bringing the total of unnamed characters to roughly 18 percent.

his opposition to her plans of marrying the maid to Chalinus. While she rants, her best friend and neighbor, Myrrhina, enters. Myrrhina, far from comforting Cleostrata, maintains that Lysidamus should be permitted to indulge his infatuation and that Cleostrata should be satisfied with her domestic situation. Their lively interchange is interrupted by the arrival of Lysidamus himself, who exuberantly delivers a few lyric verses about the powers of love. Cleostrata overhears him, and he tries to cover himself with transparent lies. As the meter shifts to trochees, the two settle into a heated exchange in which Cleostrata scolds Lysidamus for carousing and for his interference with her plans to marry Casina to Chalinus. Cleostrata exits to try to persuade Olympio to give up his claim on the girl offstage. Lysidamus meanwhile, failing to persuade Chalinus to give up his claim on the girl, proposes a lottery to determine the lucky suitor.

Matters have reached a temporary impasse, and the stalemate is marked by a conversation between Lysidamus and Olympio in plain iambs. Chalinus and Cleostrata emerge, bringing an urn, lots, and water (the water made it more difficult to see or feel the lots inside the urn, thereby minimizing the chance for cheating). In a lively scene enhanced by trochees, Chalinus and Olympio exchange curses and punches as Cleostrata and Lysidamus try to organize the proceedings. Cleostrata draws the winner, and it's . . . Olympio. A stunned Cleostrata retreats to the house, soon followed by the overjoyed Lysidamus and Olympio. The music stops as a crestfallen Chalinus reflects on his defeat in iambs. Olympio and Lysidamus soon return, affording Chalinus the opportunity to eavesdrop and overhear the whole truth: Olympio is a surrogate; Lysidamus really loves Casina; Lysidamus has made arrangements to sleep with Casina tonight at the neighbor's house. As the conspirators depart, Chalinus tells the audience that he will reveal all to Cleostrata and thereby snatch victory from the jaws of defeat. An empty stage marks a transition as a play about arranging a marriage transforms into one of intrigue.

This fresh start or second part of the play begins with the entrance of Lysidamus and his neighbor Alcesimus, who discuss in excited trochees the details of a secret rendezvous: Alcesimus will empty his house by sending everyone over to help with the wedding and Lysidamus will slip in with the maid. Lysidamus departs to spend the day at the forum. Cleostrata arrives, fuming at the news that Lysidamus intends to bed the maid that very night at the neighbor's house. Seeing Alcesimus, she throws her first wrench into their plans by denying that she needs any help with the wedding. Alcesimus therefore cannot empty his house. Lysidamus now returns, depressed at having wasted the whole day at the forum, and appropriately speaking unmusical iambs. He and Alcesimus argue fiercely until Alcesimus once again promises to vacate his house. As soon as this is resolved, Cleostrata launches her second assault. Pardalisca bursts onto the stage with tragic bombast, her lyrics claiming that Casina has gone mad, grabbed a sword, and threatens to kill the man who sleeps with her tonight. Lysidamus, fooled and terrified, sends Pardalisca away to try calming the maid. Virtually incapacitated by his lust and terror, he meets Olympio returning with the cooks for the wedding. The two cautiously enter the house, leaving the stage empty.

Pardalisca again pops out to explain, in straightforward iambs, Cleostrata's third and grandest ruse. While the cooks are making delays, Chalinus is being dressed as the bride. Lysidamus and Olympio, their excitement heightened by trochees, await the arrival of Casina. The excitement increases further, signaled by a switch to the lyric mode, when Cleostrata and Pardalisca give them their "bride," Chalinus in a wedding gown. As the three men withdraw, the lyrics change to iambs and an anxious quiet descends on the empty stage.

Cleostrata, Pardalisca, and Myrrhina take their places, chattering in lively lyrics. Soon Olympio rushes out of the house and, badgered by Pardalisca, gives a lyrical account of his mishap with the transvestite bride. Lysidamus follows delivering a similar account, until he is corraled by Chalinus. The meter changes to trochees as, accosted from all sides, he submits to the wrath of his wife. Cleostrata, triumphant, forgives him in order to end the play more quickly. A brief epilogue reveals that Casina will be found to be the long-lost daughter of the neighbors (presumably Myrrhina and Alcesimus), and that she will marry Euthynicus, the son of Lysidamus and Cleostrata.

CLEOSTRATA IN CHARGE

TRADITION AND VARIATION IN *CASINA*

CASINA is certainly among the latest of Plautus' plays, if not the very latest. This has important implications for our study: *Casina* is not the work of a novice, a playwright struggling to master the craft of turning Greek scripts into Roman plays; rather, this is the work of an old pro with over twenty years of success to draw upon. The unparalleled metrical sophistication, the rapid development and tight structure of the plot, and the robustness of the humor suggest that *Casina* is the culmination of a career, a masterwork that builds upon and reacts to the traditions of Greek and Roman Comedy, traditions that Plautus himself helped shape.

Two elements lend predictability to scripts of New Comedy: stock characters and formulaic plots. New Comic playwrights worked within a tradition of stock characters, that is, they continuously recycled a limited cast of characters with stereotyped attributes. Amidst their gallery of stereotypes we find the clever slave, the insipid young man in love, the innocent girl he loves, the sleazy slave dealer, the braggart soldier, the gullible father, the nagging wife, and the garrulous parasite. These characters operated within broadly formulaic plot structures. One traditional plot or subplot of New Comedy is that of a young man who desires a girl but cannot have her because a soldier, slave dealer, or his father obstructs him (cf. *Dyskolos* and *Phormio*). The young man seeks help from an ally, very often his clever slave, who concocts a ruse to overcome the blocking character. The audience shares in the ally's triumph and in the union of the lovers. Many of Plautus' plays have this skeletal structure, though fleshed out with different features. For example, in *Persa* the young lover is himself a slave, while in *Asinaria* the young lover is helped by two slaves and his father, and in *Curculio* the ally of the frustrated inamorato is a parasite. Such variations keep the genre fresh by enabling different characters, and different interrelations between the characters, to occupy the spotlight. Much of the humor and pleasure in New Comedy derives from the audience's familiarity with the genre and the poet's attempt to foil their expectations. The finer the balance between expectation (which produces dramatic irony) and variation (which produces suspense), the finer the structure of the play.

This essay examines how Plautus' *Casina* meets or diverges from some general expectations of New Comedy. It proceeds through the play scene-by-scene noting the ways in which characters conform to or diverge from stereotyped roles. In broad outline, the plot of *Casina* recalls the model sketched above of the frustrated young man in love; however, the action takes some unexpected turns, and this leads characters to slip in and out of traditional roles. Four characters seek to control the fate of the maid Casina: the old man Lysidamus, his wife Cleostrata, the foreman of the farm Olympio, and the squire Chalinus. As events unfold, the two slaves are relegated to subordinate roles while Cleostrata wrests control of the action from Lysidamus, who assumes progressively debased roles. A play that begins as a competition between suitors transforms into a drama of deceit, with the wife discarding her stock role of nagging matron to steal the spotlight as the trickster in charge.

The Prologue

The prologue of *Casina,* which introduces a household of anonymous stereotypes (a mother, a father, a son in love, a young girl, and two slaves), appears to forecast a traditional plot.[1] A father and his son both love the same maid, a situation paralleled in other extant ancient comedies, most notably in Plautus' own *Mercator.* The audience learns that the girl will be proven a chaste and freeborn Athenian citizen, another traditional feature of New Comedy that suggests a hackneyed plot wherein the girl's true identity is revealed and a marriage ensues. But the audience also hears that the son will not appear on stage, which suggests a divergence from the tradition, because there cannot be a happy marriage without a young man in love. More interestingly, the prologue leaves

---

1. It is unclear how much of the prologue is genuine and how much was added for the production after Plautus' death. The question of authenticity, however, is not crucial to our analysis of the script since the action is coherent and comprehensible with or without the extant prologue. At the very least, lines 5–22 were written for the post-Plautine production.

unclear which character will control the action and thereby gain the audience's confidence and sympathies.

Lines 50–51 ostensibly promise a contest between father and son, a scenario in which the audience can expect to side with the son, the traditional winner in such comedic contests. But the father has sent the son abroad and the mother has adopted her son's cause, leaving a struggle of husband versus wife. A war between the sexes has supplanted one between generations. Are spectators to side with the wife, often portrayed as the denier of pleasure yet the upholder of marital integrity? Or are they to sympathize with the husband, who might prove to be either the henpecked fellow seeking a rare bit of fun or the contemptible old fool trying to play the young lover? The prologue also leaves unclear whether husband and wife will dominate the action or if some slaves, as so often in Plautus, will step to the fore. The father has enlisted the foreman of the farm as his ally while the son is represented by his squire. These slaves do not seem to be mere tools, for at line 80 they are described as free agents working for their own interests. In effect, the prologue raises a simple question: who is the star of this show that will bring about the anticipated resolution of the plot?

In the majority of those plays of Plautus in which a young man in love must struggle to win his girl, a clever character—most often a slave—concocts one or more deceptions to overcome all obstacles. This familiar formula generates some of Plautus' slickest plots and most appealing characters. The popular play *Pseudolus* may serve as a paradigm. Therein, a young man loves a courtesan but has no money to purchase her from her owner, Ballio. Worse, she has been promised to a soldier who has already made a down payment on her. Ballio is to hand her over to the soldier's emissary, who will appear with the balance owed and a token proving that he represents the soldier. The young man's slave Pseudolus, posing as Ballio's slave, intercepts the real emissary and thus obtains the token and the money. He then directs an assistant to complete the transaction with Ballio. Thus the slave dealer is hoodwinked and the young couple is united, all this thanks to the machinations of Pseudolus. Based upon the information provided in the prologue of *Casina,* an audience might anticipate the appearance of a clever trickster like Pseudolus: there is a young man in love, as well as an obstacle blocking him, and matters have reached an apparent impasse. Yet no one is identified as the clever trickster, leaving the shape of the play indeterminate. The opening scenes heighten our curiosity by presenting us with four candidates for the role of clever trickster.

Olympio, Chalinus, and the War for Casina

The first scene's abusive confrontation between Olympio the foreman and Chalinus the squire challenges the audience to choose sides but does not make clear which side is to be favored. This is partly due to the fact that neither of the slaves conforms to traditional stock roles. At first blush, Olympio might appear to be a typical farmer. New Comedy generally celebrates urban values over rustic values and treats farmers as a source of ridicule rather than sympathy. When Chalinus scoffs at Olympio's lack of urbanity, he invites the audience to dismiss Olympio as a bumpkin, a traditional outsider and butt of jokes. If Chalinus is to be believed, then Olympio cannot be the crafty slave for whom the audience roots. But Olympio is hardly a lowly hayseed; rather, he is the foreman of the family farm, and thus holds an important position in the household. He is also the more active of the two slaves in that his arrival from the farm begins the action of the play proper, and his description of the tortures in store for Chalinus is reminiscent of the fantasizing of dominant slaves in Plautus. The farmhand Olympio apparently has the upper hand on Chalinus, who can only shadow him.

As for Chalinus, he is emphatically not the traditional urban house slave. The prologue explains that he is a squire (*armiger,* literally "arms-bearer") and perhaps his costume revealed his military background. His occupation is significant, for Chalinus becomes the focal point of the nexus of military imagery that pervades the play and gives tangible evidence of this war for Casina. Military imagery is characteristic of Plautus and particularly of his scheming slaves. The prologue introduced military terminology by stating that both son and father secretly prepare their legions, enlist soldiers, and contemplate night maneuvers (lines 50–54). The first scene augments that military imagery to make clear that this play is a struggle for possession of Casina, who is seen not as a person, but as booty (lines 113, 114; the English pun is serendipitous). But the first scene offers the audience no invitation to favor any particular faction in this war. Plautus is slow to reveal which commander is the wiliest, for although the first half of the play shows Chalinus and the wife Cleostrata on the defensive, subsequent events will prove that they possess the superior tactical expertise to triumph over Olympio and the old man Lysidamus.[2]

2. On Chalinus generally, see W. S. Anderson, "Chalinus *armiger* in Plautus' *Casina,*" *Illinois Classical Studies* 8 (1983): 11–21. Note Cleostrata's significant name ("Glory of the Army"). More military imagery: Lysidamus claims to be aware of Chalinus' javelins (line 297); defeat, for him, means falling on his sword (line 307); he sees the lottery in military terms (lines 344, 352, 357). Chalinus describes his eavesdropping as an ambush (line 436) and declares that the

Cleostrata: Martyr or Shrew?

After their heated exchange, Olympio and Chalinus depart. The audience next meets the matron Cleostrata, who bursts onto the empty stage with a lyrical flourish. Her very first word, *obsignate* ("lock up!"), an imperative, tells us much of her character. She appears to be in charge of the house, to possess foresight, and to be proactive in her defensive locking of the cupboards against her husband. When her maid Pardalisca pops out and reports that the old man has commanded a meal to be prepared, Cleostrata countermands that order. Cleostrata's word is final with the maids, in contrast to both the neighbor Myrrhina, who is ignored by her maids, and Lysidamus, who cannot control the male slaves or Pardalisca. After commanding Pardalisca to leave, Cleostrata addresses the audience as her confidant and reveals that she knows of her husband's lust (lines 150–57):

> Because he opposes his wife and his son,
> In pleasing himself and pursuing his love,
> I'll wreak my revenge on that wretch of a man:
> I'll hurt him with hunger and thwart him with thirst,
> Lambasting that lover in words and in works!
> By Pollux, I'll pain him with insults that sting,
> I'll give him the treatment he truly deserves!

While locking the cupboards may keep her husband hungry, it is unclear how she will give him "the treatment he truly deserves." Her threats are, as of yet, vague and unfocused. Lacking a clear course of action, she goes to the neighbor's to complain rather than to scheme.

How should an audience react to Cleostrata? On the one hand, she addresses the spectators in lyric verse, unlike the traditional nagging matrons in Plautus who deliver only iambs and trochees; her ability to use the lyric mode of delivery aligns her with the traditionally attractive characters. The agitated

---

vanquished will win the battle (line 509). After the women disguise the squire as Casina (line 769), he emerges with an elbow like a battering ram (line 849) and proceeds to "make war" on Olympio and Lysidamus (line 851). Some of Cleostrata's advice to the "bride" (really Chalinus in disguise) is couched in military terms (lines 819–21). Pardalisca claims that Casina has taken up a sword (two, in fact: line 691), and Chalinus, disguised as Casina, subsequently does wield a phallic "sword" (line 909) to defeat his opponents. The recurrent metaphor of a sword as a phallic symbol is increasingly charged with meaning at lines 307, 344, 629, 660, 691, 706, 750, and 909.

meters of her opening verses convey a distracted emotional state, which may invite sympathy. On the other hand, her promise to lash her husband makes her sound like a shrew and wins no sympathy, because her motives for punishing him are not strongly presented. If we believe Cleostrata, her husband is old, buzzard bait, and a sink of iniquity. But, at this point, we are not sure what he has done wrong. He has not yet slept with the chaste Casina, and unless this current infatuation is merely the latest in a string of indecencies—and there is no indication of that here—he is thus far only guilty of planning to play the role of *senex amator,* the old man in love.[3] Cleostrata's opening verses convey the emotions of anger and violence, not despair and suffering, and thus they assimilate her to the traditionally unsympathetic role of nagging matron.

The entrance of the neighbor Myrrhina further helps delineate Cleostrata's motives and isolation. Myrrhina immediately recognizes that Cleostrata is upset (line 173), is empathetic with her plight (line 180), and is explicitly identified as Cleostrata's best friend (line 182). One might expect this friend to side with Cleostrata and a denunciation of male misbehavior to ensue. But when Cleostrata explains the trouble—that Lysidamus purportedly wishes to marry her personal maid to his overseer only so that he can bed the maid himself—Myrrhina balks. Ignoring the issue of Lysidamus' lust, Myrrhina instead expresses disbelief that her friend owns a maid and implies that Cleostrata must have committed either theft or adultery to obtain the maid. Myrrhina shifts the blame from Lysidamus to Cleostrata and proceeds to advise her friend to keep quiet, accept her husband's peccadillos, and avoid divorce at all costs. She even calls Cleostrata stupid (line 204). By delivering a condemnation of Cleostrata's behavior via her best friend, Plautus sways his audience away from a sympathetic view of Cleostrata and invites them to favor old Lysidamus.[4]

Myrrhina's failure to support Cleostrata might disturb modern sensibilities, but it would have made perfect sense to a predominantly male Roman audience. Close attention to the text makes clear that Cleostrata does not center her complaint on her husband's lust for Casina, but on her loss of control over

3. Most critics assume that he is an inveterate rake: B. Williams, however, suggests that Lysidamus' incompetence in playing the part of *senex amator* implies that he is unfamiliar with this role ("Games People Play: Metatheatre as Performance Criticism in Plautus' *Casina,*" *Ramus* 22 (1993): 43).

4. See T. J. Moore, *The Theater of Plautus* (Austin, 1998), 168–70, on the contrasting initial portrayals of Cleostrata and Myrrhina. Cleostrata, for example, refuses to perform her wifely duty of cooking, while Myrrhina engages in her wifely duty of spinning.

the maid (lines 193–96; cf. line 150). Moreover, Lysidamus has not yet done anything wrong: he has not yet slept with the maid and, even if he had, there would be nothing so unusual or morally reprehensible in that. Far better that he sleep with a household slave than commit adultery with a free woman outside the household.

The key here is that Plautus presents Cleostrata's threats of vengeance before he presents Lysidamus. Had he shown a dissolute, disgusting Lysidamus first, or made clear that he had violated Casina, or emphasized Cleostrata's maternal relationship with the girl, an audience might share her outrage. The playwright's choice to put the angry Cleostrata onstage first and then have her best friend condemn her serves to mitigate whatever initial sympathy an audience may feel for her plight. Her role at the beginning seems to be that of the traditional shrew who, with limited power, attempts to thwart the pleasures of her husband.

Lysidamus: Old Man of Many Roles

Readers, like viewers of a live play, should suspend quick judgments and allow their reactions to characters to change in the course of a drama. Characters are not static, but develop through a sequence of scenes; readers who treat them as static figures that remain unchanged from beginning to end, and use passages from the end to explicate the beginning, will miss the mark. This is a particular danger in discussing Lysidamus, who is much more than a simple *senex amator*.[5] Lysidamus is better seen as a character consistently motivated by one strong emotion—lust—who, in response to changing circumstances, assumes inconsistent and progressively debased stock roles. In the course of the action this old man plays the traditional roles of *adulescens amans* (young man in love), *servus callidus* (clever slave), gullible old man, and worthless slave. His character has both unity in his lust and variety in his expression of that lust; his motivation invites us to see him as a simple stock character while his behavior shows complex variation.

After Myrrhina has counseled Cleostrata to yield to her husband, Lysidamus enters delivering a string of snappy anapests. He seems a bit tipsy and

---

5. For example, W. Forehand ("Plautus' *Casina*: An Explication," *Arethusa* 6 [1973]: 253) contends that "the old man remains a thoroughly objectionable character from beginning to end." Contrast J. Tatum's observation, based on performances of the play, that "we come to feel a wry affection" for Lysidamus (*Plautus: The Darker Comedies* [Baltimore, 1983], 89).

his lyrics are peppered with the olfactory imagery of cooks and flavors, which may recall Cleostrata's pledge to starve him. In this figurative context, the love of Casina, the "cinnamon girl," is not envisioned as the meat and potatoes in Lysidamus' diet, but rather as a condiment. The silly self-absorption of Lysidamus' lyrics echoes that of a typical Plautine young man in love. But Lysidamus is a *senex,* an old man. The *senex amator* appears in seven other comedies of Plautus and his behavior can range from laughably innocuous to offensively sleazy.[6] When presented with an enamored *senex,* an audience can either celebrate with him his escape from his bitchy wife, or condemn him as a gross and indecent old lecher. On the one hand, the joyful words and meter of Lysidamus' entry, delivered in confidence to the audience, invite the spectators to join his revelry. Plautus has already introduced his wife, and she is no sweetheart. On the other hand, his costume should make an audience hesitate, for his white hair (lines 239, 518), lack of teeth (line 550), and cane denote that Lysidamus is a very old *senex.* Moreover, this old man is married and lusts after a sixteen-year-old girl who has been raised as his daughter. If one does not feel revulsion, one at least perceives an unseemly situation as Lysidamus acts less like a father than an insipid young man in love toward a member of his own household.[7]

Before the start of the play, Lysidamus had debased himself, becoming a rival to his own son, the rightful *adulescens amans.* He then successfully removed that *adulescens amans* and thus made the role of young lover vacant and available for himself to assume. But not without competition: he, Olympio, and Chalinus all vie for the part.[8] While for those two slaves the role of young lover is a step up, for the master of the house it is a step down. Lysidamus is a man of some wealth who owns a country estate requiring a foreman and who apparently has sufficient standing in the community to serve as an advocate in a relative's court case. Although Lysidamus previously exercised some authority over his household (for example, by sending his son away), if he had been an authoritarian figure along traditional Roman lines the conflicts of *Casina* would never have arisen, for he would simply have wedded Casina to the foreman with or without his wife's consent and then bedded the maid whenever he chose.

---

6. See K. C. Ryder, "The *senex amator* in Plautus," *Greece and Rome* 31 (1984): 181–89.

7. Plautus does not belabor the prologue's claim that Casina has been raised as Cleostrata's daughter. Perhaps too much emphasis on the incestuous aspect of his lust would vilify him beyond what is acceptable to retain a lighthearted, farcical atmosphere.

8. See Williams (above, note 3), 47–48, for the old man's metatheatrical audition for the part of *adulescens amans.*

Indeed, the audience will immediately sense that Lysidamus is not in complete control as soon as he confronts his wife. This Jupiter cowers before his Juno.[9] He must ask for his wife's consent in the matter regarding Casina (lines 252–54), whereupon Cleostrata reminds him that she has been granted control of the maids (lines 260–61). He points out that his son should yield, not that the son must obey (line 265). Such remarks form a significant pattern: as Lysidamus abdicates his proper role as head of the household to play the role of lover-boy, he resorts to promises and bribes rather than imperatives in dealings with members of his household.

Neither Lysidamus nor Cleostrata clearly wins the audience's sympathy in their initial confrontation. On the one hand, Lysidamus is disingenuous, guilty, and a shameless liar. On the other hand, the *senex* is the one allowed to address the audience directly with asides that invoke the tradition of jokes at the expense of a battle-axe wife, thereby casting him as the henpecked husband and her as the nagging killjoy.[10] Evidently such spats have taken place many times before (line 318) and will be repeated in the future (line 251). Neither character emerges as wholly sympathetic, a good reminder that stock characters need not be simplistic.

As the above may have served to suggest, Plautus, in the opening scenes of *Casina,* has introduced some innovations that prevent an audience from pigeonholing the characters and the plot into hackneyed traditions of New Comedy. The first scene displaces the advertised rivalry between father and son with a rivalry between two servile surrogates. That antagonism is, in turn, replaced by antagonism between husband and wife. Husband and wife seek to manipulate the slaves, contrary to the usual practice in Plautus where slaves manipulate their masters. The wife, though shrewish, employs the lyric mode of delivery, which is usually reserved for attractive characters. The old husband may either be despised for his lechery or pitied for being henpecked. After a quarter of the play has elapsed, the sympathy of the audience is still not clearly directed toward any one character and no one yet has taken charge.

9. When Chalinus strikes Olympio during the lottery, claiming that Juno commanded him to do so, Lysidamus admits that this must be endured since his wife holds the power (lines 406–9).

10. See lines 227, 234, 326, 354, 497, and 557; compare also the joke from Caecilius Statius quoted in the introduction. There may be some truth in Lysidamus' claim that Cleostrata opposes him purely out of overzealous "meddling" (*industria,* lines 276, 278, 805), a common trait of Plautine matrons discussed by E. Segal (*Roman Laughter* [Cambridge, Mass., 1968; 2d ed. 1987], 51ff.).

A Plautine Lottery

Lysidamus proves unable to persuade Chalinus to forgo marriage with Casina. He tries to assert his authority on the squire, but, being met with insolence, quickly resorts to a bribe of an offer of freedom. He bargains with a slave rather than commanding or threatening. Because of his inability to determine the disposition of a slave in his own household, Lysidamus suggests a lottery in which fortune, not his domestic authority, will determine the maid's fate and resolve the deadlock.

The prologue's revelation that *Casina* is an adaptation of Diphilus' Greek play *The Lot-Drawers* underscores the dramatic centrality of the upcoming lottery scene. One must wonder why this is such an ingenious scheme if Olympio has only a fifty/fifty chance of winning. Surely Lysidamus does not have such faith in the gods, as he claims (line 346). Something else up must be up his sleeve, and a clue may lie in line 342, where Lysidamus declares: "I'll draw for you and Chalinus." Perhaps Lysidamus, as head of the household, plans to ensure the victory of his overseer by cheating. But as events unfold he yields that privilege to Cleostrata, ostensibly out of fairness. There is more here than meets the eye, and comparison of this scene in *Casina* with the corresponding scene in its Greek model *may* reveal a great deal about Plautus' dramatic craft. Although the following discussion is speculative because we do not possess the Greek model for comparison, it provides an example of the methods one might employ to assess Plautus' originality, and thus his dramatic priorities and the tastes of his Roman audience.

Athenian tragedy was performed with a maximum of three speaking actors (who could change masks to assume different parts). Although we cannot be certain that Greek New Comedy acknowledged such a restriction, some inscriptions suggest that troops with three speaking actors were the norm. In addition, the extant plays and fragments of Menander are all performable by three speakers, which suggests that he adhered to a tradition of having no more than three speakers onstage together in his plays.[11] *If* Menander did adhere to a limit of three speakers per scene, then whenever we find four speakers in a Plautine adaptation of a play by Menander we might have evidence of Plautine workmanship. The same might hold true for a play by Diphilus. We have no evi-

---

11. See A. Pickard-Cambridge, *The Dramatic Festivals of Athens* (2d ed., rev. J. Gould and D. Lewis; Oxford, 1968), 135–56. The fact that a script can be performed by three speaking actors does not necessarily mean it was composed with a restriction of three speakers.

dence that other Greek New Comic playwrights acknowledged a limit of three speaking actors; however, *if* Diphilus did limit his scenes to three speakers, then whenever we find four speakers onstage in *Casina* we might have evidence of Plautine workmanship.

There are four speakers in Plautus' lottery scene: Lysidamus, Cleostrata, Chalinus, and Olympio. Diphilus, if he was confined to three speaking actors, might have had the old man drawing the lots in front of the two slaves, with his wife either absent or mute. Diphilus might thereby have emphasized irony rather than suspense: the lottery would have been proposed as a charade of fairness in which the old man saw to it that his henchman won. If Plautus did add the fourth speaker, most likely Cleostrata, he gained three advantages. First, he created two balanced pairs, Cleostrata and Chalinus versus Lysidamus and Olympio, and this balance affords greater opportunity for horseplay and slapstick. Second, the scene in Plautus favors suspense over irony. The outcome of the drawing becomes uncertain for both the characters and the audience. Third, Plautus could have increased the importance of Cleostrata. By allowing her to shake the urn and draw the winner, Plautus would have made her more than a passive matron and foreshadowed her increasingly active role. Again, these remarks are speculative because Diphilus' play is not extant for comparison; however, it is plausible that Plautus was responsible for the pervasive enhancement of Cleostrata's role, this scene being indicative of a grander strategy.[12]

Is There a *Servus Callidus* in the House?

The lottery, whose winner is Lysidamus' candidate Olympio, settles the latent competition between father and son. If the play were about possession of the girl, it could end at this point. However, the play does not end, and, indeed, there is a sense that this is only the beginning, for the competition between husband and wife is just heating up. In the scenes that follow, Lysidamus, Chalinus, and Cleostrata each assume the characteristic attributes of the *servus callidus*.

As explained above, the stereotypical young man in love often turns to his clever slave for a brilliant plan to solve his dilemma. Plautus was particularly

---

12. See W. S. Anderson, *Barbarian Play* (Toronto, 1996), 55–58, which takes Plautine expansion of Cleostrata's role as a given. Using this criterion of three speakers, we might also postulate extensive Plautine aggrandizement of the final two scenes, which present six speakers onstage: Cleostrata, Myrrhina, Olympio, Lysidamus, Chalinus, and Pardalisca. It is possible that the actor portraying Pardalisca leaves the stage after her final line (line 935) in order to reappear as Chalinus (line 960), which would make *Casina* performable by five speaking actors.

fond of clever slaves like Pseudolus, and we would expect to find such a character somewhere in this script. But Lysidamus, Chalinus, and Olympio all
seem to vie for the role of lover, not trickster. Chalinus appears rather dull and
passive in the opening scene. Olympio nowhere shows a spark of genius and
Lysidamus views him as his helper and co-conspirator (e.g., line 979) rather
than as his advisor. Old Lysidamus, oddly enough, emerges as the most cunning
of the three men in that, by this point in time, he has achieved some success as
an architect of deceit. First, the prologue revealed that he began his schemes
before the play commenced by enlisting Olympio as a surrogate and by removing his main rival, his son. Second, Lysidamus himself concocted the scheme of
lot-drawing, which, through impartial fortune, awards Casina to his henchman
and also avoids a potentially embarrassing confrontation with Cleostrata. Third,
the audience now learns that he has already made arrangements for his neighbor Alcesimus to provide an empty house for his tryst (lines 477–79). The
scene in which Lysidamus reveals this scheme to Olympio is a fascinating example of how Plautus renovates the New Comic tradition, for it reverses the
motif in which a clever slave explains his ruse to his master. Here the clever
figure is the master himself (lines 480–88):

> LYSIDAMUS: I've cleverly arranged that. My wife will call her over for the wed-
> ding to be there with her, help her out, and spend the night with her. I in-
> sisted, and my wife said she'd do it. So she'll sleep there. Her husband'll be
> out of the house; I'll see to that. You take Casina to the farm, but the "farm"
> will be their house, just long enough for me to consummate the marriage with
> Casina! Then you'll take her to the real farm before dawn. Ingenious, no?
> OLYMPIO: Right clever.
> CHALINUS: Go on, construct your cunning capers! By Hercules, your craftiness
> is digging your own grave!

The descriptions of Lysidamus' ruse (here translated as "cleverly," "ingenious," "right clever," "construct your cunning capers," and "craftiness") come
straight from the lexicon of cunning Plautine slaves. But unlike those slaves,
whose aim is to aid their masters, Lysidamus plans for his own satisfaction. Indeed, his eagerness and passion are so unbridled that he makes sexual advances
to the foreman (lines 451–66). In effect, Lysidamus attempts to play two roles
at once.

Lysidamus does not usurp the role of clever slave unchallenged, for Chalinus, like many a clever slave in Plautus, has seized in this scene the advanta-
geous position of eavesdropper, which brings with it the privilege of making

asides to the audience.[13] Chalinus overhears the entire scheme, and when Lysidamus and Olympio exit basking in overconfidence, Chalinus steps out of his hiding place to address the audience:

> If I was offered my freedom three times over it couldn't keep me from cooking up big trouble for them today and telling the whole story to my mistress! I've caught my enemies red-handed! And now, if my mistress will just do her duty, the battle is ours! I'll rout them cleanly! It's our lucky day! Now the vanquished are victorious! I'll go inside to spice up what another cook seasoned. What was prepared won't turn out, and what wasn't will!
>
>   (lines 504–14)

The audience again hears lexical echoes of other scheming slaves, couched in the vocabulary of military and culinary imagery. Chalinus vacillates between seeing the victory as purely personal ("I") and communal ("our"). This suggests that he, a mere squire, may lack the cunning required to take advantage of this information. He is no Pseudolus and thus needs the tactical expertise of the general, Cleostrata.

Although Lysidamus has already made arrangements with his neighbor Alcesimus for his tryst, Plautus opts to show the audience a reconfirmation of those arrangements (lines 515–30). By inserting this logically unnecessary short scene, the playwright gains two things. First, he can again present Lysidamus as a *servus callidus* planning a ruse and directing his auxiliaries. Second, he gives Cleostrata just enough time to hear the squire's report and formulate a plan of attack. The wedding is at hand and time is of the essence. Cleostrata must think fast, not unlike Plautus' most ruthlessly improvisational slave Tranio, who in *Mostellaria* frenetically plans deceptions on the spur of the moment. Cleostrata manages to devise three schemes of increasing complexity in short shrift: she sows discord between Alcesimus and Lysidamus, fabricates a story of Casina's insanity, and disguises Chalinus as Casina. By the end of the play there will be no doubt that she has usurped the role of the scheming slave and that the audience is on her side.

Armed with the details of her husband's plans, Cleostrata swings into action.[14] First, she herself misdirects the neighbor Alcesimus by claiming that

13. See Moore (above, note 4), especially 171 and 174–75, for discussion of how eavesdroppers in *Casina* gain the upper hand and enjoy a greater rapport with the audience.

14. Some scholars believe that there is an inconsistency in Cleostrata's understanding of the situation and argue that her surprise at Chalinus' report here is incompatible with lines 58, 151, and 195, where she appears to have knowledge of Lysidamus' love for Casina. But in those

there is no need for his wife to visit and help with preparations for the wedding (lines 539–57). Alcesimus is completely fooled. Next, she tricks Lysidamus into thinking that Alcesimus has refused to lend his wife's services (lines 576–88). After an amusing shouting match, the two men iron things out and try to resume their plans; Cleostrata, however, has already launched her second assault before they can begin.

Cleostrata's first move was a mere delaying tactic, meant to give her time to prepare her maid Pardalisca for a new role. Pardalisca now enters with an overblown parody of a tragic messenger speech in which she declares that Casina has gone mad and is terrorizing the household with a sword (lines 621–29). Torn between lust and terror, Lysidamus begs Pardalisca to use her powers of persuasion (amply demonstrated in this very scene!) to calm the maid. Once again Lysidamus is unable to command a servant of his household and must resort to bribery (lines 708–12). Pardalisca's ruse is another delaying tactic rather than a final solution. Eventually Casina will be forced to marry Olympio, as Lysidamus says (lines 700–701), so the report of her madness merely causes the old man some angst and embarrassment. But this scene also marks an important shift in the development of the plot. Pardalisca reveals in an aside that she has been sent onstage by Cleostrata and Myrrhina to fool the old man (lines 685–88). This serves notice to the audience that Cleostrata is now on the offensive and scripting the action while Lysidamus is now on the defensive, playing whatever role his wife prepares for him.[15]

Here Comes the "Bride"?

When last we saw Olympio, Lysidamus was ordering him off to buy some gourmet items for the wedding feast. Now, upon his return, the two men appear to exchange roles. Olympio, dressed magnificently for his wedding, adopts the role of an aristocrat and Lysidamus plays along, even proclaiming himself Olympio's slave (lines 723–40). While the script may suggest that Lysidamus has granted Olympio his freedom (presumably in exchange for an opportunity

---

places she has only vague information; Chalinus' report gives her a "smoking gun," that is, proof that Olympio is only a surrogate and precise details about how, where, and when Lysidamus will assault the maid (so, rightly, R. C. Beacham, *The Roman Theatre and Its Audience* [Cambridge, Mass., 1991], 104).

15. See N. W. Slater, *Plautus in Performance* (Princeton, 1985), 70–93, discussing the struggle between Cleostrata and Lysidamus as one between playwrights seeking to usurp control of the plot.

to sleep with Casina), that does not mean that Lysidamus also agreed to actual servitude. Rather, this is a traditional scene of role-reversal wherein a young lover pledges his allegiance to his servile helper, who is elevated to the status of the youth's patron or father: "Oh, I beg you, Olympy! My father! My sire!" (lines 738–39).[16] Lysidamus has already abandoned his role as head of the household for that of a young man in love, which in turn, according to the traditions of the genre, requires the adoption of a servile role. This short scene marks a further stage in the debasement of Lysidamus' character.

Soon after Lysidamus and Olympio enter the house, Pardalisca pops out to give the audience an update and to announce Cleostrata's third trick, that of the false bride. While the cooks keep the men frustrated and famished, the women outfit Chalinus in a wedding gown. Lysidamus and Olympio have reached a peak of agitation when at last the "bride" emerges in a scene punctuated with dramatic irony. Cleostrata blesses the squire in a parody of conventional wedding advice laden with military and governmental imagery.[17] The men impatiently attempt to fondle Chalinus, whose disguise apparently includes breasts "as soft as a cloud" (!), but the squire defends himself with unmaidenly strength. The audience, fully aware of the trick but uncertain of when Chalinus will drop the disguise, waits on the edge of its seat as the groom, his master, and the "bride" move toward Alcesimus' house in a perverse sort of wedding procession. With the climax at hand, the meter shifts to iambs and an eerie quiet descends on the stage. A wedding looms, but not the kind traditionally found in New Comedy.

After a pause and an empty stage, the music returns as Myrrhina, Cleostrata, and Pardalisca eagerly take their places to view the results of their trickery. Myrrhina declares: "no playwright has crafted a craftier ruse / Than the snare that was crafted by us here today!" (lines 860–61). Such boasts are typical of the clever slave who pauses to admire his handiwork. The women tout their scheme with self-conscious theatricality; they seem to view themselves as playwrights better than Diphilus or Menander, or perhaps even Plautus. In retrospect, Cleostrata has evolved from a henpecking matron, to a resourceful slave, to a veritable playwright who, with help from her neighbor and her slave,

---

16. Lines 1265–66 of Plautus' *Rudens,* spoken by the young lover to his slave Trachalio, provide a typical parallel: "my soul, my Trachalio, my freedman, I mean my patron, no, indeed, my father!" See further Segal (above, note 10), 104–16.

17. The attribution of lines 814–24 is highly uncertain; I give them to Cleostrata. On the wedding ritual in general, see G. Williams, "Some Aspects of Roman Marriage Ceremonies and Ideals," *Journal of Roman Studies* 48 (1958): 16–29.

manipulates all the male characters.[18] From this point on, nothing will happen that Cleostrata has not scripted. She can relax and join the audience for the upcoming show.

Olympio bursts onto stage to deliver a hilarious lyric report of his encounter with the counterfeit Casina. Although the real target of Cleostrata's deception was Lysidamus, Olympio's sexual misadventures are a delightfully unexpected bonus that heightens our eagerness to see the old man caught in the same trap. In addition, Olympio's account makes clear that the audience can enjoy the ingenuity of Cleostrata's trickery with the added satisfaction of knowing that justice is being served. Olympio himself concedes that his punishment is deserved (line 935).[19] He also repeatedly states that he is ashamed of his behavior, a sense of propriety conspicuously absent in his master.

Lysidamus now enters with what will prove to be the final lyrical flourish of the play. Although he recognizes his disgrace, he still exhibits no sense of shame and seems more concerned with his wife's wrath than with any social taint involved in fondling the male Chalinus. In his confusion Lysidamus contemplates two courses of action: he can run away or submit to a whipping. Both are responses typical of slaves, not heads of households. The first option merely completes the play's gradual debasement of the social standing of the *senex* from head of the household to worthless, runaway slave. The second option puts his misbehavior in a broader context. He admits that his wife actually does beat him and that at times he does deserve it (lines 957–58), which confirms that we have witnessed only his latest escapade in a career of roguery. That admission vindicates Cleostrata; she is not a shrew but a woman married to a continually misbehaving husband whose shenanigans merit the punishment meted out to slaves. She has whipped him before and, one suspects, will do so again. It seems

18. Some scholars have detected an inconsistency in Myrrhina's character, claiming that the woman who earlier told Cleostrata to ignore her husband's love affairs should not become a conspirator to humiliate Lysidamus for his infidelity. Yet Myrrhina did not know in the beginning that the men planned to use *her* home as a cheap motel for Lysidamus to consummate his lust. Lysidamus thereby would involve Myrrhina in his lecherous schemes, and this makes her willingness to join Cleostrata comprehensible. That said, consistency in characterization is more a priority for Menander and Terence than for Plautus.

19. Or is it? Casina is now legitimately Olympio's bride, and there is nothing legally or morally wrong with his hasty attempt to have intercourse with her. But Olympio is a conspirator in cahoots with Lysidamus, and his agreement to lend his wife to his master on their wedding night is unseemly. Worse yet, he breaks his promise to his master. A beating from a transvestite bride is a suitable comic punishment for these transgressions of lechery and treachery.

that Lysidamus is unwilling to play the socially designated role of *senex* but not crafty enough to play the role of *servus callidus* with the success enjoyed by other Plautine clever slaves such as Pseudolus.

Resolution and Epilogue

The final scene moves very quickly. Lysidamus tries unsuccessfully to deflect the blame to others, but his co-conspirator and the women maintain the pressure. Left with no alternative, he pledges never to approach Casina again. If he does try to seduce her, he grants permission to Cleostrata to whip him like a slave. And like a powerless slave, he can only beg a patron, Myrrhina, to intercede for him. Myrrhina is actually a prudent choice on Lysidamus' part, since, if we recall her advice to Cleostrata, she is disposed to let a husband have his affairs. Cleostrata's pardon may surprise us, but her reason is a good one: she wants to end the play. This quip is more than just another aside by an actor aware of his own theatricality. It confirms the suspicion that Cleostrata has been directing the plot of this play from the moment Chalinus brought her evidence of Lysidamus' plan to sleep with the maid. Cleostrata has completed an evolution from an apparent shrew to a clever trickster who resembles a master playwright. She alone determines when and how the play will end.

This ending is abrupt and surprising. The traditions of New Comedy would lead one to expect the revelation that Casina is Myrrhina's daughter and that a subsequent vow of marriage to the son of Lysidamus and Cleostrata would bring the play to a close. Instead, there has been a charade of a wedding and the revelation that "Casina" is something other than she appears to be. Plautus has met the genre's expectations in a delightfully perverse fashion and sees no need to meet them again in a more traditional way. Instead, a two-line epilogue fills in those missing details of Casina's parentage and marriage that have been anticipated ever since the prologue. Folks expecting the hackneyed recognition scene to close the play will be caught off guard; this allows the play to end with a bang rather than a drawn-out denouement.

There is some truth to the generalization that the comic genre represents a movement toward harmony, reconciliation, and either the establishment of a new order or the restoration of the status quo.[20] Lysidamus' household was in

20. See N. Frye, "The Argument of Comedy," *English Institute Studies,* 1948, 58–73; cf. his *Anatomy of Criticism* (Princeton, 1957), 163–71; see also T. Nelson, *Comedy: An Introduction to Comedy in Literature, Drama, and Cinema* (Oxford, 1990), 19–40 and 179–86. Nelson's book is arguably the best short introduction to the genre from Aristophanes to the present.

a crisis at the start of the play because he presented a mild threat to the established order by spurning his wife, lusting after a much younger girl, and chal-
lenging his son for that girl. There was even a hint of something incestuous
about the girl being raised as Cleostrata's daughter. Most of all, his abandon-
ment of his proper role as head of the household led to upheaval in the family
structure. After the threat has been narrowly defeated, the established order
is very quickly—almost perfunctorily—restored. Lysidamus repents; Cleostrata swears that she is not even angry; Lysidamus declares his affection for her;
Cleostrata seals the reconciliation by ordering Chalinus to give Lysidamus back
his cloak and staff, a gesture which symbolically returns her humbled husband
to his rightful place. The play ends with a restoration of the status quo between
husband and wife, and the epilogue provides the promise of a new beginning
for the young lovers. Yet Plautus' attention falls mainly on the laughable, farcical events within the comedy's movement toward restoration and a new beginning. *Casina* does not focus on the young lovers and the obstacles they overcome: the two do not even appear on stage. Rather, the play revels in trickery,
bawdiness, and repeated delays of or departures from the hackneyed traditional story pattern. *Casina* is not a celebration of harmony, reconciliation, and
happiness; it is a celebration of Cleostrata's cleverness and refusal to accept the
passive role of nagging matron.

SELECT BIBLIOGRAPHY

Some Books on Roman Comedy:

Arnott, W. G. *Menander, Plautus, Terence* (Greece and Rome: New Surveys in the Classics 9). Oxford, 1975.

Beacham, R. C. *The Roman Theatre and Its Audience.* Cambridge, Mass., 1991.

Beare, W. *The Roman Stage,* 3d ed. London, 1964.

Duckworth, G. E. *The Nature of Roman Comedy.* Princeton, 1952.

Gratwick, A. S. "Roman Drama." In *Cambridge History of Classical Literature,* vol. 2, 77–137. Cambridge, 1982.

Hunter, R. L. *The New Comedy of Greece and Rome.* Cambridge, 1985.

Konstan, D. *Roman Comedy.* Cornell, 1983.

Sandbach, F. H. *The Comic Theatre of Greece and Rome.* London, 1977.

Wright, J. *Dancing in Chains: The Stylistic Unity of the Comoedia Palliata.* Rome, 1974.

Some Books on Plautus in Particular:

Anderson, W. S. *Barbarian Play.* Toronto, 1996.

Moore, T. J. *The Theater of Plautus.* Austin, 1998.

Segal, E. *Roman Laughter.* Cambridge, Mass., 1968; 2d ed. 1987.

Slater, N. W. *Plautus in Performance.* Princeton, 1985.

Some Studies of *Casina:*

Anderson, W. S. "Chalinus *armiger* in Plautus' *Casina.*" *Illinois Classical Studies* 8 (1983): 11–21.

Cody, J. M. "The *Senex Amator* in Plautus' *Casina.*" *Hermes* 104 (1976): 453–76.

Connors, C. "Scents and Sensibility in Plautus' *Casina.*" *Classical Quarterly* 47 (1997): 305–9.

Forehand, W. "Plautus' *Casina:* An Explication." *Arethusa* 6 (1973): 233–56.

Franko, G. F. "Imagery and Names in Plautus' *Casina.*" *Classical Journal* 95 (1999): 1–7.

Gold, B. "'Vested Interests' in Plautus' *Casina:* Cross-Dressing in Roman Comedy." *Helios* 25 (1998): 17–29.

MacCary, W. T. "Patterns of Myth, Ritual, and Comedy in Plautus' *Casina.*" *Texas Studies in Literature and Language* 15 (1974): 881–89.

MacCary, W. T., and M. Willcock. *Plautus: Casina.* Cambridge, 1976.

O'Bryhim, S. "The Originality of Plautus' *Casina.*" *American Journal of Philology* 110
        (1989): 81–103.
Williams, B. "Games People Play: Metatheatre as Performance Criticism in Plautus'
        Casina." *Ramus* 22 (1993): 33–59.

CASINA

OLÝMPIO, *The foreman of Lysidamus' farm*

CHALÍNUS, *The squire of Lysidamus' son*

CLEOSTRÁTA, *Lysidamus' wife*

PARDALÍSCA, *Cleostrata's maid*

MYRRHÍNA, *The neighbor, wife of Alcesimus*

LYSIDÁMUS, *The old man*

ALCÉSIMUS, *The neighbor*

COOK

MUTES:

MYRRHINA'S MAIDS

COOKS

CHARACTERS NOT APPEARING:

CÁSINA, *The foundling maid of Cleostrata*

EUTHYNICUS, *The son of Lysidamus and Cleostrata*

SCENE: A street in Athens with two houses. The house of Lysidamus is stage left (toward the forum), that of Alcesimus stage right (toward the country).

The speaker of the prologue enters.

I bid you welcome, most excellent spectators! You show the greatest devotion to good faith—as Good Faith does to you![1] If I'm right, give me a clear sign, so that I'll know right from the start that you're on my side. *(pauses for applause)*

I think people who enjoy vintage wine and vintage plays have good taste. Since old-fashioned craftsmanship and language please you, vintage plays ought to please you most of all. Nowadays the new comedies they produce are even more debased than the new coins.[2] So after we heard the

---

1. One of many deified Roman virtues, *Fides* is the goddess of good faith, trust, loyalty, oaths, etc.

2. An undatable reference to the devaluation of Roman currency, presumably by diminution of the precious metal content.

rampant rumor that you fervidly fancy Plautine plays, we dusted off an old-fashioned comedy of his that you graybeards liked. Now I realize the young bucks don't know it, but we'll make sure they learn it. This play, when it premiered, topped them all! Back then was the golden age of poets, who since have gone the way of all flesh. But though they're absent, they profit us as if still present.

Please, I would really like you all to pay close attention to our troop. Forget your anxieties and debts. Nobody should fear his creditor: it's a holiday, even for the bankers. All's quiet; it's vacation time in the forum. It's in their interest: they don't collect their money during a holiday; after a holiday they don't refund yours. Lend me your ears—if they're free. I want to give you the name of the play. This comedy is called "*Clerumenoi*" in Greek; that's "Lot-Drawers" in Latin. Diphilus wrote it in Greek, and then Plautus, with the name that barks,[3] rewrote it again in Latin.

A married old man lives here. He's got a son, who lives along with him in this house right here. He's got a slave who's resting on death's door— no, no, by Hercules! To tell you the truth, he's just resting on a bed! That slave, well, sixteen years ago he saw a baby girl being abandoned in the wee morning hours. He goes straight to the woman who's abandoning it. He begs her to give it to him. He persuades her, carries it away, brings it straight home. He gives it to his mistress, begs her to care for it and raise it. The mistress did. She raised the girl with great care, pretty much as if she were her own daughter.

After she reached that age when a girl can attract men, this old man here falls madly in love with her. And his son does, too. Now each prepares his legions against the other—father and son—without the other knowing it! The father has enlisted the foreman of his farm to ask for her hand in marriage. If she's given to the foreman, he hopes he'll go on some "night maneuvers" without his wife finding out. Meanwhile, the son has enlisted his squire to ask for her hand. He knows that if the squire gets her, he'll have his love in his own nest. The old codger's wife recognized that her husband was love-struck, so she concocted a plot with her son. But the father, after he found out that his son loved the very same girl and was blocking his way, sent the boy on a mission abroad. Knowing this, the mother is helping out her absent son. The son won't return to town in today's comedy.

---

3. The speaker puns on the name "Plautus," which could mean a dog with large, floppy ears.

Don't expect that: Plautus wouldn't allow it. He broke the bridge on the son's road home.

I imagine there are some people here saying to themselves, "By Hercules, what's this? Slave marriages? Can slaves get engaged and marry? They're making that up. It doesn't happen anywhere in the world." But I say it does happen in Greece, and in Carthage, and right here in our own land, in Apulia. Slave marriages are usually treated there with more fanfare than free ones. If that isn't so, let somebody bet me a jug of sweet wine . . . so long as the judge is Carthaginian, or even Greek, or Apulian, as far as I care. What? No takers? I get it: nobody's thirsty.

Let me return to that foundling girl, the one the slaves are trying with all their might to marry. She'll turn out to be a virgin, and freeborn—a native Athenian—and she'll certainly do nothing dirty in this comedy. But later, by Hercules, after the play's done, if someone gives her cash, I bet she'll give him a "honeymoon" without waiting for the wedding!

That's all. Farewell. Prosper and prevail with your peerless prowess, as you've done before.

Exit speaker. Enter from countryside (stage right), Olympio in rustic costume followed by Chalinus in military garb.

OLYMPIO: Can't I talk to myself and mull over my business as I see fit without your buttin' in? What the devil you followin' me for?[4]

CHALINUS: Because I'm determined to follow you all the time, wherever you go, like a shadow. Yeah, by Pollux, even if you're thinking of heading to hell, I mean to follow you. So you figure it out: can you and your schemes snatch my bride Casina without me knowing it, just like you're planning?

OLYMPIO: What d'you want with me?

CHALINUS: Say what, wise guy? Why are you slithering around town, you worthless foreman?

OLYMPIO: 'Cause I want to.

CHALINUS: But why aren't you on the farm minding your post? Why don't you take care of the job you've been assigned and leave city business alone? You came here to snatch my fiancée. Go back to the farm! Go back to your own turf, right now!

4. Olympio's rustic dialect is the translator's addition; it is not found in the Latin. The dialect is toned down in his description of his "wedding night," in accordance with the grander lyric mode.

OLYMPIO: Chalinus, I ain't forgettin' my duty. I put a fella in charge who'll look after the farm right well. If I get what I come here to town for, to marry that girl you're dyin' for, purty 'n' tender little Casina—a slave just like you—when I've married her and taken her to the farm with me, I'll hunker down on the farm and "mind my post."

CHALINUS: YOU marry HER? By Hercules, I'll hang myself before I let you have her!

OLYMPIO: She's MY booty, so YOU just go stick your head in a noose!

CHALINUS: You son-of-a-shitpile! So she's your booty?

OLYMPIO: You'll see!

CHALINUS: Go to hell!

OLYMPIO: As sure as I'm alive, I'll give you woe at my weddin' in so many ways!

CHALINUS: What'll you do to me?!

OLYMPIO: What'll I do to you? Why first off you'll hold the weddin' torch for the new bride. Then, when you get to the farmhouse, we'll give you one jug 'n' one path, one spring, one pail 'n' eight barrels: if they ain't always full, I'll tan your hide! I'll make you so hunched over from carryin' water that you'll be bent like a crupper![5] Then, when you want some grub down on the farm, 'less you eat a heap of hay, or eat dirt like a night crawler, by Pollux, I'll make you hungrier than Hunger itself! Then, when you're tuckered out 'n' starvin', I'll give you the beddin' you deserve.

CHALINUS: What'll you do?

OLYMPIO: I'll shutter you up in the window where you can listen to me kissin' Casina! When she says to me: "My little pet! My Olympio! My life! My little honey! My pride 'n' joy! Let me kiss your little eyes! My dee-light! Please, let me make love to you! My holiday! My chick-a-dee! My lovey-dovey! My honey-bunny!" When she's sayin' such to me, then you, you bastard, you'll be wrigglin' on that windowsill like a mouse! Now I'm headed in here so you won't give me any more lip; I'm sick of your jabberin'.

CHALINUS: Right behind you. You won't do a thing, by Pollux, without me butting in.

Both enter the house of Lysidamus. The stage is empty, then Cleostrata enters from Lysidamus' house, addressing maids inside.

5. A crupper is the part of a saddle curved under the horse's rump. This is a witty transformation of Chalinus, whose name means "bridle."

CLEOSTRATA:

> Lock up the cupboards and bring me the keys.
> Now I am off to the neighbor's next door.
> Send for me there, if my husband should ask.

Pardalisca begins to follow her from Lysidamus' house.

PARDALISCA:

> The Master had ordered his lunch be prepared . . .

CLEOSTRATA:

> Shhh!
> Be quiet and leave. I'm not fixing his lunch;
> Today all the cooking is canceled for him.

Pardalisca retreats into the house.

> Because he opposes his wife and his son,
> In pleasing himself and pursuing his love,
> I'll wreak my revenge on that wretch of a man:
> I'll hurt him with hunger and thwart him with thirst,
> Lambasting that lover in words and in works!
> By Pollux, I'll pain him with insults that sting,
> I'll give him the treatment he truly deserves!
> He's Fodder for Hades! A Fountain of Filth!
> A real Devotee of Debauchery's Depths!
> I'm off to my friend's to complain of my fate.
> Her door has just opened, and look, here she comes.
> By Pollux, it seems that I've picked a bad time.

Enter Myrrhina, with maids, from Alcesimus' house.

MYRRHINA:

> Follow me, ladies, I'm headed next door.
> Hey! Doesn't anyone hear what I say?
> That's where I'll be, if my husband should ask.
> When I'm at home and I'm spinning alone,
> Sleepiness slackens the speed of my hands.
> Didn't I order my spindle be brought?

CLEOSTRATA:

> Hello there, Myrrhina!

MYRRHINA:

                      Hello there, by Castor!
But why are you looking so cross, Cleostrata?

CLEOSTRATA:

For all of us women unhappily married
There's always some trouble at home and in public.
And so I was coming on over to see you.

MYRRHINA:

And I was just coming to your house, by Pollux!
But what is it now that has got you so troubled?
Whatever your trouble, I share in your sadness.

CLEOSTRATA:

By Castor, I know it, and that's why I love you:
For none of my neighbors has earned such affection,
And none of them shows me more kindness than you do.

MYRRHINA:

I love you and want you to tell me the trouble.

CLEOSTRATA:

I'm scorned in my home in the nastiest fashion!

MYRRHINA:

Oh! What do you mean? Please explain it more fully.
By Pollux, I don't understand your complaining.

CLEOSTRATA:

It's nasty the way that I'm scorned by my husband!
My rights have been wronged and I can't call for justice.

MYRRHINA:

That's certainly odd, if there's truth to your story,
Since usually wives deny rights to their husbands.

CLEOSTRATA:

The maid that I raised with my very own money—
Although she's all mine, and although I'm against it—
He keeps on insisting she'll marry his foreman,
But he really loves her, and that's my dilemma.

MYRRHINA:

Be quiet! I beg you!

CLEOSTRATA:

                      We're free to discuss it
Since now we're completely alone here.

MYRRHINA:

I guess so.

Just how did it happen that you own a servant?
No principled lady has any possession
That's privately owned and unknown to her husband.
Indeed, if she does, she indecently got it.
So either she's stealing the stuff from her husband,
Or else she's been whoring around with a lover.
I think that whatever is yours is your husband's.

CLEOSTRATA:

But all that you say is against your friend's interest!

MYRRHINA:

Be quiet, you ninny, and hear what I'm saying.
You mustn't oppose him; allow him his lovers;
And let him have fun with whatever he fancies,
Since nothing is lacking inside of your household.

CLEOSTRATA:

Those things that you say are against your own interest!
You've surely gone crazy!

MYRRHINA:

No, you are the nitwit!

Just always be careful your man never says it!

CLEOSTRATA:

What mustn't he say?

MYRRHINA:

That he wants to divorce you.

CLEOSTRATA:

Be quiet!

MYRRHINA:

What is it?

CLEOSTRATA:

Behold!

MYRRHINA:

But who is it?

CLEOSTRATA:

You see! It's my husband approaching! Oh, hurry!
Go back to your house, would you please?

MYRRHINA:

                                Yes, I'm going.

CLEOSTRATA:

As soon as we both have a little more leisure,
I'll talk with you then, but for now it's farewell.

MYRRHINA:

                                  Bye.

Exit Myrrhina into Alcesimus' house. Enter Lysidamus, from forum (stage left).

LYSIDAMUS:

The spiciest spice, according to me,
The best thing on earth is L-O-V-E.
A tastier herb? It doesn't exist!
The flavor of love's on top of the list!
I marvel at cooks when adding some zest,
Who don't use this spice, surpassing the rest.
When love's in the mix, with gusto we eat;
When love's been left out, the taste's incomplete.
Why, vinegar's tang love makes honey-sweet.
A cranky old man turns suave and elite.
I know for a fact, not just what I hear:
Since falling in love with Casina dear,
No man in the world could ever surpass
This man of the world, I'm so full of class.
I shopped for cologne; whatever smelled nice
I rubbed on my head, my love to entice.
Entice her I do, at least I surmise.
But torture awaits: my wife still survives!
I see her ahead, and all in a stew;
I'll turn on the charm to soften this shrew.
My wife, my true delight, what's new?

CLEOSTRATA:

Leave and take your hands off!

LYSIDAMUS:

Egad! It's wrong for you, my Juno dear,
To show such anger toward your Jove!
But where you going now?

CLEOSTRATA:

Let me GO.

LYSIDAMUS:

Remain!

CLEOSTRATA:

No. I'm going.

LYSIDAMUS:

By Pollux, then I'll follow you!

CLEOSTRATA:

Tell me, are you crazy?

LYSIDAMUS:

I'm crazy, dear, with love for you!

CLEOSTRATA:

I don't want your loving!

LYSIDAMUS:

You can't resist!

CLEOSTRATA:

Oh! You kill me.

LYSIDAMUS:

(aside)

I wish you spoke the truth.

CLEOSTRATA:

That remark, I'm sure you meant it.

LYSIDAMUS:

Just look at me, my dear.

CLEOSTRATA:

Dear to you as you to me. But tell me why I smell cologne?

LYSIDAMUS:

(aside)

Damn my luck! I'm caught red-handed! Hope my cloak can wipe it off.
Mercury destroy you, merchant, since you sold me this cologne!

CLEOSTRATA:

Scarcely can I keep myself from scolding you as you deserve!
Strutting through the streets at your age! Worthless, perfumed, white-
haired coot!

LYSIDAMUS:

Pollux, I was helping out a pal to purchase some cologne.

CLEOSTRATA:

    Oh, how fast he forges falsehoods! Tell me where's your sense of shame?

LYSIDAMUS:

    Anywhere you tell me.

CLEOSTRATA:

                       Where have you been whoring?

LYSIDAMUS:

                                    Whoring? ME?

CLEOSTRATA:

    I know more than you imagine!

LYSIDAMUS:

                       So, then, tell me what you know!

CLEOSTRATA:

    Out of all the old men living, none's a bigger fool than you!
    Where'd you come from, good-for-nothing? Where'd you go, and
                                where'd you whore?
    Where'd you drink? You're drunk, by Castor! See the way your cloak's a
                                         mess?

LYSIDAMUS:

    I'll be damned, and you too, woman, if I've touched a drop today!

CLEOSTRATA:

    Go ahead, indulge your pleasure! Drink and eat our home away!

LYSIDAMUS:

    Hold it, wife! Now that's sufficient! Calm yourself! You bark too much!
    Save some nagging till tomorrow.

(pauses)

                      Tell me, now your temper's cooled,
    Will you do your husband's bidding, rather than oppose him still?

CLEOSTRATA:

    What's the matter?

LYSIDAMUS:

               You've forgotten? What of Casina the maid?
    Time to make her wed our foreman: he's a good and trusty slave.
    There she'll have a lot of clothing, wood, hot water, food to eat.
    There she'll raise the boys she'll bear. She shouldn't wed that other slave,
    Worthless, good-for-nothing squire! Not a drachma to his name!

CLEOSTRATA:

    Shocking how you don't remember what's your duty at your age.

LYSIDAMUS:

What's my duty?

CLEOSTRATA:

You're supposed to let me manage all the maids.
If you hold to our agreement, I'm the one in charge of them.

LYSIDAMUS:

Why the hell are you so anxious she should wed that armor-lug?

CLEOSTRATA:

We should help our only son.

LYSIDAMUS:

But though he is our only son,
I'm no less his only father! He's the one who ought to yield!

CLEOSTRATA:

You, by God, are seeking trouble! I can smell it and it stinks!

LYSIDAMUS:

ME?

CLEOSTRATA:

YOU! Look at how you fidget! Why are you obsessed with this?

LYSIDAMUS:

All I want's for her to wed the worthy slave and not the bum.

CLEOSTRATA:

What if I persuade the foreman she should be the squire's wife?

LYSIDAMUS:

What if I persuade the squire she should be the foreman's wife?
I'm convinced that I'll persuade him.

CLEOSTRATA:

Should I call Chalinus out?
You ask him about the marriage, I will ask the foreman.

LYSIDAMUS:

Fine.

CLEOSTRATA:

He'll be here. We'll soon discover which of us is smoother tongued!

Exit Cleostrata into Lysidamus' house.

LYSIDAMUS:

Damn her, all the gods in heaven! (Now it's safe to speak my mind!)
While she pesters me with nagging, love is crucifying me!

Now the wife has got a whiff of what I'm hiding up my sleeve;
That's why she's been such a nuisance, helping out the worthless squire.

Enter Chalinus from Lysidamus' house.

Every god and goddess damn him!

CHALINUS:

YOU . . . had called me, said your wife.

LYSIDAMUS:

Yes, I asked that you be summoned.

CHALINUS:

Tell me what you want from me.

LYSIDAMUS:

First, I wish you'd wipe that scowl off; answer me with more respect.
Acting surly toward your master: surely that's a stupid move.
I've believed for quite a while that you're a good and worthy man.

CHALINUS:

Yeah? Well if you really think so, why don't you just set me free?

LYSIDAMUS:

Well, I want to. But my wishes won't come true unless you help.

CHALINUS:

Hurry up and name the favor.

LYSIDAMUS:

Listen closely, I'll explain.
I have promised to the foreman: Casina will be his wife.

CHALINUS:

But your wife and son both promised Casina to me!

LYSIDAMUS:

I know.
Rather be a slave who's married? Or a single man who's free?
These will be your only options. Pick whichever one you wish.

CHALINUS:

Free men pay their own expenses; now I'm living off of you.
Casina? I'll never yield her! Not to any man on earth!

LYSIDAMUS:

Go inside and call my wife out! Make it snappy! Bring her here!
Bring an urn, with lots and water! Set them here!

CHALINUS:

It's fine with me.

LYSIDAMUS:

Pollux, now I see your tactics! Watch me parry all your blows!
If I can't succeed by asking, maybe I'll succeed with lots.
I'll confound you, and your cronies!

CHALINUS:

Bah! The lot will fall to ME!

LYSIDAMUS:

If the lot's for crucifixion!

CHALINUS:

Go ahead and try your tricks!
I'm the one she's gonna marry!

LYSIDAMUS:

Won't you go and leave my sight?

CHALINUS:

You don't like to see my face? I guess that I can live with that.

Exit Chalinus into Lysidamus' house.

LYSIDAMUS:

Am I not a wretched fellow? Everything's against me now?
Now I'm scared my wife succeeded: she's convinced Olympio
Not to marry Casina. And if she has, my goose is cooked!
If she failed, my ray of hope is riding on the winning lot.
If the lots should turn against me, then I'll fall upon my sword.
Look! The foreman's coming forward! Excellent Olympio!

Enter Olympio from Lysidamus' house, talking to Cleostrata within the house.

OLYMPIO: By Pollux! You might as well toss me in a hot oven 'n' bake me like
a brown biscuit, ma'am, as get me to do what you're askin'!

LYSIDAMUS: I'm saved! There's still hope, from what I hear!

OLYMPIO: Why you tryin' to scare me, ma'am, with your talk about my freedom? Even if you 'n' your boy are against it, I can still buy freedom for
purty near nothin', like it or not.

LYSIDAMUS: What's that? Who are you arguing with, Olympio?

OLYMPIO: Same woman you're always arguin' with.

LYSIDAMUS: My wife?

OLYMPIO: What d'you mean *wife?* You're just like a hunter: livin' day 'n'
night with a bitch!

LYSIDAMUS: What's she doing? What's she saying to you?

OLYMPIO: She's beggin' 'n' pleadin' for me not to marry Casina.

LYSIDAMUS: And you said . . . ?

OLYMPIO: Well, I said I wouldn't give her to Jupiter himself, not if he begged me!

LYSIDAMUS: May the gods bless you, my man!

OLYMPIO: Now she's all riled up at me, just a-bubblin' with rage.

LYSIDAMUS: By Pollux, I'd like to see her bubble get pricked . . .

OLYMPIO: By Pollux, I reckon she's been pricked . . . if you're man enough! But your wooin's buggin' me, by Pollux: your wife's mad at me, your son's mad at me, the house slaves are mad at me . . .

LYSIDAMUS: What's it to you? *(pointing to himself)* As long as THIS Jupiter favors you, don't give those minor gods a second thought.

OLYMPIO: That's a lot of hooey! Like you don't know how quick them human Jupiters kick the bucket! So if you become a dead Jupiter, and your kingdom's left to those "minor gods," who'll watch my backside then?

LYSIDAMUS: You'll change your tune if we win and I sleep with Casina!

OLYMPIO: By Hercules, I don't believe you can, 'cause your wife's so dead-set against givin' her to me.

LYSIDAMUS: But here's what I'll do: I'll throw the lots into an urn and I'll draw for you and Chalinus. My summation of the situation: we've got to fight them with swords of sortition.

OLYMPIO: What if Lady Luck's against you?

LYSIDAMUS: Don't jinx me! I trust the gods: we'll rely on the gods.

OLYMPIO: I wouldn't bet a hill of beans on that! You see, everybody trusts the gods, but I've seen plenty of them god-trusters fooled.

LYSIDAMUS: Shhh! Shut up a minute!

OLYMPIO: What?

LYSIDAMUS: Look! It's Chalinus coming outside with the urn and the lots! Time to draw our weapons and fight it out!

Enter Chalinus and Cleostrata from Lysidamus' house, still a good distance from the men.

CLEOSTRATA:

What's my husband want, Chalinus?

CHALINUS:

You upon a funeral pyre!

CLEOSTRATA:

I believe he would, by Castor!

CHALINUS:

God, I know it for a fact!

LYSIDAMUS:

Never knew I owned such talent: here's a psychic right at home!
(to Olympio)
Shall we charge them? Raise the standards! Forward ho!
(to Chalinus and Cleostrata)

Hey, what's with you?

CHALINUS:

All the stuff you wanted's ready: wife, the lots, the urn, and me.

OLYMPIO:

You're an extra piece o' baggage.

CHALINUS:

Pollux, so I seem to you.
I'm a thorn to you, you bastard, digging deep into your heart.
Now you're sweating, you're so frightened!

LYSIDAMUS:

Hey Chalinus, shut your mouth!

CHALINUS:

(indicating Olympio)
He's the one who oughta stuff it!

OLYMPIO:

(to Chalinus)

You're the one he likes to stuff!

LYSIDAMUS:

Put the urn here. Pay attention. Give the lots to me. My wife,
I was sure I could convince you. Even now I think I can.
Listen, honey, reconsider: Casina should marry me!

CLEOSTRATA:

Marry YOU?!

LYSIDAMUS:

Yes, ME, of course! Uh, . . . that's not what I meant to say!
"Me" I meant, but "him" I said.[6] Indeed, I've wanted it so bad . . .
God, I'm talking like a moron!

CLEOSTRATA:

Acting like one, too, by God!

6. Lysidamus continues to misspeak.

LYSIDAMUS:
HIM. That's wrong! It's ME, by Pollux! There! I finally got it straight!

CLEOSTRATA:
Seems you blunder pretty often.

LYSIDAMUS:
When you're eager, so it goes.
Still, we know it's your decision. Both of us are begging you . . .

CLEOSTRATA:
Spit it out!

LYSIDAMUS:
Alright! I'm trying! Honey, would you be so kind,
Do our foreman here a favor: let him marry Casina.

CLEOSTRATA:
No, by Pollux, I won't do it!

LYSIDAMUS:
Then we'll let the lots decide.

CLEOSTRATA:
Who's objecting?

LYSIDAMUS:
I declare that it's the best and fairest way.
If we win, then we'll be happy. If we lose, we'll be good sports.
(to Olympio)
Take your lot and see what's written.

OLYMPIO:
"One."

CHALINUS:
No fair! He got his first!

LYSIDAMUS:
Take yours.

CHALINUS:
Got it.

OLYMPIO:
Wait a minute! I'm a thinkin' we should check—
See there ain't another hidden underneath the water there!

CHALINUS:
Think I cheat like you, you bastard?

LYSIDAMUS:
No, there's not. Just calm yourself.

OLYMPIO:

Gods almighty, grant good fortune. May my luck be . . .

CHALINUS:

. . . Really bad!

OLYMPIO:

That's the luck that you'll be gettin'! I know your ungodly kind!

Wait a minute! Sure your lot ain't made of cork?

CHALINUS:

So what's your point?

OLYMPIO:

I don't want your lot a-floatin'.

LYSIDAMUS:

Good idea! Check and see!

Ready? Set? Then throw your lots in! There. My wife, you shake the urn.

OLYMPIO:

Not your wife! Don't let 'er touch it!

LYSIDAMUS:

Calm yourself!

OLYMPIO:

I'm sure, by God,

If she'll touch the urn, she'll jinx me!

LYSIDAMUS:

Shut your mouth!

OLYMPIO:

My mouth is shut!

Gods almighty, I beseech ye . . .

CHALINUS:

. . . grant to him a ball and chain!

OLYMPIO:

Grant my lot to be the chosen . . .

CHALINUS:

. . . one for hanging by the feet!

OLYMPIO:

Why, I oughta gouge your eyes out! Then I'll pull 'em through your nose!

Scared? They oughta get the funeral started: you're already dead!

LYSIDAMUS:

You two pay attention!

OLYMPIO and CHALINUS:
                                    Yes sir!

LYSIDAMUS:
                                Cleostrata, I insist,
    So you won't declare I cheated, nor suspect it: draw the lot.

OLYMPIO:
    Boss, you've sold me out!

CHALINUS:
(aside)
                            He'd profit, if he sold you.

CLEOSTRATA:
(to Lysidamus)
                                                Fair enough.

CHALINUS:
    Gods almighty, I beseech ye, make his lot desert the urn!

OLYMPIO:
    Want the world to act like you do, just 'cause you desert your post?

CHALINUS:
    Hope your lot dissolves on contact, just like with the Heraclids! [7]

OLYMPIO:
    You'll dissolve real soon I reckon, once the bullwhip whacks your hide!

LYSIDAMUS:
    Cut it out and pay attention!

OLYMPIO:
                            Only if this "scholar" will!

LYSIDAMUS:
    May good fortune shine upon me.

OLYMPIO:
                            And on me as well, amen.

CHALINUS:
    Never!

OLYMPIO:
        Yes indeed, by Pollux!

7. In a mythical account, the descendants of Hercules divided the Peloponnesus of Greece
by lot. Cresphontes, using a lot made of baked clay, won the rich territory of Messenia when
his brother's lot of unbaked clay dissolved in the urn.

CHALINUS:

NO, by Pollux, shine on ME!

CLEOSTRATA:

(to Olympio)

He will win and *you* will suffer.

LYSIDAMUS:

Punch that bastard in the jaw!

Come on! Let me see some action!

CLEOSTRATA:

Don't you lay a hand on him!

OLYMPIO:

Uppercut or combinations?

LYSIDAMUS:

Take your pick!

Olympio hits Chalinus.

OLYMPIO:

And you take that!

CLEOSTRATA:

Where'd you get the right to strike him?

OLYMPIO:

'Cause my Jove commanded me!

CLEOSTRATA:

Hit him in the jaw, like he did!

Chalinus hits Olympio.

OLYMPIO:

Ouch! Oh Jupiter! I'm hit!

LYSIDAMUS:

Where'd you get the right to strike him?

CHALINUS:

Juno here commanded me!

LYSIDAMUS:

Sorry, you'll just have to take it: I'm alive, but she's in charge.

CLEOSTRATA:

This here slave can speak if yours can.

OLYMPIO:

Why'd he try to jinx my lot?

LYSIDAMUS:

Better watch your ass, Chalinus!

CHALINUS:

Should've warned me 'bout my jaw!

LYSIDAMUS:

Come now, wife, and draw the winner! Pay attention, both of you!
I'm so nervous, I'm all dizzy! All my nerves are shot to hell!
Now my heart is really thumping: hope it's not a heart attack!

CLEOSTRATA:

Here's the winner.

LYSIDAMUS:

Whip it out then!

CHALINUS:

Now I'm finished?

OLYMPIO:

Show it here.

Yes, it's MINE!

CHALINUS:

The devil take you!

CLEOSTRATA:

Well, Chalinus, you've been beat.

LYSIDAMUS:

I'm ecstatic! See, the gods have helped us out, Olympio!

OLYMPIO:

That's because I'm so religious, just like my ol' pappy was.

LYSIDAMUS:

Go inside, prepare the wedding, wife.

CLEOSTRATA:

I'll do as you command.

But Cleostrata stays in place.

LYSIDAMUS:

Don't you know how far away our country villa lies?

CLEOSTRATA:

I know.

LYSIDAMUS:

So then, go inside and hurry, even if it pains you.

CLEOSTRATA:

Fine.

Exit Cleostrata into Lysidamus' house.

LYSIDAMUS:

We should go inside ourselves: encourage them to hurry up.

OLYMPIO:

Time's a-wastin'.

LYSIDAMUS:

I'd prefer we didn't talk with him around.

Exit Lysidamus and Olympio into Lysidamus' house.

CHALINUS: If I hang myself now, it'd be a waste of effort, plus I'd be throwing away money on rope, and, besides, I'd give my enemies the last laugh. What's the use? I'm dead as it is. I lost the lottery; Casina will marry the foreman. It's bad enough losing to the foreman, but what's worse is seeing how badly the old man wanted that guy to marry her instead of me. Did you see how the old wretch shook and scurried around and nearly did a somersault when the foreman won! *(Lysidamus' door opens.)* Ahh! I'll go hide here; I hear the door opening. My "well-wishers" and "friends" are coming out. I'll ambush them from these bushes.

Enter Olympio and Lysidamus from Lysidamus' house. Chalinus moves upstage.

OLYMPIO: Just let 'im come to the country! I'll send that fella back to town to you with his hands tied to a pole like a milkmaid!

LYSIDAMUS: He deserves it.

OLYMPIO: And I'll make good 'n' sure he gets it!

LYSIDAMUS: If Chalinus was home, I wanted to send him shopping with you, just to rub our rival's nose in it.

CHALINUS: *(aside)* I'll make like a crab and crawl against the wall. I've got to eavesdrop! One of them flays me, the other fillets me! But this whip-magnet, this warehouse of whippings, struts in dressed like a groom. *(assuming a tragic tone)* I shall postpone my demise, yea verily, I shall send forth first this fellow Hadesward!

OLYMPIO: See how trusty I've been to you! What you hankered for most, I gave you a-plenty! Today your love'll be with you without your wife knowing!

LYSIDAMUS: Shhhhh! Lord help me, I can hardly keep my lips from kissing you for it, my darling!

CHALINUS: *(aside)* WHAT?! Kissing? For what? What's he mean "darling"? By Hercules, I think he wants to plow the farmer!

OLYMPIO: So d'you love me a little now?

LYSIDAMUS: By Pollux, more than myself! Can I hug you?

CHALINUS: *(aside)* What's he mean, "hug"?

OLYMPIO: Okey-dokey.

LYSIDAMUS: Oh! When I touch you, it's like licking honey!

OLYMPIO: Hey! Get off, lover-boy! Get away from my backside!

CHALINUS: *(aside)* That's it! That's why he made him foreman! Just like that time I came to the back door and the old man wanted to check out my backdoor!

OLYMPIO: How obliging I've been to you today, a true dee-light!

LYSIDAMUS: I swear, I'll treat you better than I treat myself!

CHALINUS: *(aside)* Hercules! I think these guys will be rubbing thighs today! This old man really chases anything, even men with beards!

LYSIDAMUS: How I'll kiss Casina today! How I'll live the high life without my wife knowing!

CHALINUS: *(aside)* Ah-hah! Now, by Pollux, I'm finally on the right track! HE'S crazy for Casina! I've got them!

LYSIDAMUS: By Hercules, I'm burning to embrace, to kiss. . . .

OLYMPIO: Hey, let 'er marry me first. What the devil's your hurry?

LYSIDAMUS: I'm in love!

OLYMPIO: But I don't reckon it can happen today.

LYSIDAMUS: Yes it can, if you really think you can get your freedom to-morrow.

CHALINUS: *(aside)* Here I really better prick up my ears; I'll cleverly kill two birds with one stone![8]

LYSIDAMUS: I've got a place all ready right next door at my buddy's. I entrusted my whole affair to him. He said he's lending me his place.

OLYMPIO: And his wife? Where'll she be?

LYSIDAMUS: I've cleverly arranged that. My wife will call her over for the wedding to be there with her, help her out, and spend the night with her. I insisted, and my wife said she'd do it. So she'll sleep there. Her husband'll be out of the house; I'll see to that. You take Casina to the farm, but

8. Literally, "catch two boars in one bush," perhaps an image with sexual overtones.

the "farm" will be their house, just long enough for me to consummate the marriage with Casina! Then you'll take her to the real farm before dawn. Ingenious, no?

OLYMPIO: Right clever.

CHALINUS: *(aside)* Go on, construct your cunning capers! By Hercules, your craftiness is digging your own grave!

LYSIDAMUS: Know what to do now?

OLYMPIO: Tell me.

LYSIDAMUS: Take my wallet. Go and get provisions—make it snappy! But I want gourmet stuff. Get some delicacies, since she's so delicate.

OLYMPIO: Okey-dokey.

LYSIDAMUS: Buy octopusseys . . . oysters . . . squidlings . . . whitefish . . .

CHALINUS: *(aside)* Make that wholewheatfish; it's better for you.

LYSIDAMUS: Sole.

CHALINUS: *(aside)* Better yet, a clog to smack you upside the head, you dirty old man!

OLYMPIO: You want snapper?

LYSIDAMUS: Why bother, when the wife's at home? She's a snapper—she never shuts up.

OLYMPIO: I can figure out what to buy when I'm down at the fish market.

LYSIDAMUS: Alright. Off with you. Spare no expense! Buy plenty of everything! Now I'd better check with my neighbor to see if he's done what I asked.

OLYMPIO: Should I go now?

LYSIDAMUS: Fly, man!

Exit Olympio toward the forum; Lysidamus exits into Alcesimus' house. Chalinus moves downstage.

CHALINUS: If I was offered my freedom three times over it couldn't keep me from cooking up big trouble for them today and telling the whole story to my mistress! I've caught my enemies red-handed! And now, if my mistress will just do her duty, the battle is ours! I'll rout them cleanly! It's our lucky day! Now the vanquished are victorious! I'll go inside to spice up what another cook seasoned. What was prepared won't turn out, and what wasn't will!

Exit Chalinus to Lysidamus' house. The stage is empty, then enter Lysidamus and Alcesimus from the latter's house.

LYSIDAMUS:

Now I'll know, Alcesimus, if you're my phony friend or pal.

Now's the acid test of friendship: time to lay it on the line!

I'm in LOVE! I don't need lectures! Save your speech, "Your hair's too
                                                                    gray!"

Curb your quip, "A man at your age!" Stuff your spiel, "A married man!"

ALCESIMUS:

Never seen a guy so lovesick!

LYSIDAMUS:

Empty out your house for me.

ALCESIMUS:

All my slaves and all my maids, I'm set to send them to your house.

LYSIDAMUS:

Oh, you crafty, crafty genius! Send them camping for the night![9]

ALCESIMUS:

I'll remember.

LYSIDAMUS:

You're a genius! Generous and genuine!

Now I'm headed for the forum. Tend to things; I'll soon be back.

ALCESIMUS:

Happy trails.

LYSIDAMUS:

Equip your rooms with open arms.

ALCESIMUS:

And why is that?

LYSIDAMUS:

Open arms are empty, plus they're primed to welcome me!

ALCESIMUS:

Be damned!

Someone has to stop you, partner! You're just having too much fun!

LYSIDAMUS:

What's the point of loving someone if I can't be clever too?

Please be sure that I can find you.

9. I omit lines 523–24, which contain a joke based on an obscure Roman proverb about a forced march: "but be sure that they come just like the blackbird sings in his songs, 'with provisions and whatever else,' as if they were marching to Sutrium." Note the military reference.

ALCESIMUS:

I'll be waiting here at home.

Exit Lysidamus toward the forum and Alcesimus to his house, just as Cleostrata enters from Lysidamus' house.

CLEOSTRATA:

That's the reason why my husband begged me on his hands and knees,
"Please invite Myrrhina over! Have her visit for the night!"
If the neighbor's house is empty, he'll go there with Casina!
No way now that I'll invite her! I won't give those fools a chance!
They won't have a place to frolic, senile ball-less billy goats!

Enter Alcesimus.

Look! The safeguard of the senate! Keeper of the commonwealth!
Builder of my husband's love nest, it's my neighbor coming out.
Wouldn't give a drachma for him: he's not worth his weight in salt!

ALCESIMUS:

I'm surprised my wife's still waiting; she's supposed to go next door.
Anxious for her invitation, all dressed up she sits at home.
Ah! At last here's Cleostrata, coming to invite her now!
Well, hello there, Cleostrata!

CLEOSTRATA:

Same to you, Alcesimus.

Where's your wife?

ALCESIMUS:

Inside the house, expecting you to send for her.
See, your husband asked if I would send her to your house to help.
Should I call her?

CLEOSTRATA:

If she's busy, please don't bother.

ALCESIMUS:

No, she's not.

CLEOSTRATA:

That's okay; I'll come by later: wouldn't want to trouble her.

ALCESIMUS:

Aren't you folks preparing for a wedding at your house today?

CLEOSTRATA:

Yes, I am. I'm almost ready.

ALCESIMUS:

Don't you need a little help?

CLEOSTRATA:

Thanks, I've got enough already. I'll come visit later on,
Once the wedding's over. Bye now! Give my greetings to your wife!

Cleostrata moves upstage to the doorway of Lysidamus' house.

ALCESIMUS:

What am I supposed to do now? Man, I'm really up the creek,
Thanks to that old horny, toothless goat who dragged me into this!
Here I promise my wife's service, like some kind of barroom mop!
First the S.O.B. assures me, says his wife will send for mine,
Then his wife says not to bother! Wonder if my neighbor here
Got a whiff of what we're planning. When I stop and think it through,
If she had the least suspicion, she'd have grilled me on the spot.
Well, I'd better go inside and tow the warship back to port.

Exit Alcesimus into his house; Cleostrata comes downstage from the doorway.

CLEOSTRATA:

This one here is wholly hoodwinked! How the codgers scurry now!
Now my worthless, withered husband: how I wish that he'd arrive!
I'd deceive him just like this one. Then I'd really get my wish:
Set them at each other's throats! But look who's coming down the street.
If you saw his stern expression, you'd believe his heart was pure.

Enter Lysidamus from the forum.

LYSIDAMUS: It's really idiotic, in my opinion, for a man in love to make a
foray to the forum on a day when the object of his love's within reach.
Well, I acted just like an idiot. I wasted the day testifying for some relative
of mine. By Hercules, I'm glad he lost that case; it serves him right for asking me to help! You see, I think a man who summons a witness ought to
find out first if his witness is witless. If he is, send the witless witness home.
But look out! My wife's outside the house. Damn my luck! I'm afraid she's
not deaf and she may have overheard this.

CLEOSTRATA: I heard it, by Castor! So much the worse for you!

LYSIDAMUS: *(aside)* I'd better go up to her. *(to Cleostrata)* What are you doing, my heart's delight?

CLEOSTRATA: Waiting for you, by Castor.

LYSIDAMUS: Is everything ready? Have you already brought your neighbor over to our house to help you?

CLEOSTRATA: I invited her, just as you insisted. But that crony of yours—your best friend—blew up at his wife for some reason. When I went to get her, he said he couldn't send her.

LYSIDAMUS: There's your greatest fault: too little charm.

CLEOSTRATA: Charming other people's husbands is a whore's job, not a wife's, my husband. You go and fetch her. I want to take care of what needs doing inside, my husband.

LYSIDAMUS: Well then, hurry up!

CLEOSTRATA: Fine. *(aside)* Now, by Pollux, I'll put some fear in his heart! Today I'll make this lover the most miserable man alive!

Exit Cleostrata into Lysidamus' house. Enter Alcesimus from his house.

ALCESIMUS: I've stopped by to see if "Lover-Boy" has come home from the forum. That madman's making a mockery of me and my wife. But look! There he is, right in front of his house. By Hercules, I was just coming to see you!

LYSIDAMUS: And I, by Hercules, was coming to see you! What's your story, you worthless bum! What did I entrust to you? What did I ask you to do?

ALCESIMUS: What's the matter?

LYSIDAMUS: Ha! You've really emptied your house for me! And you've really brought your wife over to our house! Because of you I'm ruined, and so is my big chance!

ALCESIMUS: Well go hang yourself! YOU said your wife would invite my wife over.

LYSIDAMUS: But she claims she did invite her, and you said you wouldn't send her.

ALCESIMUS: Well, she told me she didn't want her help.

LYSIDAMUS: Well, she just sent me to invite your wife over.

ALCESIMUS: Well, I don't give a damn.

LYSIDAMUS: Well, you're ruining me!

ALCESIMUS: Well, that's just fine.

LYSIDAMUS: Well, I'll have to wait even longer!

ALCESIMUS: Well, I'd like to . . .

LYSIDAMUS: Well . . .

ALCESIMUS: . . . do something that pains you . . .

LYSIDAMUS: Well . . .

ALCESIMUS: . . . and I'll do it with pleasure. And don't you ever try to slip in more "wells" than me!

LYSIDAMUS: WELL!

ALCESIMUS: By Hercules, god damn you!

LYSIDAMUS: So what now? Are you going to send your wife over?

ALCESIMUS: Take her, and go to hell with them all: my wife, your wife, and your girlie, too! Just go away and do something; I'll order my wife to cut through the garden to visit your wife.

LYSIDAMUS: Now you're really and truly being my friend. *(exit Alcesimus into his house)* What was wrong with my horoscope when I fell in love? Or what did I ever do to offend Venus to make her put so many roadblocks in the path of my love affair? *(noises from Lysidamus' house)* Whoa! What the hell's that uproar in our house?

Enter Pardalisca from Lysidamus' house, in mock-tragic tones.

PARDALISCA:

I am utterly doomed! I am utterly doomed!
With my limbs all atremble, my heart dead from fright,
I know not whence my refuge, protection, or flight,
Nor to whom I should turn, nor whose succor to seek.
I saw dastardly deeds done in dastardly ways,
With audacity strange and unheard of these days.
Cleostrata, I warn thee, withdraw from that maid,
Lest, aroused in her fury, she do thee some harm!
Wrest the sword from her grasp! She is out of her mind!

LYSIDAMUS:

Why in the world is this maid in a tizzy,
Bursting out here in a fright? Pardalisca!

PARDALISCA:

I am expiréd! But whence comes yon tumult?

LYSIDAMUS:

Look just behind you! I'm here!

PARDALISCA:

Oh my master!

LYSIDAMUS:

What is your problem and why the hysterics?

PARDALISCA:

I am expiréd!

LYSIDAMUS:
                    Say what? You're "expiréd"?
PARDALISCA:
I am expiréd. And you are expiréd.
LYSIDAMUS:
Huh? I'm expiréd?
PARDALISCA:
                    Oh, woe unto thee!
LYSIDAMUS:
There'll be some woe unto THEE in a minute!
PARDALISCA:
Hold me, I beg you; I think that I'm fainting!
LYSIDAMUS:
Tell me it quickly, whatever the trouble!
PARDALISCA:
Please, put your hand 'round my waist to support me!
Take off your mantle and fan me a little.
LYSIDAMUS:
This is beginning to look a bit scary,
Could she be drunk by the power of Bacchus?
PARDALISCA:
Give me your mouth for some resuscitation!
LYSIDAMUS:
Leave me alone! And to hell with your waist!
Same with your mouth, and the rest of your body!
Tell me the truth in an instant, you serpent,
O, I will bludgeon your brains with my cane!
Scum! You have made me your fool long enough!
PARDALISCA:
Master . . .
LYSIDAMUS:
                    Well, what do you want from me, slave?
PARDALISCA:
Master, your wrath is so rabid!
LYSIDAMUS:
                              It's growing!
Out with the story! Just give me the highlights!
What was that ruckus inside of the house?

PARDALISCA:

    Listen; I'll tell you: 'twas terrible, horrid!

    Right in our presence, your maid starting acting

    Unlike a girl that's been brought up in Athens.

LYSIDAMUS:

    What was she doing?

PARDALISCA:

                    My tongue ties with terror!

LYSIDAMUS:

    Can I discover from you what's the trouble?

PARDALISCA:

    Let me explain it. Your maid that you want to . . .

    Marry your foreman, well she's in the house and . . .

LYSIDAMUS:

    What is she doing? And how is she acting?

PARDALISCA:

    Acting depraved, like a villainous woman,

    Muttering threats that the life of her husband . . .

LYSIDAMUS:

    What did she threaten?

PARDALISCA:

              Oh!

LYSIDAMUS:

             What was she saying?

PARDALISCA:

    Threats that she wants to extinguish his life! A . . .

    Sword . . .

LYSIDAMUS:

       Huh?

PARDALISCA:

       A sword.

LYSIDAMUS:

            There's a sword?

PARDALISCA:

                  Yes, she has one.

LYSIDAMUS:

    Oh! My misfortune! But why does she have one?

PARDALISCA:

> She's been pursuing us all through the building!
> No one's permitted to even get near her!
> Everyone's hiding in chests and 'neath couches,
> Frightened to mutter the tiniest murmur!

LYSIDAMUS:

> Death and damnation! But what sort of sickness
> Seized her so suddenly?

PARDALISCA:

>   Madness has seized her!

LYSIDAMUS:

> I'm the accursedest man in existence!

PARDALISCA:

> Wait till you hear all the things she was saying!

LYSIDAMUS:

> What was she saying? I'm desperate to know it!

PARDALISCA:

> Listen: she swore by the gods, one and all, to
> Murder the man that she sleeps with tonight.

LYSIDAMUS:

> Murder for me?

PARDALISCA:

>   Does it somehow affect you?

LYSIDAMUS:

> Ack!

PARDALISCA:

> Why does it matter to you what she's saying?

LYSIDAMUS:

> Slip of the tongue; I had meant to say "foreman."

PARDALISCA:

(aside)

> Trying to lead me off course with his lying.

LYSIDAMUS:

> Surely I wasn't the one that she threatened!

PARDALISCA:

> You, above all, bear the brunt of her anger.

LYSIDAMUS:

> Why?

PARDALISCA:
>Since you're making her marry that foreman,
>Neither her own life, nor yours, nor her husband's,
>Shall she allow to extend until morning!
>I have been sent to forewarn you about her.

LYSIDAMUS:
>Pollux! I'm wretchedly wrecked!

PARDALISCA:
>You deserve it.

LYSIDAMUS:
>Never on earth was an old man in love as
>Wretched as I am!

PARDALISCA:
(aside)
>I fooled him completely!
>All of that stuff I just said was a fiction,
>Bait from the mistress, along with our neighbor.
>I have been sent to delude the old codger.

LYSIDAMUS:
>Hey, Pardalisca!

PARDALISCA:
>What is it?

LYSIDAMUS:
>There's something . . .

PARDALISCA:
>What?

LYSIDAMUS:
>There's a question I wanted to ask you.

PARDALISCA:
>How you delay me!

LYSIDAMUS:
>And how you dismay me!
>Tell me, does Casina still have a sword?

PARDALISCA:
>Yes.
>Two of them.

LYSIDAMUS:
>Why's she have two?

PARDALISCA:

                                        She will murder
  You with the one, with the other the foreman.

LYSIDAMUS:

  I am the deadest of everyone living!
  Maybe it's best that I put on some armor.
  What of my wife? did she try to disarm her?

PARDALISCA:

  Nobody dares to approach any nearer.

LYSIDAMUS:

  Well, she should try to persuade her!

PARDALISCA:

                                        She's trying.
  Casina says she won't lower her weapon,
  Not till she knows that the wedding is canceled.

LYSIDAMUS:

  Even unwilling—because she's unwilling—
  She will be forced to get married today.
  Why should I cancel the plans that I've started?
  Shouldn't she marry me? Make that the foreman?
  That's what I meant.

PARDALISCA:

                        You misspeak a bit often.

LYSIDAMUS:

  "Terror has tied up my tongue!" But I beg you,
  Please tell my wife she should plead with the maid to
  Put down the sword and allow me to enter.

PARDALISCA:

  I will inform her.

LYSIDAMUS:

                        You plead with her also.

PARDALISCA:

  Right. I will plead with her also.

LYSIDAMUS:

                                        But sweetly,
  As is your habit. And listen to this:
  If you can do this thing,
  I'll give to you a ring

Of gold, and fancy shoes,
And other prizes too.

PARDALISCA:

I'll try to do the deed.

LYSIDAMUS:

Be sure that you succeed.

PARDALISCA:

I'm leaving now, unless
You have some more requests.

LYSIDAMUS:

Just go, and do your best.

Exit Pardalisca into Lysidamus' house. Enter from forum Olympio and cooks.

Look! A parade!
It's my partner returned from his shopping, at last!

OLYMPIO:

(indicating the assistant cooks)

Watch it, you thief! Cover your thorns!

COOK:

What do you mean? Why are they thorns?

OLYMPIO:

'Cause they snag in a jiffy whatever they touch;
And they rip you to shreds if you try to escape!
So wherever they go, and wherever they're at,
Why the fella that hires 'em gets torn into two!

COOK:

HEY!

OLYMPIO:

(seeing Lysidamus)

Well, ahoy!
I should fix up my frock like some blue-blooded lord,
Then I'll go to my master and greet him like this.

LYSIDAMUS:

Greetings, good sir!

OLYMPIO:

Ain't it the truth!

LYSIDAMUS:

What's going on?

OLYMPIO:

You're in love, but I'm dyin' of hunger 'n' thirst.

LYSIDAMUS:

What delightful provisions you've put on parade!

OLYMPIO:

Yesiree, for today I'm the real upper crust.

LYSIDAMUS:

Well just hold it a minute, you Toast of the Town.

OLYMPIO:

Peeeee-YEW!

MAN, your breath STINKS!

LYSIDAMUS:

What do you mean?

OLYMPIO:

That's what I mean!

LYSIDAMUS:

Won't you be still?

OLYMPIO:

Yesiree, me estás jodiendo a mí! [10]

LYSIDAMUS:

Y te doy un tortazo, unless you stand still!

OLYMPIO:

Vaya con Dios!

Could you gimme some room, 'less you want me to puke!

LYSIDAMUS:

Don't run away!

OLYMPIO:

What the heck? Who are you to give orders to me?

LYSIDAMUS:

I am the boss!

OLYMPIO:

You are the boss?

10. These lines in colloquial Spanish translate Greek phrases. Greek in Plautus is not retained from the original Greek scripts and generally occurs in the speech of slaves; thus, it con-
notes servile origins rather than educated nobility. Mildly translated, Olympio says, "You're
being a pain in my butt"; Lysidamus replies, "And I'll give you a beating, unless you stand still";
Olympio swears, "God, get lost!"

LYSIDAMUS:

 You are my slave.

OLYMPIO:

 I am a slave?

LYSIDAMUS:

 Yes, and you're mine!

OLYMPIO:

 Ain't I been freed? Don't you recall?

LYSIDAMUS:

 Stand over here.

OLYMPIO:

 Hey! Lemme go!

LYSIDAMUS:

 I am your slave.

OLYMPIO:

 That sounded good.

LYSIDAMUS:

 Oh, I beg you, Olympy! My father! My sire!

OLYMPIO:

 Now you got smarts!

LYSIDAMUS:

 Take me, I'm yours!

OLYMPIO:

 And just what would I want with a slave that's so bad?

LYSIDAMUS:

(pointing to kitchen)

 So, how long will you wait to replenish my strength?

OLYMPIO:

 Well, if only our supper were ready to eat.

LYSIDAMUS:

 Get them to work.

OLYMPIO:

(to cooks)

 You, make haste to the kitchen and hurry it up!
 Get along! In a minute I'll join you myself.
 And you better make sure that my plate runneth over.
 But I want somethin' fancy and elegant, see?
 I don't care for barbarian spinach today!

Exit cooks into Lysidamus' house.

You're still around?

LYSIDAMUS:

You go ahead. Here's where I'll stay.

OLYMPIO:

Is there somethin' outside here to make us delay?

LYSIDAMUS:

Pardalisca says Casina's holding a sword!

And she's waiting inside to destroy you and me!

OLYMPIO:

Oh, I see. Let 'er have it. They're foolin' around.

Them cantankerous women, I've seen 'em before.

You just stick by my side when we enter the house.

LYSIDAMUS:

But by Pollux I'm scared! Why don't YOU go ahead?

You can check for yourself what they're doing inside.

OLYMPIO:

'Cause I value my life just like you value yours.

Just move along.

LYSIDAMUS:

If you insist. Please, after you.

Exit Lysidamus and Olympio into Lysidamus' house. The stage is empty. Enter Pardalisca from Lysidamus' house.

PARDALISCA: By Pollux, I don't think the Nemean games or the Olympic games or any other games are half as fun as the fun-tastical games they're playing inside here with our friends, the old man and Olýmpio the fore-man! The whole house is buzzing with activity. The old man's clamoring in the kitchen, pestering the cooks: "Why don't you get on with it? If you're going to do something, do it! Hurry up! Dinner should've been cooked by now!" The foreman, now he's parading around, all spiffy in his wedding suit and a crown. Meanwhile the two women are in the bedroom, dressing up Chalinus to marry HIM to our foreman, instead of Casina! They've got on a perfectly straight face as if they don't know what's going to happen. Meanwhile the cooks are playing their part perfectly by making sure the old man goes without dinner. They're knocking over pots and pouring wa-ter on the fire just like the women told them to do. See, the women want to kick the old man out unfed so that THEY can stuff their bellies. I know those gluttonesses: they could eat a whole freighter of food! Ah, the door's opening!

Enter Lysidamus, from his house.

LYSIDAMUS: If you're smart, wife, you'll all dine when dinner's ready. I'll dine on the farm. See, I want to follow the newlyweds to the farm; I know the nefarious nature of folks. I don't want anyone to kidnap her. You all enjoy yourselves. But hurry up and send the couple out at once so we can get there before dark. I'll come back tomorrow, dear, and join the party then.

PARDALISCA: It's happening just as I said: the women are kicking the old man out unfed.

LYSIDAMUS: What are YOU doing here?

PARDALISCA: I'm on an errand for the mistress.

LYSIDAMUS: Really?

PARDALISCA: Seriously.

LYSIDAMUS: Why are you here spying?

PARDALISCA: I am NOT spying!

LYSIDAMUS: Get lost! You're loafing out here while the others are busy inside.

PARDALISCA: I'm going.

LYSIDAMUS: So GO already, you scum! *(exit Pardalisca into Lysidamus' house)* Has she gone yet? Now I can speak openly. If a man in love is starving, by Hercules, he's not starving for food. But look! Here he comes with a crown and a wedding torch, my cohort, co-conspirator, co-groom: the foreman.

Enter Olympio from Lysidamus' house.

OLYMPIO:
Come on piper, start your playin' while they're bringin' out my bride.
Fill the street with joyful music! Let 'em hear my wedding march!
Here comes the bride! All dressed in white!

LYSIDAMUS:
How's my savior?

OLYMPIO:
                          Starvin', dammit! Not a scrap to savor yet!

LYSIDAMUS:
I'm in LOVE, Olympio!

OLYMPIO:

Well, frankly, I don't give a damn!

You've been feastin' on your lovin', I've been fastin' all day long!

LYSIDAMUS:

Can't they speed it up, the slowpokes? What the hell could take so long?

Seems the more I want to hurry, things go slower out of spite!

OLYMPIO:

Think they'll move a little faster if I sing the wedding march?

LYSIDAMUS:

Good idea! I'll assist you: since the wedding's mine as well!

LYSIDAMUS AND OLYMPIO:

Here comes the bride! All dressed in white!

LYSIDAMUS:

Hercules! I'll pull a muscle belting out the wedding song.

Still, I haven't got the chance to pull the muscle down below!

OLYMPIO:

Damn! If you'd been born a stallion, no one'd ever break you in!

LYSIDAMUS:

How so?

OLYMPIO:

You're too hard to handle!

LYSIDAMUS:

Ever try me for a ride?

OLYMPIO:

Lord forbid it! Wait! The door's a-creakin'! Someone's comin' out!

LYSIDAMUS:

Hercules! The gods in heaven finally want to rescue me!

Enter Chalinus, dressed as bride, from Lysidamus' house, accompanied by Cleostrata and Pardalisca.

PARDALISCA:

(aside)

Now the scent of Casinus has reached the old man from afar.[11]

---

11. The meaning and attribution of this line is much disputed. I attribute the following lines, with their echoes of traditional legal language, to the matron Cleostrata based on the arguments of G. Williams, "Some Aspects of Roman Marriage Ceremonies and Ideals," *Journal of Roman Studies* 48 (1958): 16–29.

CLEOSTRATA:

Carefully lift your foot over the threshold.
Start your trip safely, my newlywed maiden.
See that you always stand over your husband;
See that your power is always more potent;
Master your husband, and you be the mistress.
You have authority; your word is final.
Let him adorn you, while stripping him naked.
Promise by day and by night to deceive him.

OLYMPIO:

Soon as she slips in the tiniest fashion,
Hercules knows that she's in for a thrashin'!

LYSIDAMUS:

Quiet!

OLYMPIO:

     I ain't being quiet!

LYSIDAMUS:

          And why?

OLYMPIO:

               That
Devil delivers divisive directions!

LYSIDAMUS:

You will unsettle the plans that I settled!
That's what they're hoping: to undo our doings!

CLEOSTRATA:

Come now, Olympio, here is your bride; so,
Take her from us if you want to be married.

OLYMPIO:

Gimme my bride if you're fixin' to give 'er.

LYSIDAMUS:

(to women)

You go inside.

CLEOSTRATA:

         She's an innocent virgin;
Please treat her gently.

OLYMPIO:

         I certainly will.

CLEOSTRATA:

Bye.

LYSIDAMUS:

Leave us already!

CLEOSTRATA:

Bye.

(The women exit.)

LYSIDAMUS:

Now has the wife gone?

OLYMPIO:

She's in the house, so don't worry.

LYSIDAMUS:

Eureka!

Finally, by Pollux, I'm free for my darling!

My little honey pie! My little sweetheart!

OLYMPIO:

Hey there, she's my bride; you'd better be careful!

LYSIDAMUS:

True, but the first fruits belong to the master.

OLYMPIO:

Take this here torch.

LYSIDAMUS:

(grabbing "Casina")

But I'd rather take THIS one.

Venus almighty, you gave me a bonus,

When you bestowed this here present upon me!

OLYMPIO:

Oh! What a soft little delicate body!

My little wifey is . . . What in tarnation?

LYSIDAMUS:

What?

OLYMPIO:

She just stomped on my foot, like a mammoth!

LYSIDAMUS: Quiet, please! Her breast is as soft as a cloud!

OLYMPIO: By Pollux! A purty little titty! OUCH! Damn!

LYSIDAMUS: What's the matter?

OLYMPIO: She walloped my chest with an elbow like a battering ram!

LYSIDAMUS: Well, what do you expect when you handle her so rough? But with me, she doesn't struggle when I snuggle. OW!

OLYMPIO: What's your problem?

LYSIDAMUS: My God! How strong the little dear is! Her elbow almost laid me out!

OLYMPIO: That means she wants to get laid!

LYSIDAMUS: Well, why don't we move along?

OLYMPIO: Come along, my comely lass!

Exit Lysidamus, Olympio, and Chalinus into Alcesimus' house. The stage is empty. Enter Myrrhina, Pardalisca, and Cleostrata.

MYRRHINA:
After grand entertainment inside of the house,
We have come to the street for the nuptial games!
Well, by Castor, I never have laughed like today,
And I doubt that I'll laugh so much ever again!

PARDALISCA:
It would sure be delightful to know the details,
What the new bride Chalinus has done with the groom!

MYRRHINA:
And no playwright has crafted a craftier ruse
Than the snare that was crafted by us here today!

CLEOSTRATA:
It would thoroughly thrill me to see the old man
Walking out of the house with his face rearranged!
He's a worthless old man, even worse than the scum
Who provided the place for unleashing his lust.
Pardalisca, I want you to stand here on guard,
So that you can make fun of whoever comes out.

PARDALISCA:
I will do it with pleasure. I've done it a lot.

CLEOSTRATA:
From behind me, you watch what they're doing inside.

MYRRHINA:
And from there you can fearlessly say what you please.

PARDALISCA:
But be quiet! The door of your house has just creaked!

Enter Olympio from Alcesimus' house, addressing audience.

OLYMPIO:

> There's nowhere to run and there's nowhere to hide!
> There's no way I know of to cover my shame!
> The master and me, with the greatest disgrace,
> Sank lower than low at our weddin' today!
> I feel all ashamed, and all rattled right now,
> With both of us treated like toys on a string.
> I'm totally green at this sort of affair:
> I never felt shame but I'm feelin' it now.
> You folks pay attention; I'll tell you my tale.
> It's well worth the effort to prick up your ears.
> It's crazy to hear and it's crazy to tell,
> The mess of confusion I stirred up inside.
>
> I led my new bride on inside of the house,
> And carried her straight to the "honeymoon suite."
> Inside, it was darker than pitch in a well.
> The gaffer was gone, so I told her, "Lay down."
> I pamper her, cushion her, flatter, and coax,
> To join her in "wedlock" before the old man.
> I started out slow, 'cause [I wasn't at ease,] [12]
> I kept checkin' over my shoulder to see,
> [Make sure] the old man didn't [sneak up behind.]
> I asked for a kiss, to excite her a bit,
> She shoved back my hand and refused me the kiss.
> So now I'm [all flustered.] The faster I go,
> The greater my itchin' to jump on her bones.
> I hanker to have her before the old man.
> I bolted the door so he couldn't come in.

CLEOSTRATA:

(to Pardalisca)

> The time has come! Approach him now!

---

12. Square brackets indicate a conjectural restoration. Our manuscripts contain fairly sizeable lacunae from here through line 990.

PARDALISCA:

Excuse me sir, but where's your bride?

OLYMPIO:

I'm damned, by God! The jig is up!

PARDALISCA:

It's only fair to tell us all.

So what occurred inside the house?

And how did Casina behave?

Did she oblige you well enough?

OLYMPIO:

I'm too ashamed to even speak.

PARDALISCA:

From start to finish, tell it all!

OLYMPIO:

By Hercules, I'm too ashamed.

PARDALISCA:

Be brave and tell the tale to us.

Begin with when you laid her down:

I want to hear the whole account.

OLYMPIO:

I feel defiled . . .

PARDALISCA:

A lesson for

The audience.

OLYMPIO:

[The shame's too] great!

PARDALISCA:

You're wasting time. Just move along.

OLYMPIO:

[I reached my hand down] underneath . . .

PARDALISCA:

And what?

OLYMPIO:

Oh God!

PARDALISCA:

AND WHAT?

OLYMPIO:

OH LORD!

PARDALISCA:

    [A big surprise?]

OLYMPIO:

                The BIGGEST! Oh!

    I feared she had [a sword in hand.]

    I started feeling [up her dress—]

    To see if she had kept that sword—

    I grabbed a shaft! And then I thought:

    "That ain't no sword! A sword is cold!"

PARDALISCA:

    Continue, then!

OLYMPIO:

                I'm too ashamed!

PARDALISCA:

    Perhaps it was a radish?

OLYMPIO:

                Nope.

PARDALISCA:

    Perhaps it was a cucumber?

OLYMPIO:

    It wasn't any vegetable.

    But what it was, by Hercules,

    It wasn't wilted, that's for sure!

    No matter what it was, 'twas huge.

PARDALISCA:

    What happened next? Reveal it all!

OLYMPIO:

    I call to her sweetly, "My wifey," I say,

    "Just why are you being so cruel to your man?

    This god-awful treatment I sure don't deserve!

    I'm pinin' for you!" Not a peep in reply.

    She walls off her womanly parts with her dress.

    So seeing her front door is closed to my love,

    I ask her to show me the "alternate route."

    I want her to face me; she elbows [my groin,]

    She doesn't say nothin', [but tries to escape.]

    I leap to my feet and I [chase] her [about,]

    She [runs like a rabbit, and me like a hound!]

PARDALISCA:

Delightful narration! [Continue it please!]

OLYMPIO:

[At last I corral her, and try for] a kiss:
A beard like a pricker bush punctures my lips!
I get on my knees, and she kicks at my ribs.
I fall from the couch and I land on my head,
She jumps on my chest and she pummels my face!
I ran from the house, all undressed as you see,
But haven't said nothin' to warn the old man,
So he gets a taste of this medicine, too!

PARDALISCA:

Oh yes, that's just perfect. But where is your cloak?

OLYMPIO:

I left it in there.

PARDALISCA:

                              And so what do you think?
We've hoodwinked the two of you smartly enough?

OLYMPIO:

The way we deserved. But the door made a noise.
She still isn't followin' me even now?

Enter Lysidamus, from Alcesimus' house, addressing audience.

LYSIDAMUS:

Branded am I, with the greatest disgrace!
What am I going to do in this mess?
How will I look at my wife in the face?
More than just dead, I'm completely destroyed!
All my dishonor is out on display:
Wretched, I'm ruined in numberless ways!
[Now] I've been caught with my leg in the trap;
[. . .] How will I ever explain to the wife?
Wretched [I stand here decaned] and decloaked,
[All has been lost in this] wedding charade.
[What should I do when I can't even] think!
Best thing for me [is to sound a retreat.]
[Maybe instead] I'll go in to my wife,

Give her my backside to pay for my sins.
Anyone willing to stand in my place?
I'm at a loss as to what I should do:
Act like a renegade, runaway slave?
Whips will be waiting for when I return.
YOU might be thinking that this is a joke;
Really, I'm whipped! And I hate it, by God,
Even when whipping is what I deserve.
Time I got moving and made my escape.

Enter Chalinus from Alcesimus' house.

CHALINUS:
HEY!
Hold it there, lover-boy.

LYSIDAMUS:
Damn! I'm caught!
I'll pretend not to hear and I'll run.

CHALINUS:
Where you hiding, filthy faggot? Now's your chance to fondle me!
Come back to the bedroom, won't you! Hercules, you're finished now!
Please approach the judge's chambers: we can settle out of court!

LYSIDAMUS:
Damn, he's gonna use his "gavel," and my ass will be the bench! [13]
This ship better change direction: there's a dickwreck up ahead!

CLEOSTRATA:
Lover-boy, I bid you welcome!

LYSIDAMUS:
                                   Wife ahoy! She's off the prow!
Caught between a rock and hard place: no escape that I can see.
Wolves ahead, and dogs behind me. Seems the wolf has got a club.
Now I think I'll test that proverb: try my luck and face the bitch.

CLEOSTRATA:
What's your story, you two-timer? Tell me, husband, where you've
                                                                   been.
Aren't you underdressed a little? Where'd you leave your cloak and cane?

13. Literally, "now that man will strip the wool [*defloccabit*] from my loins with his stick."

MYRRHINA:

    I believe he lost them whoring, while seducing Casina!

LYSIDAMUS:

    Ruined!

CHALINUS:

        Shall we go inside the bedroom? Casina is . . . ME!

LYSIDAMUS:

    Go to hell, you!

CHALINUS:

        Don't you love me?

CLEOSTRATA:

            Well, what happened to your cloak?

LYSIDAMUS:

    Dear, I swear, the Bacchae . . .

CLEOSTRATA:

        Bacchae?

LYSIDAMUS:

          Yes, the Bacchae, dear, I swear . . .

MYRRHINA:

    That's just nonsense and he knows it! No more Bacchae revel now!

LYSIDAMUS:

(aside)

    I forgot.

(to Cleostrata)

        Why, yes, the Bacchae . . .

CLEOSTRATA:

          What about the Bacchae, then?

LYSIDAMUS:

    Sure, it sounds a bit outlandish . . .

CLEOSTRATA:

        You're afraid, by Castor.

LYSIDAMUS:

            Me?

CLEOSTRATA:

    Hercules! I know you're lying! See the way you're growing pale?
    Where's your sense of shame, my husband?

LYSIDAMUS:

          Why would I be telling lies?

CLEOSTRATA:

Even now, you dare to ask me? [I know all about your schemes!]¹⁴

LYSIDAMUS:

[I've been framed! They're out to get me! Please, believe me. Here's the
truth:]

[I had hid their wedding present over in the neighbor's house.]

[So we stop. I wish them joy and go inside to get my gift.]

[Then I hear a ruckus coming from the bedroom. Thumps and cries!]

[Thinking old Alcesimus is needing help, I try the door.]

[Locked! And] when I peer inside the keyhole, I can see the girl,

[Standing naked with our foreman! Only thing: she's NOT a girl!]

[Then they see me; "We're in trouble! Lysidamus caught a glimpse!]

[Get him! Quick!" I try to run, but they're too fast. They knock me down.]

[Then they beat me. Worse, they steal my cloak and cane. Believe me,
dear.]

OLYMPIO:

[That's a lot of bull he's talkin'! Hercules, he's full of lies!]

See the way that his pree-versions made a jerk of me as well!

LYSIDAMUS:

SHUT UP!

OLYMPIO:

No, I won't by Pollux! YOU begged ME on hands and knees,
Made me marry Casina, and just to satisfy your lust!

LYSIDAMUS:

I did that?

OLYMPIO:

No, Trojan Hector!

LYSIDAMUS:

. . . Would have given you the shaft!

Did I do what you're alleging?

CLEOSTRATA:

Oh, the nerve to even ask!

14. Lines 983–90 are essentially lost. We cannot even be sure of which, or how many,
characters spoke these lines. This conjectural restoration relies upon a handful of decipherable
letters that seem to spell words for "badly," "me," "I congratulate," "old man," "now," and "Casinus." A medieval scholar records a part of line 987: "When I saw the girl from my watching
place."

LYSIDAMUS:

If I did, I acted badly.

CLEOSTRATA:

Get yourself inside the house.

I'll remind you what just happened, if your memory starts to fade.

LYSIDAMUS:

Hercules, on second thought, I guess I'll take your word for it.

Please, my wife, forgive your husband. Plead with her, Myrrhina, please.

If I henceforth ever after, either sleep with Casina,

Or I even flirt a little (since I'll never sleep with her),

Hang me up, with my permission, whack my back with bullwhips, wife.

MYRRHINA:

I propose you grant him pardon.

CLEOSTRATA:

Then I'll follow your advice.

Yes, I'll grant your pardon freely: let me tell the reason why:

Let's not drag the play out longer; this has gone on long enough.

LYSIDAMUS:

You're not angry?

CLEOSTRATA:

I'm not angry.

LYSIDAMUS:

That's a promise?

CLEOSTRATA:

On my word.

LYSIDAMUS:

No man's wife is more delightful than the one I've got right here!

CLEOSTRATA:

Come, Chalinus, now's the time to give him back his cloak and cane.

CHALINUS:

Here you go. By Pollux, really, I'm the biggest loser here:

I just married these two guys, and never got my honeymoon!

Now we'll brief you on the ending, if you'll pay attention, folks:

Casina's the neighbor's daughter! Soon she'll wed Euthynicus.[15]

---

15. The speaker here names the son of Cleostrata and Lysistrata "Euthynicus," meaning "victorious."

Now it's right to pay the actors: give them well-earned, loud applause.
He who does will ever after bed the whore he likes the best,
And his wife will never know it! He who doesn't clap so hard,
He won't get the whore he wanted, just a goat all smeared with shit! [16]

16. I wish to thank those colleagues who generously read and commented on drafts of this chapter: S. O'Bryhim, T. Moore, D. Olson, A. Becker, R. Mondi, C. Salowey, D. Murphy, and J. Cunningham. Misinterpretations and infelicities of translation should be attributed to my own obstinancy.

TERENCE
AND ROMAN
NEW COMEDY

TIMOTHY J. MOORE

INTRODUCTION

Terence's Life

ACCORDING to the ancient Roman biographer Suetonius, Publius Terentius Afer was born in Carthage, in modern-day Tunisia in North Africa. If Suetonius' sources can be trusted (they are not always reliable), Terence may himself have been a Carthaginian, and therefore Semitic. Given his cognomen Afer ("African"), however, he also may have been of an ethnicity native to Africa: probably a relative of modern North Africans, but it is not beyond the realm of possibility that he is the world's first extant black author. Suetonius also tells us that Terence was later a slave at Rome—whether he was born a slave or became a slave is not certain—but was freed by his master, the Roman senator Terentius Lucanus. He died, according to the biographical tradition, a young man, while on a trip to Greece in 159 B.C. In the decade before his death he wrote six plays, all of which survive: *The Girl from Andros* (produced in 166 B.C.), *The Mother-in-Law* (produced unsuccessfully in 165 and 160, successfully at a third attempt in 160), *The Self-Tormentor* (163), *The Eunuch* (161), *Phormio* (161), and *The Brothers* (160).

Terence and His Contemporaries

Two features of Terence's life are especially interesting, and especially controversial: his alleged association with Publius Scipio Aemilianus and other Roman aristocrats, and his relationship with his audience and fellow playwrights. Both controversies derive ultimately from the prologues of Terence's six plays, the earliest extended passages of literary criticism in Latin.

In two of his prologues, Terence responds to charges allegedly made by his critics that "he relies on the genius of his friends, rather than his own talent" (*The Self-Tormentor*), and that "aristocrats help him and are continually writing together with him" (*The Brothers*). In neither prologue does Terence explicitly rebut these charges. In *The Self-Tormentor* he merely has his prologue-speaker say to the spectators, "You be the judges." In *The Brothers,* the speaker says: "What they think is a powerful charge, he (Terence) considers the highest praise, that he pleases those who please all of you and the people, and whose talents each of us has used when the opportunity has arisen." The supposed charges, and Terence's refusal to rebut them, have led many since antiquity to assume that Terence had help in writing his plays from members of the Roman upper class.[1]

The most common candidates for Terence's high-born helpers are Publius Scipio Aemilianus, arguably the leading Roman statesman of the mid-second century B.C., and his best friend, Gaius Laelius. Although ancient biographies of Terence preserve anecdotes about the two aristocrats helping the young playwright, the entire tradition about aristocratic helpers is without any firm evidence and may well be apocryphal. Nevertheless, it is quite likely that Scipio had some association with Terence, as a friend and/or as a patron. Terence's *The Brothers* and *The Mother-in-Law* were offered at funeral games held by Scipio and his brother for their father. Scipio and many of his friends were known for their attachment to Greek culture. Any connection must remain speculative, but the philhellenism of his aristocratic friends may have helped inspire Terence to be more faithful to his Greek originals than his predecessor Plautus had been.

If we are to believe Terence's prologues, he was persecuted throughout his career by critics, especially Luscius Lanuvinus, a fellow playwright. In addition to the charges that others helped write his plays, Terence claims that Luscius and others censured him for mixing two Greek plays together while creating one Roman play (*contaminatio*), for adapting Greek plays that other Latin playwrights had already adapted, and for writing plays "weak in diction, anemic in style." Terence's presentation of competitors trying to ruin his career is probably rhetorical exaggeration.[2] Nevertheless, the polemics of the prologues suggest that the mid-second century B.C. was a time of lively controversy regarding how Greek comedies could best be adapted to the Roman stage.

How those controversies, and Terence's reactions to them, affected Terence's audience as a whole is not certain. Terence himself reports that one of his plays, *The Mother-in-Law,* faced great difficulties: its first performance was

1. Compare the many attempts to attribute Shakespeare's plays to more well-bred authors.
2. See S. M. Goldberg, *Understanding Terence* (Princeton, 1986), 31–60.

disrupted by persons hoping to see rope-dancers and boxers; a second attempt failed in the face of confusion caused by rumors that there were to be gladiatorial games. These difficulties, however, do not imply that Terence was an unsuccessful playwright. Those who disrupted the two performances of *The Mother-in-Law* were evidently not the spectators themselves, discontent with what they were watching, but others entering the theater from elsewhere in the belief that they were going to see a different form of entertainment.[3] *The Mother-in-Law* was performed to completion when it was offered for a third time, and there is no evidence that any of Terence's other plays met with anything less than success. Indeed, Suetonius reports that for *The Eunuch,* honored with an encore performance, Terence received the highest fee that had ever been paid for a comedy at Rome.

Characteristics of Terentian Comedy

The question of Terence's popularity not only is of significance for Terence's own career, but has bearing on one of the central questions of Roman cultural history: Rome's response to the culture of Greece. Shortly before Terence produced his first play, Rome had emphatically confirmed her control over most of the Greek world with the defeat of Perseus, king of Macedon (168 B.C.). This victory accelerated a process that had been going on in Rome for centuries: the importation and adaptation of things Greek. In her visual arts, rhetoric, philosophy, science, and literature Rome had long turned to Greece for inspiration and models. Seldom, however, were the Romans slavish imitators. They took what they admired in Greek culture and made it their own, and they vehemently maintained their own unique identity even as they created what has justly been called the "Greco-Roman" world.[4]

Roman comedy is the quintessential example of Rome's response to Greek culture in the middle Republic. Terence's predecessors, most notably Plautus, had found models for their own plays in the Greek New Comedy of Menander and his contemporaries. In adapting Greek New Comedy, however, Plautus and his colleagues made it Roman. They added allusions to Roman institutions, replaced the relatively subdued language of New Comedy with rollicking lin-

3. H. N. Parker, "Plautus vs. Terence: Audience and Popularity Re-examined," *American Journal of Philology* 117 (1996): 592–601.

4. On Rome's response to Greek culture in this period, see especially E. S. Gruen, *Studies in Greek Culture and Roman Policy* (Leiden, 1990), and *Culture and National Identity in Republican Rome* (Ithaca, N.Y., 1992).

guistic exuberance, exaggerated the stock features of characters to the point of absurdity, made the plays more musical, removed the Greek plays' divisions between acts, added characters, and changed the plays they adapted in numerous other ways. Their most conspicuous change was to make the plays more immediately and uproariously funny. That is, they broadened the plays' farce, probably in response to the Romans' own traditions of farcical performance.[5]

In some ways, Terence followed the patterns set by his predecessors. In two of the three plays where we know he added scenes from a second Greek play to the main play he was adapting, the changes make the plays considerably more farcical: Terence added a lively chase scene from a play of Diphilus to Menander's *The Brothers,* and he added a stock braggart soldier and parasite — both very funny characters—from another play of Menander to the same author's *The Eunuch.* Terence's plays, like those of Plautus, were performed without regular act breaks and included many more lines accompanied by music than did those of New Comedy.

More often, however, Terence's tendency was to take Roman comedy in the opposite direction, making it closer to Greek New Comedy in tone and style. Most of Terence's stock characters are far less exaggerated than those of Plautus. Although Terence followed Plautus in increasing the musical element of the plays, he virtually eliminated from his plays many of the widely varied meters used by Plautus. Whereas Plautus' characters approach their audience with great self-consciousness, always reveling in the fact that they are onstage performing, Terence keeps these "metatheatrical" elements to a minimum. His language is far more restrained than that of his Roman predecessors: less alliteration and assonance, far fewer outrageous similes and allusions, fewer digressions, neologisms, and comic long words. Indeed, Julius Caesar praised Terence as a *puri sermonis amator,* a lover of pure language.[6]

Terence also made his own unique contribution to the history of theater, for in a number of ways he seems to have diverged from New Comedy as well as from his Roman predecessors. Four adjustments he made to his Greek originals are particularly significant: the double plot, an increase of suspense and surprise at the expense of dramatic irony, greater verisimilitude, and the universal humanity of his characters.

Most plots of New Comedy seem to have centered around one love affair.

---

5. See the discussion of Plautus' methods of adaptation in the essay on Plautus above.

6. On the differences between Terence and his Roman predecessors, see especially J. Wright, *Dancing in Chains: The Stylistic Unity of the Comoedia Palliata* (Rome, 1974), 127–51.

Five of Terence's six plays, however, involve two sets of lovers, both important to the plot. Although in several plays Terence must have found both sets of lovers in his Greek originals, he appears to have expanded the role of the second pair of lovers; and in one play, *The Girl from Andros,* he added the second couple to a play of Menander. This emphasis on two couples adds richness to Terence's plots, and it allows him to paint significant contrasts between the two pairs, as when one young man loves a marriageable maiden, the other a prostitute. One need only consider the inevitable two (or more) sets of lovers that inhabit Shakespeare's comedies, or the contrasted couples of many American musicals, to appreciate the influence of this Terentian innovation.[7]

In contrast to the suspense sought by most modern writers of drama and cinema, writers of New Comedy relied to a far greater extent on dramatic irony. Spectators at plays of Menander and his colleagues usually had a pretty good idea how things on stage would work out. Their pleasure came less from suspense than from the discrepancy between their own knowledge and the ignorance of the characters. Many plays of New Comedy had prologues spoken by gods, who could reveal much of what would happen in the plot (note, for example, Pan's introduction to *Dyskolos*). Terence removed the divine prologue-speakers from his originals and pointedly refused to discuss the plot of his plays in his prologues. Therefore, although dramatic irony is still present on many occasions, the audience is frequently in suspense as to what will happen, and a number of the most effective moments in Terence's comedies are surprises. These surprises are particularly potent when Terence reverses the expectations of stock characters: when the prostitute, for example, proves to be generous and kind, or the "clever" slave proves himself incompetent.

Menander was praised for his imitation of life, and in general New Comedy seems to have been considerably closer to a reflection of reality than was Old Comedy. Terence appears not only to have reduced some of the more fantastic features of his Roman predecessors, but in some ways to have increased the relative verisimilitude he found in his Greek originals. His characters are more likely than those of Menander to disguise their addresses to the audience as "thinking aloud," and on several occasions Terence replaced a monologue from his Greek original with a dialogue. His language is not only restrained, but is filled with the interjections, colloquialisms, and ellipses (leaving out of words)

---

7. Terence did not invent the so-called duality method: some Greek comedies also had two sets of lovers. His additional emphasis on the second pair of lovers is nevertheless significant. See G. E. Duckworth, *The Nature of Roman Comedy* (Princeton, 1952), 185–90.

one might hear in everyday conversation. This naturalism must not be exaggerated: with its masked[8] actors, its many scenes accompanied by music, its verse, its numerous monologues, and its stock characters, Terence's comedy is a long way from modern naturalistic theater (e.g., the plays of Chekov as interpreted by Stanislavski, or the later plays of Ibsen). Nevertheless, within the conventions of ancient drama, Terence achieved an unusual degree of naturalism that allowed his audience to find his characters both believable and familiar.

Those characters in fact have a remarkable relevance well beyond the world of Greece or Rome, for Terence shows great skill in portraying universal human characteristics and foibles. The most famous line from his plays, *homo sum: humani nil a me alienum puto*—"I am a human being: I consider nothing foreign to myself that pertains to humans"—may well be ironic in its context, since it is spoken by an incorrigible busybody (*The Self-Tormentor* line 77). Nevertheless, the line expresses an important aspect of Terence's comedies. The plays are acutely concerned with the human weaknesses we all share. In Terence's fathers, for example, there is a bit of every parent, struggling, often unsuccessfully, to find the best way to raise children. Terence's sympathetic prostitutes advertise the common humanity of a class often dismissed. Minor characters, such as the slave Davus who begins *Phormio,* display personality and psychological plausibility well beyond what is required by their roles in the plot. Indeed, even Terence's pimps are portrayed with a surprising degree of sympathy. Although we may laugh at Terence's characters—or even find them distasteful—we are continually reminded of the humanity we share with them.

Terence's Reputation

Terence's refined language gave him an important place in the ancient Latin school curriculum, even after his plays—and those of the other Roman comic playwrights—ceased to be performed regularly in the centuries after his death. Since the end of the Roman era, the literary and dramatic history of Europe and the Americas might be divided into "Terentian" and "Plautine" periods. The Middle Ages were decidedly Terentian: Terence remained one of the authors most frequently taught in schools, and the twelfth-century German nun Hrostvit even looked to Terence as her model when she created comedies with Christian themes. Renaissance playwrights and scholars continued to ad-

8. Probably, though there is some controversy about whether Roman actors wore masks in Terence's day. See the discussion in W. Beare, *The Roman Stage,* 3d ed. (London, 1964), 192–94, 303–9.

mire Terence, but turned more often to Plautus as they produced, translated, and adapted ancient comedies. Shakespeare's Polonius offers Plautus as the paradigm of comedy (*Hamlet,* Act 2, Scene 2). Molière, however, drew inspiration from both Plautus and Terence, and his *Les Fourberies de Scapin* is an adaptation of *Phormio.* We live today in a largely Plautine age (witness the recent revival of the 1962 Broadway musical *A Funny Thing Happened on the Way to the Forum,* an adaptation of a number of scenes from Plautus' comedies). Terence, however, remains a valued author in schools, and his position as one of the founders of what is now known as "high comedy" is undeniable.

The Plot of *Phormio*

In the first scenes of *Phormio* we learn that two brothers, Demipho and Chremes, have both been gone from Athens for some time. In their absence, each brother's son has fallen in love. Chremes' son, Phaedria, has fallen for a female lyre player. Unfortunately, the lyre player is owned by the pimp Dorio, so the penniless Phaedria can do nothing but watch the girl wistfully from a distance. Demipho's son, Antipho, has fallen in love with Phanium, a poor Athenian girl whose father is unaccounted for and whose mother has just died.

Knowing that his father will scarcely allow him to marry a penniless orphan, Antipho has turned to the resourceful parasite Phormio. Phormio has taken advantage of a peculiar Athenian law. In Athens, if a woman was left fatherless, it was the legal obligation of her father's nearest living male relative either to marry her himself or to provide a dowry and marry her to someone else. Phormio, therefore, has sued Antipho, pretending to be a friend of the girl's deceased father and claiming that Antipho is the girl's closest living relative, and Antipho has been "forced" to marry Phanium. When the play begins, both Antipho and his slave Geta, who was left in charge of Antipho and Phaedria, are in terror at the prospect of Demipho's return.

While Antipho and Phaedria are arguing about whose lot is more pitiable, Geta reports that Demipho has in fact returned to Athens. Antipho prepares to face his father, but in the end his fear overcomes him, and he flees. Phaedria and Geta are left to confront Demipho, and they blame the whole affair on Phormio the parasite, whom Demipho demands to see. Heated debate between Phormio and Demipho leaves Demipho outwitted and flustered.

Antipho finally returns when Demipho has left the stage: Terence and/or Apollodorus (the author of the Greek play he adapted) has taken pains that the sons never meet their respective fathers during the course of the play. After Geta explains to Antipho what has happened, the two learn that Dorio the pimp has sold Phaedria's beloved lyre player. She is to be taken from Athens unless Phaedria can come up with her purchase price within the day. Antipho and Phaedria persuade the reluctant Geta to help procure the money, and he comes up with a plan: Phormio will pretend that he is willing to marry Phanium himself, in exchange for a substantial dowry. The "dowry" will be used to pay Dorio for the lyre player, until Phaedria can borrow the money he needs from his friends.

Demipho enters next with his brother Chremes, who has also returned from abroad. Chremes, we learn, is a bigamist. He had gone to Lemnos to find a woman he had secretly married there, and their daughter. His Lemnian wife, however, had gone to seek him in Athens before his arrival in Lemnos. Chremes hopes that by marrying his Lemnian daughter to Antipho he can keep the whole affair hidden, especially from Nausistrata, his wealthy Athenian wife. He is therefore most upset by Antipho's marriage to Phanium.

Geta then enters and tells Demipho and Chremes of Phormio's willingness to marry Phanium. Demipho is reluctant to pay the dowry, but Chremes offers to pay most of the necessary money, using the resources of Nausistrata. Geta leads Demipho with the money to Phormio. Chremes, left alone onstage, comes upon Sophrona, Phanium's nurse, who recognizes Chremes as Phanium's father by his Lemnian wife. Antipho has married the woman his father and uncle wanted him to marry after all.

Geta overhears Chremes and Demipho discussing Phanium's parentage, and he tells Antipho and Phormio. Phormio decides that he will blackmail Chremes and Demipho so that Phaedria can keep the money from Phanium's dowry. When Demipho and Chremes return, Phormio refuses to return the dowry, and he reveals that he knows the truth. Chremes is inclined to give in, but Demipho admonishes him to have courage, and the two threaten Phormio. Not to be intimidated, Phormio calls Nausistrata onstage and tells her the entire story. The angry Nausistrata decides not only that Phaedria can keep the money for his lyre player, but that he will decide what is to happen now to his humiliated and powerless father. A happy ending, then, for both youths, and the happiest of all possible endings for the parasite: Nausistrata invites him to dinner.

A Note on Meter

Unlike Plautus, Terence did not use a wide variety of lyric meters in his plays. Nevertheless, he made very sophisticated use of the meters he did employ.

Two metrical distinctions are especially important: the difference between unaccompanied iambic senarii and accompanied meters, and that between trochaic and iambic lines. I have tried to imitate these distinctions in my English translation.

About one-half of Terence's lines are written in iambic senarii (see the description of iambic senarii in Franko's introduction to Plautus above). In all likelihood, these iambic senarii were unaccompanied, while the player of the *tibia* (a reed instrument with two separate pipes) played during lines performed in all other meters. In this translation, iambic senarii have been translated into prose, all other meters into verse. Terence achieves a number of effects by switching from accompanied to unaccompanied verse and back. For example, the meter switches from unaccompanied to accompanied verse (from prose to verse in the translation) to underline the anger of Demipho when he first enters, but it changes back to unaccompanied iambic senarii (prose in the translation) when Phaedria seeks to calm him. Perhaps most striking is the meter accompanying Nausistrata's refusal to address Chremes at the end of the play: the meter switches from iambic senarii to an accompanied meter as she turns to Demipho in disgust:

> Has anything more foul ever been done? And when they come to their wives, then they become old men.
>
> (prose: unaccompanied verse in original)

> Démipho, yoú I'm addréssing. I dón't want to tálk to *hím:* it disgústs me
>
> (trochaics: accompanied in original).

Almost all the accompanied meters Terence uses (all of them in *Phormio*) are based either on the trochee (a heavy syllable followed by a light) or on the iamb (a light syllable followed by a heavy). As English prosody is based on stress, rather than "weight" of syllables, I have used English trochees (a stressed syllable followed by an unstressed syllable) and iambs (an unstressed syllable followed by a stressed syllable) in my translation. To recreate the feel of the Latin trochaic lines, I have used lines made up of seven trochees or dactyls (a stressed syllable followed by two unstressed syllables):

> Loók what I've cóme to. My fáther ónly wánts to seé me háppy.[9]

---

9. Exceptions: lines 183 and 191, where I have followed Terence's use of very short trochaic lines.

For the iambic lines, I have used lines consisting of seven iambs or anapests (two unstressed syllables followed by a stressed syllable), with an extra syllable at line's end:

I'm álways wóndering: whén will my fáther come báck and énd my márriage?

The trochaic meters, because their heaviest syllable comes at the beginning of the foot, encourage a sense of motion: they are sometimes called "falling" meters. Iambic meters, on the other hand, are "rising" meters: the need to pronounce the heavier syllable at the end of the foot introduces a certain restraint in comparison with the trochees. Terence often juxtaposes trochees and iambs to great effect. Note, for example, Geta's first entrance as a "running slave," when he has seen Demipho at the harbor:

Fínished, Géta! Thát's what you áre, if you dón't think of sómething quíckly.
   (trochaic)

Óverwhélmed, and caúght by surpríse, and fáced with súdden disáster.
   (trochaic)

There's nó escápe, no wáy to get oút from únder áll these troúbles.
   (iambic)

If yoú don't thínk of sómething quíck, you're dóne for: yoú and your máster.
   (iambic)

Geta enters in a panic: the trochees reinforce his haste and confusion. As he ponders his fate, however, he slows down somewhat and uses iambs.

WHO IS THE PARASITE?

GIVING AND TAKING IN *PHORMIO*

T ERENCE'S prologues concern themselves principally with literary and theatrical polemics, not with the plays to come. The prologue of *Phormio,* however, includes one piece of information that
is of great significance to the play as a whole. Terence informs his audience that
the Greek play he adapted (we know from other sources that it was by the
playwright Apollodorus) was called *Epidicazomenos,* or "The One Being Sued."
Terence's Latin play, however, is called *Phormio,* "because the parasite Phormio
will play the lead role, and will instigate most of the action." *Phormio* is the only
play in which Terence changed the name of his Greek original. The change of
title is indicative of the emphasis Terence has placed on the character Phormio
throughout the play. Phormio not only sets the play's plot in motion through
his bogus lawsuit against Antipho, but he dominates the action throughout. His
machinations bring about the happy ending for both Phaedria and Antipho, and
he provides the play's liveliest moments: his humorous self-description, his argument with Demipho, and his revelation to Nausistrata of Chremes' bigamy.[1]

Not only does the prologue establish Phormio's importance—it also makes
clear the stock character type to which he belongs: the parasite. The parasite
first appeared in Greek comedies of the fifth century B.C. and was a common
feature of the plays of New Comedy (Chaireas in Menander's *Dyskolos* is an ex-

---

1. On the role of Phormio, especially his remarkable language, see W. G. Arnott, "*Phormio
Parasitus:* A Study in Dramatic Methods of Characterization," *Greece and Rome* 17 (1970): 32—57.

ample of the type). Plautus incorporated the character in several of his plays, and Terence also used one in his *The Eunuch*.[2] As his name implies, the parasite's central characteristic is that he depends on someone else for his livelihood. Comic parasites, who are usually ravenously and continually hungry, employ various methods to persuade their patrons to keep feeding them. Sometimes, especially when their patron is a braggart soldier, they rely upon flattery. Elsewhere they entertain with jokes and witty stories or perform various services, most notably, as here in *Phormio,* assistance in romantic affairs and in deception. In spite of these services, however, the relationship between a comic parasite and his patron is almost always emphatically one-sided: the parasite gets valuable sustenance from his patron though he offers little of real value in return.

Although it is impossible to reconstruct Apollodorus' lost *Epidicazomenos* with certainty, we can be reasonably sure that Terence reworked his model to call extra attention to Phormio's status as a parasite. Furthermore, Terence created in Phormio a most unusual parasite: one who gives more than he receives. This oddity combines with other ironies surrounding the exchange of favors in the play to make *Phormio* a humorous but pointed commentary on giving and taking in human relationships.

Terence's special interest in Phormio as parasite becomes clearest at Phormio's first entrance. Unlike his predecessor Plautus, Terence generally avoided giving his characters long speeches that did not contribute directly to the plot. This lack of digression is particularly evident in *Phormio*.[3] After the brief first scenes dedicated to exposition, the action of *Phormio* almost never stops, as the audience is led rapidly through a never-ending series of new developments. At Phormio's entrance, however, Terence pauses for several minutes, as Phormio gives a long discourse on his ways as a parasite. He begins with an admonition to himself, using just the kind of language the audience would expect from a hungry parasite: "Well then, Phormio, it's up to you. You cooked this dinner. You're the one who must eat it, every bite, so get yourself ready." When Geta says he fears that Phormio's audacity will get him into legal trouble, Phormio responds that he never fears being sued for his actions, for, like any good parasite, he has no property of his own with which he could pay fines. Nor, he says, does he fear that his enemies will enslave him to pay off the fines, for it would

2. On the parasite in New Comedy and Roman comedy, see C. Damon, *The Mask of the Parasite: A Pathology of Roman Patronage* (Ann Arbor, 1997), 23–101.

3. Donatus, an ancient scholar who wrote a commentary on Terence's plays, described *Phormio* as a play "almost always in motion" (*prope tota motoria*).

be not a punishment but a great benefit for someone else to feed him. When Geta exclaims that Antipho will never be able to repay Phormio for what he has done for him, Phormio counters that it is patrons who can never be repaid, and he sings the praises of the parasite's life:

> Thanks to your patron you get to come home from the baths, oiled, washed,
> and carefree.
> You pay nothing, while he gets eaten up with expense and worry.
> You get whatever you want: he grins and bears it, while you're laughing.
> You drink first. You get the best seat. He gives you a doubtful dinner.
> GETA:
> Doubtful? What do you mean?
> PHORMIO:
> I mean it's doubtful what I should eat first!
> Once you start to think how nice this is, and how expensive,
> Don't you think a patron's like a god in mortal's clothing?

In providing this long digression, Phormio is like the other comic parasites of Greek and Roman comedy, who almost always take time to describe themselves and their lives as parasites at their first entrance.[4] Much (if not all) of this discourse derives from Terence himself, rather than from Apollodorus. The ancient scholar Donatus reports that Terence derived part of Phormio's description of the parasite's life from a satire by the Roman poet Ennius. Terence therefore must have at the very least embellished this section of the play, and he may have added Phormio's entire digression.

Phormio's role as parasite comes to the fore again in the play's last scene. After he has revealed the truth about Chremes to Nausistrata, and has made sure that Phaedria will be able to keep both his beloved and the money Phormio swindled from Chremes and Demipho, Phormio asks for, and receives, an invitation to dinner from Nausistrata:

> NAUSISTRATA:
> Well then, Phormio, I'll make a promise to you. I swear by Castor,
> From this moment I'll say and do whatever I can to please you.

---

4. Peniculus, for example, the parasite of Plautus' *Menaechmi,* first enters with a discourse on how food works like chains for him, binding him to his patron. The parasite Gelasimus first enters in Plautus' *Stichus* complaining about his inability to find patrons, and he offers to sell his jokes to one of the spectators. Terence's other parasite, Gnatho of *The Eunuch,* begins his time on stage with a long lecture on the advantages of gaining sustenance through flattery.

PHORMIO:

That's very kind.

NAUSISTRATA:

You've earned it.

PHORMIO:

Well, then, I can think of something
You could do right now to make me happy—and vex your husband.

NAUSISTRATA:

Say the word.

PHORMIO:

Invite me to dinner.

NAUSISTRATA:

Why certainly: you're invited.

The last image the audience receives of Phormio, therefore, is the quintessential picture of the successful parasite, achieving his greatest end, an invitation to dinner.

It is probable that here as well Terence himself added the stereotypical behavior of the parasite to his Greek original. The last scene of the play requires four speaking characters: Demipho, Chremes, Phormio, and Nausistrata. We have no firm evidence that Apollodorus always used only three speaking characters on the stage, but it seems likely that he did not employ a fourth speaking actor, as Apollodorus was a close follower of Menander and none of the surviving scenes of Menander require more than three speaking actors.[5] If this is the case, Terence must have added the revelation to Nausistrata and the ensuing dinner invitation.

Terence thus appears to have enlarged the role of the parasite in the play as a whole, and to have taken pains to call attention to Phormio's status as parasite in both his first and last scenes.[6] Why such attention to this parasite? One

5. See the discussion of this question in Franko's essay on *Casina* above, with respect to Diphilus and Plautus. On Apollodorus and Menander, see T. B. L. Webster, *Studies in Later Greek Comedy* (2d ed., Manchester, 1970), 225–37.

6. If we can believe Donatus, Terence also encouraged stock parasitic behavior in the actor playing Phormio. Commenting on the line where Phormio first enters (315), Donatus reports the following story regarding preparations for the play's first performance: "A story is still told about Terence and Ambivius [the lead actor in the company producing the play]: Ambivius was drunk when he was getting ready to perform this play, and he spoke these verses of Terence with his mouth wide open, in a drunken manner, and picking at his ear with his little finger. When

reason is obvious: parasites are fun. From their prevalence in the plays of Plautus and Terence, it is clear that parasites brought great delight to the Roman audience. Such delight is not surprising, for parasites belong to that class of roguish freeloaders who have enchanted and amused audiences from the beginnings of comedy through the modern sitcom. One need only think of Shakespeare's Falstaff, Wilde's Algernon, or the onscreen personality of Groucho Marx. There is a great sense of wish-fulfillment in watching the arrogance and success of one so completely irresponsible—especially when, like Phormio, he lords it over those who are much more "respectable" than he.

Within the context of *Phormio,* however, the antics of the title character have a greater significance. To appreciate that significance, we need to consider one of the play's major themes, that of favors given and received.

The central element of the play's plot, the deception of Demipho and Chremes, involves an unusual amount of cooperation and mutual benefit. Antipho and Phaedria each love to complain about how his own lot is worse than his cousin's, but in fact they help each other out a great deal in the play: when Antipho is afraid to face his father, Phaedria joins Geta in defending him to Demipho; and when Phaedria is in need of money, it is Antipho who insists that Geta come up with a plan to get it. The slave Geta helps Phaedria in his argument with Demipho, masterminds the plan to gain additional money for Phaedria, and reveals to Antipho and Phormio the truth about Phanium's parentage. Indeed, Geta's role shows the extent to which even the resourceful Phormio depends on others. While arguing with Demipho, Phormio forgets the name of Phanium's alleged father, and Geta must whisper it to him.

Just as a network of mutual benefaction allows the deception to occur, a similar network acts in response to the deception. In countering Phormio's machinations, Demipho thinks he is helping his brother, Chremes, get a husband for his daughter. Chremes offers money to help Demipho pay off Phormio. Nausistrata helps Demipho, first with money and then by agreeing to talk to Phanium.

In the midst of all this benefaction, the greatest benefactor of all is Phormio the parasite. At considerable risk to himself (in spite of his protestations to the contrary), Phormio brings about the marriage of Antipho and Phanium. When Demipho returns, it is Phormio who takes him on, bringing all the onus for the

---

the playwright heard the lines he shouted that this was just the way he had envisioned the parasite, and his anger at finding the actor drunk and stuffed with food was immediately softened."

marriage upon himself. He then executes Geta's plan to get money for Phaedria by pretending he himself is willing to marry Phanium in exchange for a dowry.

It is in the play's last scenes that Phormio's role as extraordinary benefactor becomes clearest. The plot easily could have ended happily after Phormio and his comrades have learned that Phanium is Chremes' daughter. Antipho will get to keep Phanium, and in a few days Phaedria's friends will lend him the money with which Phormio can repay what he has received from Demipho and Chremes. Phormio, therefore, need do nothing, except hold off Chremes and Demipho for a few days until Phaedria gets his loans. Terence, however, has Phormio deliver a monologue at this point, his first in the play. The monologue, spoken without musical accompaniment to encourage greater intimacy with the audience, marks the moment at which Phormio goes "above and beyond the call of duty." He tells the audience that he will use his knowledge to get Phaedria his money for keeps. In the final scenes, he first tries blackmail, and when that fails he tells all to Nausistrata.

Why does Phormio do all this? As a parasite, he wants to keep the goodwill of the young men, so that they will continue to feed him. Yet he appears to go well beyond what is required to maintain that goodwill, especially when he risks a lawsuit at play's end in order to make Phaedria free of debt. Part of Phormio's motivation may be the pure joy of outwitting the old men: there can be little doubt that, like the other tricky slaves and parasites who mastermind the deceptions of Roman comedy, Phormio enjoys trickery for its own sake. One cannot escape the impression, however, that there is something selfless in Phormio's benefaction. His helpfulness goes beyond his own self-interest to a concern that he benefit Antipho and Phaedria.[7]

Herein lies the play's greatest irony. By definition, the parasite is one who takes much and gives little in return. Yet the parasite Phormio is the most determined and successful benefactor in a play filled with benefaction. Contributing to this irony is Terence's manipulation of the audience's expectations, language used to describe Phormio, and the context of Phormio's long self-description.

As we have seen, the audience would have a firm set of expectations sur-

---

7. On Phormio's altruism, see D. Parker in *The Complete Comedies of Terence: Modern Verse Translations by Palmer Bovie, Constance Carrier, and Douglass Parker,* ed. P. Bovie (New Brunswick, N.J., 1974), 229–31, though I do not agree with Parker's view that Phormio abandons that altruism at play's end.

rounding Phormio from his identification as a parasite in the prologue. The first scenes of the play reinforce those expectations. When Geta first describes Phormio, he calls him "an arrogant fellow" and implies that he is nothing but a troublemaker. Geta goes on to philosophize: "I have only myself to rely on," implying that he can expect no help from the parasite. In the next scene, as Antipho laments his lot, we hear little about Phormio, only that Antipho wishes Phormio had never persuaded him to accept his plan. Phaedria, in his defense of Antipho before Demipho, presents Phormio as a charlatan. When Geta returns with Phormio, however, he is no longer the stoic dependent only on himself, but he relies upon Phormio, pleading: "We need you," "Please help us!" Against the audience's expectations, the parasite has become the savior. The same pattern occurs later in the play. Asking Geta to help Phaedria win his beloved, Antipho says, "only you can save him." Yet again Geta relies not on himself but on Phormio to gain the money for Phaedria.

Roman ideals of friendship (*amicitia*) placed heavy emphasis on the reciprocal exchange of favors. Because comic parasites so dramatically skew the balance in that reciprocal exchange, they are almost never described as *amici* (friends).[8] Yet Geta praises the parasite for being such a good friend at Phormio's first entrance, and Phaedria later describes Phormio as "the very best friend in the world." Geta reports in a monologue that Phormio, when approached about helping Phaedria, "thanked the gods that he'd gotten the chance to show himself no less a friend to Phaedria than he was to Antipho;" and Phormio, identifying himself to Nausistrata, calls himself, "a great friend to your family and Phaedria."

The parasite becomes not only *amicus,* but even *patronus* (patron), one who would normally be just the opposite of a parasite. Demipho calls Phormio the "woman's patron" (*patronum mulieris*) when he discusses Phormio's legal maneuvers on behalf of Phanium. Although Demipho means to use the word in its restricted sense of "legal advocate," the use of the word *patronus,* rare in Terence,[9] to describe a parasite is nevertheless striking. Still more striking is Phormio's language as he prepares to tell Demipho and Chremes that he knows about Chremes' second marriage: "Perhaps you think I act as patron only for women without dowries. I also like to help women *with* dowries." Phormio's use of the word *patrocinari* (act as a patron) provides a verbal reminder that he

8. Cf. Damon (above, note 2), 78–79.
9. The word occurs only three other times in Terence's corpus.

is in fact acting like a patron toward both the women and the youths, even as he is about to prove himself most the parasite, asking Nausistrata for a dinner invitation.

The other moment in which Phormio acts most like a stock parasite, his self-description, also is made ironic by its context. Parasites' self-descriptions are almost always monologues, as the parasite divulges to the audience his own ability to get something for nothing or next-to-nothing. Phormio, however, discourses on being a parasite to Geta, who is thanking him effusively for the benefits he is bringing to Antipho. This is typical Terentian technique: the playwright frequently achieved greater verisimilitude by using a dialogue where one of his predecessors might have written a monologue. Here, however, the use of dialogue also has additional significance: the presence of the fervently grateful Geta underlines the fact that even while he boasts of his life as a parasite, Phormio is really giving more than he is receiving.

Phormio's role, then, makes problematic the concepts of parasitism, friendship, and the exchange of favors. As a parasite, Phormio by definition should be the least giving and most taking of the characters; but he is instead the greatest benefactor in a play filled with benefaction. In spite of Phormio's own description of his life as a parasite and his successful request for a dinner invitation at play's end, the spectator is encouraged to ask, "Is this parasite really so parasitic after all?"

Parallel to this irony are ironies surrounding favors given and received by Phormio's opponents, Demipho and Chremes. Geta assumes in the first scene that Demipho will disapprove of Antipho's marriage to Phanium because of his greed: Phanium brings no dowry. The impression is reinforced by Geta's story that Demipho went to Cilicia because his friend there offered him mountains of money.[10] Antipho provides a somewhat more favorable impression of his father as he enters: he says his father had always looked out for his (Antipho's) interests. Still, he does nothing to dispel the audience's impression that Demipho's objection to the marriage would be based on his own financial interests. Nor does Demipho himself change that impression when he enters in anger, or when he argues with Phaedria, Geta, and Phormio. Only halfway through the play does the audience learn Demipho's real motivation for objecting to Antipho's marriage to Phanium. True, Demipho is tight-fisted (note his reluctance

10. Davus' reaction to the story is particularly interesting in this context: he says *o regem me esse oportuit* (If only *I* were rich), using for "rich man" the word *rex* (king), usually used in comedy for a parasite's patron.

to hand over money to Phormio), but he objects to the marriage not because of money, but because he is trying to help out his brother.

The audience thus is initially deceived about Demipho in the same way they are initially fooled about Phormio. Just as they expected Phormio would have little to offer in return for what his patrons give him, so they are made to believe that Demipho is looking out only for his own interests when actually he is working to help his brother. In all likelihood, Terence himself brought this false perception to the play. Most (if not all) plays of Greek New Comedy, as far as we can tell, had prologues that described some of the background to the plot. Many of these prologues were spoken by a god, who could reveal some of what would happen in the play to come, as Pan does in Menander's *Dysko-los*.[11] Apollodorus' *Epidicazomenos* probably had such a divine prologue, which revealed, among other things, that Phanium was Chremes' daughter. Apollodorus' audience, therefore, would have known from the beginning of the play that Demipho was concerned not with his own purse, but with helping his brother. The Greek audience would have enjoyed the resulting dramatic irony, as they knew the truth and Geta, Antipho, and the other characters did not. This dramatic irony, however, would have had nowhere near the same effect as the surprise Terence produces by keeping this information hidden until the middle of the play.

A still greater effect would have resulted from the audience's delayed knowledge about Chremes. Apollodorus' audience would have known from the beginning that Chremes had a skeleton in his closet. Terence's audience, however, would assume through the first half of the play that Chremes was the epitome of propriety. Geta introduces Chremes as Demipho's older brother: as he is the elder, the audience will expect that Chremes will look out for the younger Demipho. Demipho gives the same impression when his argument with Phormio has ended in an impasse: he will wait for the return of his brother to decide what to do. Nor is Chremes only an older brother: in all his relationships, he is the one the audience would expect to be the provider of the most benefits, the one on whom others can rely. He is Phaedria's father, and Nausistrata's husband. Perhaps most significantly, he is Antipho's paternal uncle: in Roman society, the paternal uncle (*patruus*) was expected to be a source of stern and fatherly advice.[12]

11. R. L. Hunter, *The New Comedy of Greece and Rome* (Cambridge, 1985), 24–25.

12. M. Bettini (trans. J. Van Sickle), *Anthropology and Roman Culture: Kinship, Time, Images of the Soul* (Baltimore, 1991), 14–38.

As soon as Chremes comes on the stage for the first time, however, the audience learns that their impression of him has been mistaken, for he went to Lemnos to seek his own daughter by another woman. Demipho was waiting for Chremes' advice not because Chremes is the wiser elder brother, but because it is in Chremes' interest that he wants Antipho not to marry Phanium, so that Antipho can marry Chremes' daughter. Chremes, who appeared to be the greatest potential benefactor, is of all the characters most dependent on the favors of others.

In the next scenes Chremes begins to look still worse. He tells Demipho that he especially wants Antipho to marry his daughter so that his wife does not find out about the daughter's parentage. He fears her anger, for he is completely dependent on her financially ("for the only thing I have that's my own is myself"). Nevertheless, he offers without hesitation to pay twenty of the thirty minae required to pay off Phormio. The money, as he states clearly, will come from the fruits of his wife's property on Lemnos. Later Nausistrata reveals that this is not the first time Chremes has pilfered her estates for his own ends: she has received much less money from the farms than she had when they were in her father's hands. She learns at the end of the play that the profits have been smaller because Chremes has been supporting his Lemnian wife and daughter with the proceeds. Chremes uses his wife's voice the same way he uses her income, prodding Demipho to get Nausistrata to talk to Phanium about her new marriage. Nor has Chremes been much of a benefactor to his Lemnian wife and daughter: his own admission of negligence with respect to them is confirmed by the fact that they have had to come to Athens seeking him because he waited so long to see them, and the mother's travails have led to her death.

Who, then, is the real parasite in this play? Not the stock parasite, who performs substantial services in return for his dinners, and who goes beyond the expected services in helping his patrons; but the character who appears at play's beginning to be the pinnacle of society. The elder brother, husband, father, and paternal uncle, on whom it first appears that everyone can rely, is in fact living off of his wife's income, providing no service in return, and pilfering in secret as well.

The parasite, then, brings much of the play's fun, but he also is the key element in a problem examined by the play as a whole: the difficulty of determining who really is a parasite. Phormio, who according to his stock characteristics, his description by others, and his own self-description would seem to be the parasite par excellence, in fact appears almost altruistic, bringing benefits, with only vague or limited rewards for himself, throughout the play.

Chremes, who would seem at first to be just the opposite of a parasite, the bulwark of society and family, turns out to be far more parasitic than Phormio or any other character of the play.

The problems surrounding who gives and who takes in relationships would have been of special significance to Terence's Roman audience. Romans were particularly concerned with the exchange of benefits within human relationships. The importance of mutual benefits in Roman discourse about friendship was noted above. The same kind of language pervades Roman discussion of kinship relationships, politics, and religion. Central to Roman discourse about all these kinds of relationships was an ethic of reciprocity: relatives, friends, political allies, even mortals and gods, developed relationships of *gratia* (goodwill), based to a great degree on mutual exchange of *officia* (duties) and *beneficia* (favors).[13] Furthermore, central to Roman society was the system of patrons and clients, in which the wealthy and powerful provided benefits (e.g., help in legal cases, political favors, and sometimes sustenance) to their poorer neighbors in exchange for benefits they could provide (e.g., votes, accompaniment when a crowd of supporters was needed, and gratitude).[14]

In any system where reciprocity is an important ideal, anxiety regarding proper exchange inevitably occurs. Absolute balance is impossible when the items exchanged are often intangibles like favors and gratitude. Participants in any relationship are always open to the charge that they are not performing their expected duties to kin, friends, patrons, and clients. Ambiguity about relative giving and taking thus shows up throughout Roman discourse about human relationships.[15] Questions surrounding reciprocity in the patronage system in particular appear to have become more acute in Terence's day, as vastly increased resources brought from Rome's conquests undermined traditional networks of dependence between patrons and clients.[16] Terence himself, if we are to believe his prologues, suffered from the anxieties surrounding patronage, as his critics accused him of depending on his patrons to write or help write his plays.

The comic parasite offered an unparalleled opportunity for comment on the uncertainties surrounding mutually beneficial relationships; for the parasite

13. R. P. Saller, *Personal Patronage under the Early Empire* (Cambridge, 1982), 7–29.

14. See especially P. A. Brunt, *The Fall of the Roman Republic and Related Essays* (Oxford, 1988), 382–442; A. Wallace-Hadrill, "Patronage in Roman Society: From Republic to Empire," in A. Wallace-Hadrill, ed., *Patronage in Ancient Society* (London, 1989), 63–87.

15. Saller (above, note 13), 16–17.

16. Brunt (above, note 14), 414–24; Wallace-Hadrill (above, note 14), 70–71.

was a client seen through the most jaundiced eyes, a dependent who offered little of worth in exchange for his sustenance.[17] In *Phormio,* Terence created a superb example of this "client-gone-wrong," but then made him the play's greatest benefactor; and he surrounded the play's other relationships with ironies and surprises regarding who is benefiting whom. He thus produced a most effective discourse on the uncertainties surrounding Rome's important ethic of reciprocity.

Yet we do not need to be Romans to appreciate the questions raised by *Phormio.* Every society, including our own, has its own ethic of reciprocity. As much as we may wish to believe that our relationships with one another are based only on affection and selflessness, we too have anxiety about reciprocity and its lack in our friendships, ties of kinship, and other relationships; it is not only in Rome that sometimes those who most appear to be "givers" are really the "takers" and vice-versa. *Phormio,* like all of Terence's plays, deals with issues that are universal. The uncertainties surrounding who gives what and who receives what in human relationships affect us all. In *Phormio* Terence has offered not only a delightful comic romp, but also an invitation to ponder those uncertainties.

17. Damon (above, note 2), 1–10 and passim.

SELECT BIBLIOGRAPHY

See also the bibliography on Roman Comedy in general provided with the Plautus bibliography above.

Arnott, W. G. *"Phormio Parasitus:* A Study in Dramatic Methods of Characterization." *Greece and Rome* 17 (1970): 32–57.

Forehand, W. E. *Terence.* Boston, 1985.

Goldberg, S. M. *Understanding Terence.* Princeton, 1986.

Ludwig, W. "The Originality of Terence and His Greek Models." *Greek, Roman, and Byzantine Studies* 9 (1968): 169–82.

Norwood, G. *The Art of Terence.* Oxford, 1923.

Parker, H. N. "Plautus vs. Terence: Audience and Popularity Re-examined." *American Journal of Philology* 117 (1996): 585–617.

PHORMIO

ANTIPHO, *Demipho's son*

CHREMES, *Demipho's brother, Phaedria's father*

DAVUS, *a slave, Geta's friend*

DEMIPHO, *Antipho's father, Chremes' brother*

DORIO, *a pimp*

GETA, *slave of Antipho and Demipho*

HEGIO, CRATINUS, and CRITO, *Demipho's friends*

NAUSISTRATA, *Chremes' wife, Phaedria's mother*

PHAEDRIA, *Chremes' son*

PHORMIO, *a parasite*

SOPHRONA, *handmaid of Phanium, Antipho's wife*

SCENE: A street in Athens. Off stage left, the street leads toward the forum; off stage right, it leads toward the harbor.[1] *Behind the street are two houses: Demipho's at stage right and Chremes' at stage left.*

PROLOGUE: *(spoken by an anonymous actor)* Well, that *old* playwright[2] is at it again. He's tried before to discourage *our* playwright and force him to retire, but he hasn't succeeded. So now he's decided to scare him off with insults. He's been going around saying that what our playwright has written up to now has been weak in diction, anemic in style. Well, I suppose that's because *our* playwright has never put onstage a young man hallucinating, convinced he sees a deer pursued by dogs, begging and pleading with him to rescue her.[3]

You know, that old playwright wouldn't be so brazen in insulting our playwright if he realized the truth: back when *his* play succeeded at its first performance, it was more because of the chief actor than because of anything *he* did. Now perhaps there's somebody out there who's saying or

---

1. I have followed here the arguments of G. E. Duckworth in *The Nature of Roman Comedy* (Princeton, 1952), 85–87, that the Roman convention of wing entrances was opposite to the convention in Athens, where the harbor was off stage left, the agora off stage right.

2. Luscius Lanuvinus, one of Terence's rivals.

3. Terence refers to a scene from a recently produced play of Luscius Lanuvinus.

thinking: "If the old playwright hadn't insulted him, your new playwright wouldn't be able to come up with a prologue of his own, since he wouldn't have anybody to abuse." Here's what our playwright says to that: "The prize is available to anyone who writes poetry." *He* has tried to drive *him* off the stage, to starvation: our man only wants to respond, not to insult him. If he had competed with kind words, he would have received kind words in return. Just let him think of it this way: he has gotten as good as he gave. For my part, I'll lay off talking about him now, even though for his part he never lays off doing wrong.

Now, listen to what I want. I am bringing you a new comedy. It's called *Epidicazomenos* in Greek. In Latin it's called *Phormio,* because the parasite Phormio will play the lead role, and will instigate most of the action—that is, as long as you are well disposed to our playwright. Pay attention, and give the play a fair hearing in silence, so we don't have the same bad luck we had before, when our company was driven from the stage by confusion. Only the excellence of our lead actor—with the help of your goodness and fairness—has brought us back.[4]

He exits. Davus enters stage left and approaches Demipho's house.

DAVUS: My best friend and fellow slave Geta came to me yesterday. For a long time I've had a little bit of his money in my possession. He wanted me to get it for him. I got it, and I'm bringing it to him. I hear his young master has taken a wife. I guess he's scraping together a gift for her. You know, it's really not fair: those who have less are always giving something to those who have more. Poor Geta just barely managed to save up some cash, bit by bit, from his allowance,[5] cheating himself. Now she's going to snatch all of it right out of his hands. And she won't have any thought for how much work it took to get it. Not only that, but Geta will be hit up for another present, when his mistress has a baby; and still another, when it's the child's

---

4. The speaker refers to the first performance of Terence's *The Mother-in-Law,* where excitement about alleged exhibitions of rope-walking and boxing nearby caused such confusion that the performance was broken off. At a second performance, rumors of gladiatorial competition caused similar chaos, and *The Mother-in-Law* was not performed from start to finish until its third production.

5. Theoretically slaves in Rome could own no property, but many slaves were permitted to use money they had earned and saved at their own discretion. This "allowance" was called their *peculium.*

birthday; and another when they get it initiated.[6] The mother will get all this: the child will only be an excuse. *(Geta enters from Demipho's house.)* But is that Geta I see?

GETA: *(Speaking back to someone inside the house)* If a guy with red hair asks after me. . . .

DAVUS: Wait a minute, Geta! I'm right here.

GETA: Davus! I was just going to look for you.

DAVUS: Look, here's your money. It's all there: exactly what I owe you.

GETA: You're a true friend, Davus, and I'm grateful that you haven't let me down.

DAVUS: Especially the way things are now: nowadays, it's so hard to get your money back, you really have to be grateful if anybody repays what he owes you. But what are you so down-in-the-mouth about?

GETA: Davus, you have no idea how frightened we are, and what danger we're in.

DAVUS: What is it?

GETA: I'll tell you, but only if you can keep it secret.

DAVUS: Don't be silly! Are you afraid to trust me with words, when I just proved you can trust me with your money? What good would it do me to deceive you?

GETA: Alright, then: listen.

DAVUS: I'm all ears.

GETA: Do you know Chremes, our old master's older brother?

DAVUS: Of course.

GETA: What about his son, Phaedria?

DAVUS: I know him as well as I know you.

GETA: Well, it just so happened that both Demipho and Chremes needed to take trips at the same time. Chremes went to Lemnos. Our master went to Cilicia to an old friend of his, who enticed the old man with letters, virtually promising him mountains of money.

DAVUS: But he's already rolling in it!

GETA: Never mind. That's just the way he is.

DAVUS: If only *I* were rich.

---

6. Athenian youths were regularly initiated into various religious cults. The ancient scholar Donatus reports that Apollodorus, the author of Terence's Greek model, referred specifically to the mysteries of the island of Samothrace here.

GETA: When they left, both fathers put me in charge of their sons, as if I were their tutor.

DAVUS: Geta! That's a tough assignment you took on!

GETA: So I found out, the hard way. Looking back on it, I see that I was cursed when I was left behind. First I tried to stand up to them. Need I say more? So long as I was faithful to the old man, I ended up black and blue.

DAVUS: That reminds me of the old saying: "Only a stupid horse fights against the whip."

GETA: So I started to give in and do whatever they wanted.

DAVUS: You saw the lay of the land.

GETA: At first, our young master didn't get into any trouble; but that Phaedria met a girl right away: a lyre player. He fell madly in love with her. She belonged to a really foul pimp, and there was no money to pay him: their fathers had taken care of that. He couldn't do anything except feast his eyes on her, follow her around, and walk her to and from her music school. We didn't have anything better to do, so we tried to help him out. Right across from the school where she was studying was a barber shop. We would often wait there for her to start her walk home. Once, while we were sitting there, a young man came in, all in tears. That seemed strange to us, and we asked him what was up. He said: "I never realized until just now what a pitiable and heavy burden poverty is. I just saw, not far from here, a poor girl weeping for her dead mother. The body had been laid out just inside the door, and no friend or relative or neighbor was around to help with the funeral, except for one little slave woman. I felt so sorry for her. And the girl herself is very beautiful." Need I say more? We were all moved. Right away Antipho says, "Do you want to go see her?" Somebody else says, "Sure, let's go. Please, take us there." We go, we get there, we see her. The girl *was* beautiful, all the more, because she had nothing to help her look beautiful: her hair was disheveled, her feet bare, she was crying, and she wore messy, tattered clothing. If she hadn't had her own inner beauty, these things would have made her ugly. Phaedria, who was in love with that lyre player, just said, "She's pretty enough." But Antipho. . . .

DAVUS: I know. He fell in love with her.

GETA: Did he ever. Just listen to what happened then. The next day he goes straight to the old slave woman. He begs her to let him have access to her. She refuses, and says it's not right for him to do that: the girl is an Athenian citizen, a good girl from a good family. "If you want a wife," she says, "you can have her legally. Otherwise, forget it." Antipho didn't know what to do: he wanted to marry her, but he was afraid of his absent father.

DAVUS: Wouldn't his father give him permission, when he came home?

GETA: Him? Let him marry a girl without any family or dowry? He'd never do that!

DAVUS: So what happened then?

GETA: Well you might ask. There's this parasite named Phormio, an arrogant fellow. May all the gods damn him!

DAVUS: What did he do?

GETA: Here's the advice he gave: "There's a law that says that orphaned maidens should marry their closest relatives. The same law says their relatives must marry them.[7] I'll claim that you're her relative, and I'll take you to court. I'll pretend that I'm a friend of the girl's father. We'll go to court. Father, mother, how she's related to you, I'll make it all up, whatever seems to fit best. You won't refute any of this, so I'll win, of course. Your father will come home. He'll sue me. What do I care? She'll be ours."

DAVUS: What a scam!

GETA: Well, Phormio persuaded him. It was done. There was a trial. We lost. He married her.

DAVUS: What are you saying?

GETA: Just what you're hearing.

DAVUS: Oh Geta, what's going to happen to you?

GETA: Hercules, I don't know. I only know this (pompously): Whatever happens, I will endure it with fortitude.

DAVUS: Good. That's being a man.

GETA: (still pompous) I have only myself to rely on.

DAVUS: Excellent!

GETA: I suppose I could get somebody to plead for me. Something like this: "Please, let him go this time. But if he does anything after this, I won't plead for him again." But he may as well add, "As soon as I'm gone, go ahead and kill him."

DAVUS: And what of the lyre player's escort? How's he faring?

GETA: Not well.

DAVUS: I suppose he doesn't have much he can pay.

GETA: Not much? He has nothing at all, except pure hope.

---

7. This was the law in Athens: the closest relative of an orphaned woman had to marry her himself or find her a husband and provide a dowry for her.

DAVUS: Has his father come back?

GETA: Not yet.

DAVUS: And when do you expect your old master?

GETA: I'm not sure, but I just heard that the customs officers have gotten a letter from him: I'm going after it.

DAVUS: Anything else you want from me, Geta?

GETA: Only that you stay well. *(Davus exits stage left.)* Hey, boy! Won't somebody come out here? *(A slave comes out of Demipho's house; Geta gives him the money he received from Davus.)* Take this and give it to Dorcium.[8]

Geta exits stage right; the slave exits into Demipho's house; Antipho and Phaedria enter from Chremes' house.

ANTIPHO:

Look what I've come to. My father only wants to see me happy,
Phaedria, but I just panic whenever I think of him returning.
Frightened of my father! Oh, if only I'd used my brain more.
Then I'd want my father home: then I'd feel the way I ought to.

PHAEDRIA:

What is it, Antipho?

ANTIPHO:

You have to ask? You know very well what's the matter.
I just wish that Phormio never had gotten the idea to persuade me
Or that I hadn't been so much in love that I listened: that was my downfall.
Then I'd be without her. For a few days that would be painful.
At least I'd be without this daily anguish, though.

PHAEDRIA:

I hear you.

ANTIPHO:

I'm always wondering: when will my father come back and end my
marriage?

PHAEDRIA:

For others, it's the lack of what they love that makes them suffer,
But you've got lots of love: too much, in fact. That's why you're whining.
You've got what everybody wants. Your life's what people long for.
So help me, I'd give life and limb to have the girl that I love

8. Geta's wife (or rather, the equivalent of a wife: slaves were not legally allowed to marry).

As long as you've had yours. Why, just compare our situations.
Observe what you've got: everything. And then what I've got: nothing.
And that's not all. You're with the one you love; what's more, she's
                                                    freeborn.
And she's your wife, out in the open, just the way you wanted.
You didn't have to spend a thing, you kept your reputation.
You ought to be so happy, but there's only one thing missing:
The character to relish what you've got without complaining.
If you had business with that pimp I deal with, then you'd get it.
It's human nature, I suppose: "the grass is always greener . . ."

ANTIPHO:

No, Phaedria, there you're wrong. I say it's you, not me, who's lucky.
You have the power to ponder what you want to do about her:
To keep her, love her, leave her. Me, I've lost that power completely.
I don't know how to keep her, but there's no way I could leave her.

Geta enters stage right, running frantically. He does not see Antipho and Phaedria.

But look. What's this? I see somebody running. Is it Geta?
It is: I'm scared to death, to think what news he might be bringing.

GETA:

Finished, Geta! That's what you are, if you don't think of something
                                                    quickly.
Overwhelmed, and caught by surprise, and faced with sudden disaster.
There's no escape, no way to get out from under all these troubles.
If you don't think of something quick, you're done for: you and your
                                                    master.
We can't keep what we've done from being found out any longer.

ANTIPHO:

What's he so stirred up about?

GETA:

I've only got a minute: the master's coming!

ANTIPHO:

                                    What's gone wrong here?

GETA:

Soon he'll know the truth. What then? Then how will you calm his anger?
With words? I'll ignite him. Mute? I'll incite him. Excuses? A waste of
                                                    effort.

So much for me. And not just me. There's Antipho, too, poor fellow.
He's the one I feel for. He's the one I fear will suffer.
He's the one who's holding me back. If he weren't in the picture,
Then, I'd see to my own needs, and make the old man pay for his anger:
Steal some stuff: that's what I'd do, then hurry across the border.

ANTIPHO:

What's he planning? Theft, or flight?

GETA:

But where on earth is Antipho? I don't know where to find him.

PHAEDRIA:

He's saying your name.

ANTIPHO:

                       He's got some really awful news, I know it.

PHAEDRIA:

Don't be silly.

GETA:

                Home—that's where I'll go, where I usually find him.

PHAEDRIA:

Let's call him back.

ANTIPHO:

(shouting to Geta)

                   Hey! Stop right there!

GETA:

(he does not see Antipho)

                           What is it? Listen to this guy!
Arrogant, aren't you, whoever you are? You'd think that you were my
                                        master.

ANTIPHO:

Geta!

GETA:

(he sees Antipho)

        Oh! It's him! The very one I wanted to find here!

ANTIPHO:

Tell me, please, what news you've got. And briefly, if you're able.

GETA:

Alright.

(he pauses)

ANTIPHO:
> Tell.

GETA:
> Just now, at the harbor . . .

ANTIPHO:
>   My . . .

GETA:
>   Right.

ANTIPHO:
>   Oh no! I'm dead!

PHAEDRIA:
>   What?

ANTIPHO:
> What will I do?

PHAEDRIA:
>   Geta, what are you saying?

GETA:
>   His father, your uncle, I saw him.

ANTIPHO:
> Oh no! What can I do? I'm doomed. I'm done for. It's a disaster.
> Phanium, if I'm torn from you, I'm dead: life's not worth living.

GETA:
> All the more reason to be alert: "Fortune helps the brave," remember.

ANTIPHO:
> I'm in a panic.

GETA:
>   But now's when you most need to keep yourself calm and collected.
> If your father sees you're frightened, then he'll start suspecting,
> Thinking you're guilty.

PHAEDRIA:
>   He's right.

ANTIPHO:
>   But I can't change: I'm just not able.

GETA:
> What would you do if you had to do something else? Something harder
>   than this was?

ANTIPHO:
> Well, since I can't do this, I could do that less.

GETA:

Oh, just forget it.
Phaedria, why are we wasting our time? I'm leaving.

PHAEDRIA:

Me too.

ANTIPHO:

No! Wait!
What if I pretend?
(He tries to look calm.)
Will this do?

GETA:

Nonsense.

ANTIPHO:

Watch my expression.
Won't this do?

GETA:

Nope.

ANTIPHO:

How about this, then?

GETA:

Close.

ANTIPHO:

This?

GETA:

That will do it.
Now: hold on to that, and answer him word for word. No matter
How much he rages, what angry words he says, hold your own.

ANTIPHO:

I got it.

GETA:

Just remember: against your will you were forced . . .

PHAEDRIA:

By the law, and the jury.

GETA:

Got it? But who's that man I see at the end of the street? He's coming!

ANTIPHO: I can't stay.

He begins to leave.

GETA: Hey! What are you doing? Where are you going, Antipho? Wait!

ANTIPHO: I'm just too guilty, and I know it. I hand over my life and my Phanium to you.

He exits stage left.

PHAEDRIA: What now, Geta?

GETA: Unless I'm mistaken, you're going to get yelled at, and I'm going to be strung up and beaten. But, Phaedria, it's imperative that you and I do ourselves what we just told Antipho to do.

PHAEDRIA: Forget that "imperative" stuff. Just tell me what to do.

GETA: Do you remember that speech you made in our defense when we started this business? "This case is fair, it's easy, we can win it, and it's the best thing to do."

PHAEDRIA: I remember.

GETA: Well, now we need that speech. Or, if you can, come up with one even better and more clever.

PHAEDRIA: I'll do my best.

GETA: You go to him first. I'll wait here in ambush, and come to your rescue, if you need me.

PHAEDRIA: Right.

Demipho enters stage right, in a huff; he has not seen Geta or Phaedria.

DEMIPHO:

So then, Antipho's got himself married without asking my permission?
All my authority . . . Forget my authority! What about my anger?
He felt no fear, no shame at all. What impudence! And Geta!
Some guardian you turned out to be.

GETA:
(aside to Phaedria)

At last, he comes to my part.

DEMIPHO:

I wonder what excuse they'll give.

GETA:
(aside to Phaedria)

I'll find one. Don't you worry.

DEMIPHO:

"I had to. It was the law." I hear you. Sure.

GETA:

(aside to Phaedria)

I rather like that.

DEMIPHO:

But why'd they have to yield without a word to their opponents?
The law made them do that?

PHAEDRIA:

(aside to Geta)

That's a tough one.

GETA:

Relax. I'm ready for him.

DEMIPHO:

I don't know what to do—I'm caught off guard. I don't believe it!
I'm so damn mad, I'm all churned up inside. I can't even think straight.
(suddenly waxing philosophical)
It just goes to show, when things are going well, that's when you most need
To think about the troubles that may come, and how to bear them.
Like danger, loss, or exile. When you come home from abroad,

remember,
Your son may sin, your wife may die, an illness may strike your daughter.
Such bad things happen to everyone. Let nothing be unexpected.
Expect the worst, and if it doesn't happen, count it as profit.

GETA:

You know, it's amazing, Phaedria, how much quicker I am than the

master.
I've already pondered all the things that would happen to me when he

got here.
The labor at the mill,[9] the crack of the whip, the chains on my ankles,
The farm work breaking my back: of these things nothing is unexpected.
I expect the worst, and if it doesn't happen, I'll count it as profit.
Alright. Approach him now, with soothing words.

DEMIPHO:

Why look, it's Phaedria.

PHAEDRIA: Hello, uncle.

DEMIPHO: Hello. Where's Antipho?

---

9. A standard punishment for recalcitrant Roman slaves was hard labor in flour mills.

PHAEDRIA: I'm so glad you've come ho. . . .

DEMIPHO: Right. Answer my question.

PHAEDRIA: He's fine, and he's around. Is everything alright?

DEMIPHO: I wish it were.

PHAEDRIA: What's the matter?

DEMIPHO: You have to ask? You boys conjured up a fine marriage while I was gone.

PHAEDRIA: Oh, are you angry at him for that?

GETA: *(aside)* What a good liar!

DEMIPHO: How could I not be angry? I'm itching to get him in my sight. I want him to know what he's done: how he's turned me from a gentle, easygoing man into the harshest of fathers.

PHAEDRIA: But uncle, he hasn't done anything you should be angry at.

DEMIPHO: Just look! They're all the same! They're all in it together. When you know one, you know them all.

PHAEDRIA: That's not true.

DEMIPHO: That one is in the wrong, so this one is here to defend him. When this one does wrong, the other will plead his case. "You scratch my back, I'll scratch yours."

GETA: *(aside)* The old man paints these two more true to life than he knows.

DEMIPHO: That's the way things are, Phaedria. If it weren't, you wouldn't be standing up for him now.

PHAEDRIA: Uncle, if Antipho did anything wrong, if he gave too little thought to the family property, or to his reputation, then I won't defend him. He should get the punishment he deserves. But if somebody ambushed us, relying on his own wickedness and our youth, and won, is it our fault or the jurors'? You know jurors: they're always ruling against the rich because they're jealous, or giving things to the poor because they pity them.

GETA: *(aside)* If I didn't know the real story, I'd swear he was telling the truth.

DEMIPHO: But how can any juror know you're in the right, when you don't say a word, like he did?

PHAEDRIA: He acted the way a freeborn youth should: when it came time to address the jury, he couldn't get the words out. He was struck dumb with shame and fear.

GETA: *(aside)* This guy is great! Now it's my turn. *(to Demipho)* Hello, Master! I'm glad to see you home safe and sound.

DEMIPHO: Well, hello, my fine guardian, true bulwark of my family, protector of my son while I was away.

GETA: For some time now I've been listening to you accusing us all wrongly, especially me. What did you expect *me* to do about all this? The law doesn't allow a slave to plead a case or give testimony.

DEMIPHO: Forget all that. I grant you your "The young man was caught off guard and was frightened." I grant you your "I'm just a slave." But even if she were the closest possible relative, he didn't have to marry her. You could have done what the law orders: give her a dowry, and let her find another husband. What lack of sense made him marry a pauper instead?

GETA: It wasn't sense he lacked, it was money.

DEMIPHO: He should have borrowed it from somebody.

GETA: Borrow it? That's easier said than done.

DEMIPHO: Well, if he couldn't get it any other way, he should have taken out a loan at interest.

GETA: Sure! As if anyone would lend him money while you're still alive.

DEMIPHO: No! No! This is not going to happen! This will not stand! Do you think I'll allow her to stay married to him for one more day? This is no time to be gentle. I want you to show me that man, or tell me where he lives.

GETA: You mean Phormio?

DEMIPHO: The woman's advocate.

GETA: I'll see that he's here in a minute.

DEMIPHO: And where's Antipho now?

GETA: Out.

DEMIPHO: Phaedria, go find him and bring him here.

PHAEDRIA: Alright. I'll go straight there.

He exits stage left.

GETA: *(aside)* Straight to Pamphila,[10] he means.

He exits stage left.

DEMIPHO: I'll go inside to greet my household gods.[11] Then I'll go to the forum and call together some friends who can assist me in this business. I want to be ready when Phormio comes.

He exits into his house. Phormio and Geta enter stage left.

10. The lyre player.

11. Demipho refers to the *Penates,* Roman gods who protected the household. A shrine inside the house was dedicated to them.

PHORMIO:

So. You say when he heard his father was here he panicked and ran?

GETA:

You got it.

PHORMIO:

Phanium's left all alone, then?

GETA:

Right.

PHORMIO:

And the father: you say he's angry?

GETA:

Very.

PHORMIO:

Well then, Phormio, it's up to you. You cooked this dinner.
You're the one who must eat it, every bite, so get yourself ready.

GETA:

Please, I beg you.

PHORMIO:

(pondering how he will deal with Demipho)

What if he should ask . . .

GETA:

We need you.

PHORMIO:

(still pondering)

That's it!

What if he answers . . .

GETA:

You compelled him.

PHORMIO:

(still pondering)

That's what I'll say!

GETA:

Please, help us!

PHORMIO:

Bring on the old man. All my plans are ready, in battle formation.

GETA:

What will you do?

PHORMIO:

          Why, everything: Phanium stays here, Antipho's blameless,
All the old man's anger falls on me. What more could you ask for?

GETA:

You're so brave! And such a good friend! But, Phormio, often you

                                  scare me.
All that courage of yours, I fear, is likely to land you in prison.

PHORMIO:

No way! I've been through this before. I'm perfectly sure of my footing.
How many men do you think I've practically beaten to death? And not

                                    just
Foreigners. Citizens, too. The better I know them, the more I beat them.
Tell me, though, have you ever seen me taken to court for violence?

GETA:

Never. Why?

PHORMIO:

        'Cause people don't put out nets for birds that can hurt them,
Hawks and eagles, and birds like that. They catch the birds that are

                                  harmless.
Harmless birds bring profit, but hawks and eagles bring only trouble.
Own some property, then you're at risk. You have something: your

                              victim can fine you.
I've got nothing, as everyone knows. "But suppose they enslave you?"

                              you ask me.
What? And feed me? Certainly not. They won't, and with good reason.
Punishment's what they want, but that would be the greatest kindness.

GETA:

After all you've done for him, Antipho won't know how to repay you.

PHORMIO:

Nonsense. No one can ever repay a patron for all that *he's* done.
Thanks to your patron you get to come home from the baths, oiled,

                              washed, and carefree.
You pay nothing, while he gets eaten up with expense and worry.
You get whatever you want: he grins and bears it, while you're laughing.
You drink first. You get the best seat. He gives you a doubtful dinner.

GETA:

Doubtful? What do you mean?

PHORMIO:

I mean it's doubtful what I should eat first!
Once you start to think how nice this is, and how expensive,
Don't you think a patron's like a god in mortal's clothing?

Demipho enters stage left, followed by Hegio, Cratinus, and Crito.

GETA:

(to Phormio)

Here comes the old man. Watch what you're doing. The first encounter
is hardest.
Handle him now, and later on you can play however you want to.

DEMIPHO: *(to Hegio, Cratinus, and Crito)* Did you ever hear of anything more
insulting, more outrageous, than what's been done to me? Please, help me
out in this.

GETA: Ooh, he's mad.

PHORMIO: Sh! Pay attention. I'm going to stir him up. *(in a loud voice)* By the
immortal gods! You say Demipho denies that our Phanium is his relation?
He actually denies that she's his relation?

GETA: That's right.

PHORMIO: And he claims he doesn't know who her father was?

GETA: That's right.

DEMIPHO: *(to Hegio, Cratinus, and Crito)* I think this guy must be the one I was
telling you about. Follow me.

PHORMIO: And that he doesn't know who Stilpo was?

GETA: That's right.

PHORMIO: Because the poor girl was left a pauper, her father is suddenly a
stranger, and she is neglected: just look at what greed does.

GETA: If you insult my master, you'll hear insults in return.

DEMIPHO: *(to Hegio, Cratinus, and Crito)* The nerve! He even comes here on
his own to accuse me?

PHORMIO: You see, there's no reason for me to be angry at the young man
for not knowing who Stilpo was. He was rather old, and poor. His life was
nothing but work, and he generally kept himself in the country. That's
where he had some land our father left him to farm. He often used to tell
me that he ought to pay more attention to this relative of his. Ah, but what
a man he was. The best I've ever known.

GETA: Then he's sure a far cry from you.

PHORMIO: Go to hell! If I didn't think he was such a great man, I never would have taken on so much hostility from your family on account of his daughter, whom he's treating so badly.

GETA: Will you go on speaking ill of my master when he's not here to defend himself, you scum?

PHORMIO: It's only what he deserves.

GETA: Will you shut up, you jail bait?

DEMIPHO: Geta!

GETA: *(to Phormio)* Conman! Shyster!

DEMIPHO: Geta!

PHORMIO: *(softly)* Answer him.

GETA: Who is it? Oh!

DEMIPHO: Be quiet.

GETA: This guy wouldn't stop insulting you in your absence, saying things he deserved to hear, not you.

DEMIPHO: That's enough. *(to Phormio)* Young man, first I ask this favor of you, a fair one, I think. Would you please answer this question: just who is this friend of yours, who said that I was related to him?

PHORMIO: Oh, sure. As if you didn't already know.

DEMIPHO: Already know?

PHORMIO: That's right.

DEMIPHO: I say I don't know. Since you're the one making the accusation, you jog my memory.

PHORMIO: What do you mean? You don't know your own cousin?

DEMIPHO: Damn you, just tell me his name.

PHORMIO: His name? Of course. *(he pauses)*

DEMIPHO: Well?

PHORMIO: *(aside)* Hercules, I'm finished! I can't remember the name.

DEMIPHO: Well? What is it?

PHORMIO: *(aside to Geta)* Geta, if you remember the name we used, pitch it to me. *(aloud)* No! I won't say it: you're just testing me, as if you didn't know it.

DEMIPHO: *Me? Testing you?*

GETA: *(aside to Phormio)* Stilpo.

PHORMIO: But what's that to me? It's Stilpo.

DEMIPHO: Who?

PHORMIO: Stilpo, I say. You knew him.

DEMIPHO: I did not know him, nor have I ever had a relative with that name.

PHORMIO: Really? Aren't you ashamed to say such things in front of these gentlemen? But if he had left ten talents' [12] worth of property . . .

DEMIPHO: Damn you!

PHORMIO: Then you'd be the first to remember. You'd call up your common ancestry, all the way back to your grandfather and great-grandfather.

DEMIPHO: Alright, suppose that were the case. If it were, I would explain, when I made my claim, how she was related to me. Now you do the same. Well, how is she related to me?

GETA: Well done, master. *(to Phormio)* You watch out now.

PHORMIO: I explained everything clearly to the jurors, as I was supposed to. If what I said then was false, why didn't your son refute me?

DEMIPHO: My son, you say? I can't begin to describe how stupid *he* is.

PHORMIO: Alright, then. Since *you're* so smart, you go to the magistrates and get them to make another ruling in this case. Obviously you're the king here, and you alone can get two rulings on one case.

DEMIPHO: I've been wronged, but rather than go to court and listen to you, I'll do what the law orders and give her a dowry, just as if she were my relative. Take 5 minae [13] and get her out of here.

PHORMIO: Ha ha ha! You're a fine fellow!

DEMIPHO: What is it? Don't you think that's fair? Or don't I even get what everyone knows the law allows?

PHORMIO: Oh, really? Tell me, does the law allow you to pay a fee and send her away after you've used her like a prostitute? Doesn't the law demand that an orphan be given to her closest relative, so that no citizen woman is shamed on account of her poverty, and so that she can live her life with one man? You're certainly not obeying that law.

DEMIPHO: Alright, she marries her closest relative. But how did we become her relatives? And why?

PHORMIO: Wait a minute! You know what they say: "The battle's over, so stop fighting."

DEMIPHO: Stop fighting? Oh, no. I'm not going to stop fighting until I finish this.

---

12. A talent is 60 minae (see next note).

13. The *mina* is an Athenian unit of currency, equal to 100 drachmas. Note that Phaedria's beloved is considered very expensive at thirty minae.

PHORMIO: You're wasting your time.

DEMIPHO: Just watch me.

PHORMIO: Really, Demipho, we have no quarrel with you. It's your son who was convicted, not you. You're too old to marry her.

DEMIPHO: Just assume, then, that he agrees with everything I'm saying now. If he doesn't, I'll throw him out of my house right alongside his wife.

GETA: *(aside)* Ooh, he's mad.

PHORMIO: You'd do better to throw yourself out.

DEMIPHO: So the gloves are off, then, you scoundrel?

PHORMIO: *(aside to Geta)* He's afraid of us, even though he puts on a good act.

GETA: *(aside to Phormio)* You've made a good start.

PHORMIO: Why don't you just accept the inevitable? Wouldn't it be better to do what's honorable, so we could be friends?

DEMIPHO: Friends? Do you think I'd ever want to be friends with you? Or even to lay eyes on you again?

PHORMIO: If you make peace with her, you'll have somebody to bring you pleasure in your old age. Think about it: you're not getting any younger.

DEMIPHO: Let her bring *you* pleasure. *You* take her.

PHORMIO: Just calm down.

DEMIPHO: Listen to me: unless you take that woman away immediately, I'm going to throw her out. Enough said, Phormio.

PHORMIO: Listen to me: if you so much as touch her in any way other than as a free woman deserves, I'll lay a huge lawsuit on you. Enough said, Demipho. *(aside to Geta)* Hey, if you need anything, I'll be at home.

GETA: *(aside to Phormio)* Gotcha.

Phormio exits stage left.

DEMIPHO: What pain and trouble my son brought me, when he loaded this marriage on himself and me! And he hasn't even put in an appearance, so at least I could know what he has to say, or what he thinks about all this. Geta, go see whether he's returned home yet.

GETA: Alright.

Geta exits into Demipho's house.

DEMIPHO: You see what a predicament I'm in. What should I do? Tell me, Hegio.

HEGIO: Me? I think you should ask Cratinus, if you think that's a good idea.

DEMIPHO: Well, Cratinus?

CRATINUS: You want my opinion?

DEMIPHO: Yes.

CRATINUS: Well, I think you should do what benefits you. This is what seems
best to me: it is right and good for you to undo what your son did while
you were absent, and you can do that. That's what I think.

DEMIPHO: Now you, Hegio.

HEGIO: I think Cratinus here spoke sincerely. But you know how it is. Everybody has a different opinion. To each his own. I don't think that what's been
done by law can be undone, and it would be dishonorable to try.

DEMIPHO: What about you, Crito?

CRITO: I think you should think about it more. This is an important matter.

CRATINUS: Is there anything else you want from us?

DEMIPHO: You've done a fine job. I'm a lot less sure what to do now than I
was before.

The three friends exit stage left. Geta reenters from Demipho's house.

GETA: They say he hasn't come back.

DEMIPHO: I need to wait for my brother. Whatever advice he gives me about
this business, I'll follow. I'll go to the harbor to find out when he's due in.

Demipho exits stage right.

GETA: And I'll look for Antipho, so he can know what went on here. *(Antipho
enters stage left.)* But look: there he is. Perfect timing.

ANTIPHO:

Really, Antipho. That was shameful. You ought to be thoroughly
chastised.
Think of it! You took off, and left your life in the hands of others.
What were you thinking? That others would see to your own affairs
better than you could?
Worst of all, you didn't look out for your wife, who's counting on you.
All the poor girl's hopes reside in you: you're her only salvation.

GETA:

That's right, master. While you've been absent, we've been blaming you
for leaving.

ANTIPHO:

You're just the man I've been looking for.

GETA:

> But still, we didn't fail you.

ANTIPHO:

So tell me, Geta, please, where are we now? Is my fate decided?
My father? Has he sniffed us out?

GETA:

> He hasn't.

ANTIPHO:

> Then there's hope still?

GETA:

Who knows?

ANTIPHO:

> Oh dear!

GETA:

> But Phaedria never gave up.

ANTIPHO:

> That's what I expected.

GETA:

And Phormio likewise showed himself as enterprising as always.

ANTIPHO:

What's Phormio done?

GETA:

> His arguments left your angry dad in confusion.

ANTIPHO:

Well done!

GETA:

> And me, I did what I could.

ANTIPHO:

> Oh, Geta! You're all terrific!

GETA:

That's the way the beginning has gone: so far things are calm and peaceful,
Now your father's waiting for your uncle.

ANTIPHO:

> Why?

GETA:

> As he told me,

He wants to do whatever his brother advises in this matter.

ANTIPHO:

Oh! I'm frightened now to think of my uncle arriving home safely.
For now it seems that whether I live or die is his decision.

Phaedria enters stage left, pursuing Dorio. They do not see Antipho and Geta.

GETA:

Phaedria's here.

ANTIPHO:

                         Where?

GETA:

                                   Look: He's made an exit from his playground.

PHAEDRIA: Dorio.

Just hear me, please. . . .

DORIO:

                         No. I'm not listening.

Phaedria grabs onto Dorio's cloak.

PHAEDRIA:

                                                   Just a bit . . .

DORIO:

                                                             Release me!

PHAEDRIA:

Listen to me.

DORIO:

                    I'm tired of listening. A thousand times, it's the same thing.

PHAEDRIA:

No. What I've got to say now, you'll like, I'm sure.

DORIO:

                                                   Alright. I'm listening.

PHAEDRIA:

Can't I persuade you to wait just three more days?

Dorio starts to leave.

                                             Now where are you going?

DORIO: I wondered whether you really had anything new to say.

ANTIPHO: *(aside to Geta)* Oh, dear.

I fear that pimp may. . . .

GETA:

(aside to Antipho)

get his head bashed in? I fear the same thing.

PHAEDRIA:

You still don't trust me?

DORIO:

Brilliant deduction.

PHAEDRIA:

What if I promise?

DORIO:

Nonsense!

PHAEDRIA:

Do me this favor, please. I'll repay you many times over.

DORIO:

Words, words!

PHAEDRIA:

Trust me, you'll be glad you did. I'm telling the truth.

DORIO:

You're dreaming.

PHAEDRIA:

Try me. It's not long.

DORIO:

You always sing the same old chorus.

PHAEDRIA:

You'll be my kinsman, father, friend . . .

DORIO:

Talk all you want. It's babble.

PHAEDRIA:

How can you be so hard, so heartless, that pity and prayers won't move
you?

DORIO:

How can you be so dumb, so shameless, to think that you can deceive me
with
All your fine-sounding words, and walk away with my property, scot-free?

ANTIPHO:

(aside)

Poor guy.

PHAEDRIA:
    That's the truth, I'm afraid. You win.

GETA:
                            How predictable this is.

PHAEDRIA:
    And just to think, while Antipho is freed from all his worries
    I have to face this. It's not fair!

ANTIPHO:
                   What is it, Phaedria? Tell me.

PHAEDRIA:
    Antipho, you're so lucky.

ANTIPHO:
                Me? Why?

PHAEDRIA:
                  You've got your beloved.
    You never had the kind of trouble I've been forced to deal with.

ANTIPHO:
    What do you mean? A tiger by the tail: that's what I've got.
    I don't know how I can send her away, but I can't hold on to her, either.

DORIO:
    That's how I feel about *him*.
    (pointing to Phaedria)

ANTIPHO:
             No danger of *you* being too unpimplike.

To Phaedria.

    What's he done?

PHAEDRIA:
    What's he done? He's done what only the worst of fiends would:
    Sold my Pamphila, right out from under me!

ANTIPHO:
                    What? He sold her?

GETA:
                                Sold her?

PHAEDRIA:
    Sold her.

DORIO:
    How awful to sell the girl I bought with my very own money.

PHAEDRIA:

    No matter how I beg, he won't cancel his bargain and give me a respite.
    Three days! That's all I need 'til my friends give all the money they've
                                          promised.
    And if you don't get the money by then, then don't wait one more
                                            minute.

DORIO:

    Go on.

ANTIPHO:

        But Dorio, he's not asking much. Let him persuade you!
    Just grant him this one favor, and he'll pay you back twice over.

DORIO:

    Words, words, words.

ANTIPHO:

            Then you'll see Pamphila dragged away from this city?
    How can you bear to let these lovers' hearts be torn asunder?

DORIO:

(sarcastically)

    No. I just can't bear it, no more than you can, Antipho.

PHAEDRIA:

                                Damn you!

DORIO:

    Several months I've waited for you, against my better judgment.
    Promises. Tears. That's all you brought. Well, now there's someone here
                                          who
    Pays instead of weeps. So yield the field to those who are better.

ANTIPHO:

    Wait just a minute! I'm sure I remember that once you set a date for
    Payment. Did you not?

PHAEDRIA:

                We did.

DORIO:

                That's right. Have I denied it?

ANTIPHO:

    Well? Has that day come and gone?

DORIO:

                No, but this day got here sooner.

ANTIPHO:

>   Aren't you ashamed of this nonsense?

DORIO:

>   Not if it brings me profit.

GETA:

>   Shithead!

PHAEDRIA:

>   How can you act this way?

DORIO:

>   That's how I am, so take it or leave it.

ANTIPHO:

>   Damn! You're such a cheat!

DORIO:

>   Oh, no. I'm not the cheat here: *he* is.
>   He knew what kind of person *I* was, but I thought *he* was different.
>   He deceived me. I treated him no different from all the others.
>   Nevertheless, in spite of all this, here's what I'll do: tomorrow
>   Morning the soldier promised the money. If you can pay before then,
>   Phaedria, I'll follow my usual practice: the first cash gets her. Good-bye
>   now.

Dorio exits stage left.

PHAEDRIA:

>   What do I do now? Where can I drum up that much money in one day?
>   I've got less than nothing! Oh! If only I'd talked him into
>   Three more days. Then I'd have the loans my friends have promised.

ANTIPHO:

>   Geta,
>   How can we let him suffer like this, when he's just now been such a good
>   friend?
>   He's done me a kindness. Won't we try to repay the favor?

GETA:

>   That's the fair thing to do, I know.

ANTIPHO:

>   Yes, and only you can save him.

GETA:

>   Me? But what can *I* do?

ANTIPHO:

Find some money.

GETA:

I want to, but where from?

ANTIPHO:

Father is home.

GETA:

I know. So what?

ANTIPHO:

A word to the wise is sufficient.

GETA:

You mean that?

ANTIPHO:

Yes, I mean that.

GETA:

Oh, great! Get out of here, will you?
Don't you know, with you getting married I've barely avoided a beating?
Now you want me to find a cross to hang myself on for this guy? [14]

ANTIPHO:
(to Phaedria)

Yes, I'm afraid he's telling the truth.

PHAEDRIA:

What? Geta, am I a stranger?

GETA:

No, but still, don't you think the old man's angry enough already?
Should we really goad him on, 'til we've lost all hope of forgiveness?

PHAEDRIA:

Somebody else will take her away to some unknown place without me?
Well, then, Antipho, while you still can, talk to me, gaze upon me,
While I'm still here.

ANTIPHO:

Why? What is it? What are you planning? Tell me.

PHAEDRIA:

Anyplace, wherever she's taken, I'll follow, or I'll perish.
That's my decision.

---

14. Geta fears the ultimate punishment handed out to slaves in Rome: crucifixion.

GETA:

The Gods forbid! Slow down!

ANTIPHO:

Geta, isn't there something

You can do to help him?

GETA:

What?

ANTIPHO:

I don't know, but try, I beg you.
I'm afraid of what he'll do if we don't help him.

GETA:

Alright.

I'll put on my thinking cap.

He ponders a moment.

He's saved, I think. *(he pauses)* But I'm frightened.

ANTIPHO:

Don't be afraid. Whatever may happen, we'll all be in it together.

GETA:

Tell me, how much cash do you need?

PHAEDRIA:

Just 30 minae.

GETA:

30!?

Whew, she's expensive, Phaedria!

PHAEDRIA:

No, for her that price is nothing.

GETA:

Alright, then. Consider it done. I'll find the money.

PHAEDRIA:

Terrific!

GETA:

Now just scram.

PHAEDRIA:

I need it *now.*

GETA:

You'll have it *now,* I promise.
I'll need Phormio, though. He needs to help me manage this business.

PHAEDRIA:

He'll be here. Just give him your orders. No matter what, he'll do it.
He's the very best friend in the world.

GETA:

Alright, then, let's go get him.

ANTIPHO:

Anything else you need from me, then, Geta?

GETA:

Nothing. Go home.
Go inside to your wife: I'm sure she's practically dead from terror.
You must console her. Well?

ANTIPHO:

There's nothing on earth I'd rather be doing.

Antipho exits into Demipho's house.

PHAEDRIA:

What's the plan?

GETA:

I'll tell you on the way. Now get a move on.

Geta and Phaedria exit stage left; Demipho and Chremes enter stage right.

DEMIPHO: Well? Did you get what you went to Lemnos for, Chremes? Did
you bring your daughter back with you?

CHREMES: No.

DEMIPHO: Why not?

CHREMES: Her mother saw that I was here for too long, and her daughter was
growing older, not waiting for me to act. So she herself set out with her
whole household to find me. Or so they told me.

DEMIPHO: Well then, why did you stay there so long, after you heard that?

CHREMES: I got sick.

DEMIPHO: How? What was it?

CHREMES: You have to ask? Old age itself is a sickness. But I heard from the
sailor who brought them that they got here safely.

DEMIPHO: Have you heard what happened to my son while I was gone,
Chremes?

CHREMES: Yes, and that's really put my plans in jeopardy. If I arrange this
marriage with somebody who's not in the family, I'll have to explain in detail where she came from and how it all happened. I knew that *you* were as

loyal to me as I am to myself. Somebody not in the family, if he wants to be my relative, will keep quiet, as long as our friendship continues. But if he spurns my offer, then he'll know more than he should. And I'm afraid my wife will find out about this business somehow. If that happens, the only thing left for me is to clear out and leave home, for the only thing I have that's my own is myself.

DEMIPHO: I know that's how it is, and I'm worried about that, too. So I'm not going to give up trying until I get you what I promised.

Geta enters stage left.

GETA: I never saw anybody more clever than that Phormio. I went to him to tell him about the money we needed and how we could get it. I'd hardly told half the story, when he understood everything. He was thrilled. He praised me, and he asked where the old man was. He thanked the gods that he'd gotten the chance to show himself no less a friend to Phaedria than he was to Antipho. I told him to wait at the forum; I'd bring the old man there. But look! There's the old man himself. Who's that with him? Oh, dear. It's Phaedria's father, come home. Wait a minute, you ass! Why should I be afraid of him? I've got two to deceive instead of one, that's all. I think it's better to double my chances. I'll try to get the money from this one, the one I started with. If he comes through, fine; if I can't get anything from him, then I'll go after this newcomer.

Antipho enters from Demipho's house.

ANTIPHO: I wonder how long it will take Geta to get back? But I see my uncle standing there with my father. Oh dear, I'm frightened. What will my father do now that *he's* come home?

Antipho eavesdrops on the following conversation.

GETA: I'll go up to them. Chremes! . . .
CHREMES: Hello, Geta.
GETA: I'm so glad you've arrived home safely.
CHREMES: Thank you.
GETA: How are you? As usual, quite a bit has happened while you were gone, hasn't it?
CHREMES: A whole lot.
GETA: Yes. Did you hear about what happened to Antipho?
CHREMES: Everything.

GETA: *(to Demipho)* You told him, huh? It's such a crime, Chremes, for us to be deceived in this way. We don't deserve it.

CHREMES: That's what we were saying just now.

GETA: Hercules! I was just thinking really hard about this business myself, and I think I've found a solution.

CHREMES: What is it, Geta?

DEMIPHO: What solution?

GETA: When I left you, I happened to bump into Phormio.

CHREMES: Who's Phormio?

DEMIPHO: He's the one who . . .

CHREMES: Oh. That's right.

GETA: I decided I should feel out what he was thinking. I took him aside alone, and I said, "Phormio, why don't you let us arrange this matter between ourselves as friends rather than as enemies? My master is a gentleman: he doesn't want lawsuits. All his friends, you see, were unanimous: they said he should throw her right out."

ANTIPHO: What's he up to? Where's all this leading?

GETA: "So you say the law will punish him if he throws her out? He's already looked into that. Whoa! You'll really sweat if you go to court against him: he knows how to argue a case. But suppose he loses: he's only risking money, not his civic status." After I saw that he was starting to soften at what I was saying, I said, "Alright, we're alone now. Tell me: how much do you want, so my master can avoid a lawsuit, she gets out of here, and you stop being a pest?"

ANTIPHO: Is he out of his mind?

GETA: "For I'm sure, given the good man my master is, if you name some price that's anywhere near just and fair, you won't have three words of argument about it."

DEMIPHO: Who told you to say such things?

CHREMES: Wait! This is the best way to get what we want.

ANTIPHO: I'm ruined!

DEMIPHO: Go on.

GETA: First the man was completely crazy.

CHREMES: Well, what did he ask for?

GETA: Way too much: outrageous.

CHREMES: Tell us.

GETA: He wanted somebody to give him a whole talent.

DEMIPHO: Somebody's more likely to give him a thrashing. What impudence!

GETA: That's just what I told him: "I ask you, what if he were finding a husband for his only daughter? It didn't do him much good that he didn't raise a daughter: one was found for him who would demand a dowry." To make the matter brief, and skip all his nonsense, this was what he finally said: "From the beginning I wanted to marry my friend's daughter myself, as was right. For I realized that it would be bad for her, a poor girl, to be handed over to be slave to a rich man. But to be frank, I needed a little money to pay off some debts. Here's what I'll do. I'm engaged to another woman. If Demipho wants to give me as much money as I would receive in dowry from her, I'd like nothing better than to marry Phanium myself."

ANTIPHO: What is this? I can't tell whether it's stupidity or viciousness. Is he off his head, or is he deliberately trying to do me in?

DEMIPHO: What if he owes his very soul?

GETA: Here's what he said: "I've mortgaged some land for 10 minae . . ."

DEMIPHO: Alright, alright, let him marry her. I'll give him the money.

GETA: " . . . and there's a little house mortgaged for 10 more . . ."

DEMIPHO: Whoa! That's too much!

CHREMES: Calm down. You can get the other 10 minae from me.

GETA: " . . . and I have to buy a slave-girl for my new wife. I need a little bit for furniture, and I need money for the marriage ceremony. For these things," he said, "I need about 10 minae."

DEMIPHO: Let him sue me a million times: I'm not giving him anything. Am I going to let that bastard mock me?

CHREMES: Please, I'll pay it. Calm down. You just make sure your son marries the girl we want him to.

ANTIPHO: Oh no! Geta, you've killed me with your tricks.

CHREMES: It's for my sake that she's being thrown out, so it's right for me to lose this money.

GETA: He said, "Let me know as soon as possible, if they're going to give her to me, so I can get rid of the other girl. I don't want things up in the air. For they've already promised to give me a dowry."

CHREMES: Let him take her away, give notice that the other engagement is broken, and marry her.

DEMIPHO: And may it bring only trouble to him!

CHREMES: By chance I've brought some money with me: profit from my wife's estates on Lemnos. I'll go get it, and I'll tell my wife you needed it.

Demipho and Chremes exit into Chremes' house.

ANTIPHO: Geta!

GETA: Huh?

ANTIPHO: What have you done?

GETA: I've swindled the old men out of some money.

ANTIPHO: Are you satisfied?

GETA: I don't know. I got as much money as I was ordered to.

ANTIPHO: Damn you! I ask you one thing and you answer another.

GETA: What's this all about?

ANTIPHO: What do you think? It's obvious that thanks to you there's nothing left for me but to go hang myself. As for you, may all the gods and goddesses, those above and those below, damn you right to hell! If you want anything done, if there's anything you want taken care of well, ask this guy to do it. What could have been less useful than to open up this wound, or even to mention my wife? Now my father's got hopes that he can throw her out. So tell me. If Phormio accepts the dowry, he has to marry her: what happens then?

GETA: But he won't marry her.

ANTIPHO: Sure. And I suppose when they demand the money back, he'll just go to prison for our sake.

GETA: Antipho: there's nothing that can't be made to look bad when it's told badly. You take out what's good, and you only say what's bad. Now listen to the other side. Alright, if he takes the money, he has to marry her, just as you say. I grant you that. Still, there will be a little time, while he gets the marriage arrangements ready, issues invitations, makes the necessary sacrifices. Meanwhile, Phaedria's friends will give the money they promised: he'll pay back the money from that.

ANTIPHO: For what reason? What excuse will he give?

GETA: You have to ask? "What horrible things happened to me, right after I made that agreement! Someone's black dog came into my house; a snake fell from my roof tiles into my fish pond; a cock crowed; a soothsayer decreed against it; a seer forbade me to do it; I can't start any new business before the winter solstice." Those are all perfectly legitimate reasons. Things like that are going to happen.

ANTIPHO: If only they would happen!

GETA: They'll happen, trust me. *(Demipho and Chremes enter from Chremes' house.)* Here comes your father: get out of here. Tell Phaedria his money is ready.

Antipho exits stage left.

DEMIPHO:

    Relax, I say. I'll make damn sure he won't be able to trick us.
    I'll never let this money out of my hands without a witness.
    I'll state the payment and its cause.

GETA:

(aside)

                    How careful, when there's no reason!

CHREMES:

    That's good. That's how it needs to be done, and hurry, while he's still
                                        willing.
    For if that other woman presses him, he might refuse us.

GETA:

    You're right about that.

DEMIPHO:

             So take me there.

GETA:

                  I'm ready.

CHREMES:

                       And when you've finished,
    Go get my wife, and have her visit the girl before she leaves us.
    I want her to tell her we're giving her to Phormio: she shouldn't be angry.
    He'll make a better spouse for her: after all, she knows him better.
    And we've not shirked our duty, either: he'll get plenty of dowry.

DEMIPHO:

    Well, dammit, why should you care about that?

CHREMES:

                      I care because it's important.
    It's not enough to do what's right, if no one gives you credit.
    I don't want her saying we've kicked her out: she must leave of her own
                                      volition.

DEMIPHO:

    But I can do that on my own.

CHREMES:

                  But women do better with women.

DEMIPHO:

    Alright, I'll ask her.

Demipho and Geta exit stage left.

CHREMES:

I wonder where I'll ever be able to find them?

Sophrona enters from Demipho's house. She does not see Chremes.

SOPHRONA:

What do I do now? Where can I find a friend? And who can help me?
I'm so afraid my mistress, because she took my advice, will suffer.
Antipho's father has borne this news so violently, they tell me.

CHREMES:

What? Who's this? Who is that old woman at Demipho's all in a tizzy?

SOPHRONA:

It's poverty that made me do it, although I knew this marriage
Was risky, still I thought that at least for a while it might bring safety.

CHREMES:

Surely, unless my mind's playing tricks, or my old eyes just don't see well,
That's my daughter's nurse.

SOPHRONA:

And not a trace of . . .

CHREMES:

What do I do now?

SOPHRONA:

Him: her father.

CHREMES:

Should I approach her, or hear more of what she's saying?

SOPHRONA:

I wouldn't have to be frightened if only I found him.

CHREMES:

It really is her.

Time to speak to her.

SOPHRONA:

Who's that talking?

CHREMES:

Sophrona.

SOPHRONA:

He knows my name, too!

CHREMES:

Look at me.

SOPHRONA:

My goodness! Is that Stilpo?

CHREMES:

No.

SOPHRONA:

You deny it?

CHREMES:

Sophrona, come over here if you please, away from that door a little.
I don't want you to call me by that name.

SOPHRONA:

Why not? Are you not

The one you always said you were?

CHREMES:

Sh!

SOPHRONA:

What's to fear in this doorway?

CHREMES:

I have a savage wife closed up inside. But about that name there:
I used it falsely once, for fear someday in a thoughtless moment
You women might reveal my name, and then my wife would find out.

SOPHRONA:

So that's why we poor women could never find you.

CHREMES:

Yes. But tell me,

What business brings you to this house, the one you've just come out of?
Your mistresses—where are they?

SOPHRONA:

Oh!

CHREMES:

What is it? Are they living?

SOPHRONA:

Your daughter lives. Her mother died from grief at all she'd suffered.

CHREMES:

Oh dear.

SOPHRONA:

But I, alone and old, impoverished, in a strange land,
I did as much as possible: I got the girl a husband,
The youth who's master in this house here.

CHREMES:

Antipho?

SOPHRONA:

Exactly.

CHREMES:

What's that? He has two wives?

SOPHRONA:

No, please! His only wife is this one.

CHREMES:

But what about that other one, the counterfeit relation?

SOPHRONA:

That's this one.

CHREMES:

What?

SOPHRONA:

We made that story up, so he could wed her
Without a dowry. He's in love with her.

CHREMES:

Great gods above us!
How often things work out by chance you never would have hoped for!
I've now come home to find the girl has married the man I wanted.
And not just that: he loves her, too; it's just the thing I wished for.
We worked so hard, my brother and I, to make this happen, and now

look:

He's done it on his own, without our help, through his own efforts.

Demipho and Geta enter stage left.

SOPHRONA:

Now see to what you have to do: here comes the young man's father.
They say he's awfully angry at all this.

CHREMES:

No need to worry.
But by the gods, please, don't let anyone find out she's my daughter.

SOPHRONA: Nobody will find out from me.

CHREMES: Follow me. We'll discuss the rest inside.

Sophrona and Chremes exit into Demipho's house.

DEMIPHO:

It's all our fault. We make crime pay, we're too soft on the culprits.
It's all because we worry too much about our reputation.
But you know what they say: "It's out of the frying pan, into the fire."
It's bad enough he wronged me. Now on top of that I've paid him,
So he can live on that 'til he can dream some other scheme up.

GETA:

You're right.

DEMIPHO:

And so the bad ones get rewards for being immoral.

GETA:

Exactly.

DEMIPHO:

Oh how stupidly we've handled all this business.

GETA:

I only hope this works, and that he takes her away and weds her.

DEMIPHO:

You hope? But aren't you sure?

GETA:

Who knows? Perhaps he'll change his mind yet.

DEMIPHO:

What? Change his mind?

GETA:

I only said he might, that's all I'm saying.

DEMIPHO:

Well, I'll go do what my brother advised. I'll bring his wife to see her,
So she can talk with her. Go on inside and say she's coming.

Demipho exits into Chremes' house.

GETA:

We've found the money for Phaedria: not a word about a lawsuit;
And as for now, the wife will stay right here. So what's the next step?
What happens now? Well, Geta, now you're right back where you
started.
You'll pay for this with interest, though you've delayed the day of
reckoning.
The beating you'll get is only growing worse, if you don't watch out.

I'll go inside and reassure the girl about what's coming.
I'll tell her not to be afraid of anything from Phormio.

Geta exits into Demipho's house. Demipho and Nausistrata enter from Chremes' house.

DEMIPHO:

Go on inside, Nausistrata, and use your skill in speaking.
Make sure she does what's needed of her own will.

NAUSISTRATA:

Yes, I'll do it.

DEMIPHO:

I'm grateful for your actions now, just as I was for your money.

NAUSISTRATA:

I'm glad. But I can't help as much as I'd like because of my husband.

DEMIPHO:

What's that?

NAUSISTRATA:

He's been so careless with my father's good investments.
My father used to make two talents every year from his holdings.
He's not the man my father was.

DEMIPHO:

Each year, two talents? Really?

NAUSISTRATA:

That's right. Two talents, even back then, when prices were all much
lower.

DEMIPHO:

Astounding.

NAUSISTRATA:

What do you think of that?

DEMIPHO:

It's obvious. You're right.

NAUSISTRATA:

Oh,
If only I'd been born a man. I'd show . . .

DEMIPHO:

I know.

NAUSISTRATA:

How they ought to . . .

DEMIPHO:

Calm down, please, save your strength for the girl. She's young. She may
fatigue you.

NAUSISTRATA:

Alright. I'll do as you say.

Chremes enters from Demipho's house.

But look! My husband's coming from your house.

CHREMES:

Oh! Demipho! You've paid the man?

DEMIPHO:

At once.

CHREMES:

I wish you hadn't.

(aside)
Oh, no! My wife. I almost said too much.

DEMIPHO:

Why? What's the matter?

CHREMES:

It's alright now.

DEMIPHO:

And you? You've told her why your wife is coming?

CHREMES:

It's settled now.

DEMIPHO:

Well? What's she say?

CHREMES:

She can't be taken.

DEMIPHO:

Why not?

CHREMES:

Because they love each other.

DEMIPHO:

What is that to us?

CHREMES:

A great deal.

Besides, I've found she *is* related to us.

DEMIPHO:

What? You're crazy!

CHREMES:

You'll see. I'm not speaking rashly: I've remembered.

DEMIPHO:

You've gone crazy!

NAUSISTRATA:

Wait, please! Make sure you don't mistreat your kin.

DEMIPHO:

We're *not* related.

CHREMES:

Don't say that. It's the name: they gave the wrong name for her father,
And that's where you went wrong.

DEMIPHO:

You mean she didn't know her own father?

CHREMES:

She knew him.

DEMIPHO:

Well, then, why'd she give another name?

CHREMES:

Oh! Will you
Not give this up and try to understand me just a little?

DEMIPHO:

How can I, when you tell me nothing?

CHREMES:

Oh! You're going to kill me!

NAUSISTRATA:

I wonder what this is all about.

DEMIPHO:

Well I sure couldn't tell you.

CHREMES:

You want to know? Then I will swear, with Jupiter as my witness,
That we're her closest relatives on earth.

DEMIPHO:

Great gods almighty,
Let's go inside and see: I want us all to know — or not know —
Together.

CHREMES:
　　　No!
DEMIPHO:
　　　　What?
CHREMES:
　　　　　　Can't you trust me just a bit?
DEMIPHO:
　　　　　　　　　　　　Alright, then.
You want me to believe you? And you want an end to questions?
Alright. But what about our friend? What happens to his daughter?
CHREMES:
She's taken care of.
DEMIPHO:
　　　　　　This one's sent away, then?
CHREMES:
　　　　　　　　　　Why?
DEMIPHO:
　　　　　　　　　　　She'll stay?
CHREMES:
　　　　　　　　　　　　　　Right.
DEMIPHO:
Then you can go, Nausistrata.
NAUSISTRATA:
　　　　　　　I think it will be better
For everyone for her to stay than what you two were planning.
I saw her once: she seemed to me a very respectable woman.

Nausistrata exits into Chremes' house.

DEMIPHO:
What is all this?
CHREMES:
　　　　She's closed the door?
DEMIPHO:
　　　　　　　　Yes.
CHREMES:
　　　　　　　Jupiter in heaven!
The gods are looking after us: your son has wed my daughter.

DEMIPHO:

    What? How could that have happened?

CHREMES:

                                It's not safe here: I can't tell you.

DEMIPHO:

    Alright, let's go inside.

CHREMES:

                   Look here: not even our sons must know this.

Chremes and Demipho exit into Demipho's house.

Antipho enters stage left.

ANTIPHO:

    I'm happy, whatever happens to me, that my cousin has what he wanted.
    How wise he is to want what he could fix with little trouble
    When things went wrong. As soon as he found money, his cares were
                                    over.
    But me! I'm stuck! There's no way I can twist myself out of these
                                  troubles,
    If it's kept in the dark, I'm frightened, if it's known to the world, I'm
                                  guilty.
    I wouldn't be coming home now if I hadn't seen a glimmer
    Of hope that I might keep her. But where is Geta? I need to ask him
    What time he thinks is best for me to go and meet my father.

Phormio enters stage left.

PHORMIO:

    I got the money, gave it to the pimp, and took the woman.
    I made sure Phaedria has her to himself: she's got her freedom.
    And now there's just one thing that must be done: to get some leisure
    Away from these old men: I want to spend a few days drinking.

ANTIPHO:

    It's Phormio. What's up?

PHORMIO:

                How's that?

ANTIPHO:

                            What's Phaedria going to do now?
    What plan's he got for burning up his amatory surplus?

PHORMIO:

He plans to play your part.

ANTIPHO:

What part?

PHORMIO:

To flee the sight of his father.
He asked that you in turn take up his part, and be his lawyer.
He's off to drink at my house. I'll just say I'm going to market,
To Sunium,[15] to buy the maid that Geta said I'd purchase.
I don't want them to see me here and think I'm wasting their money.
But listen, it's your door.

ANTIPHO:

Tell me: who's coming out?

PHORMIO:

It's Geta.

Geta enters from Demipho's house. He does not see Antipho or Phormio.

GETA:

Fortune! Great and Lucky Fortune! What divine munificence!
What an unexpected boon you've granted to my master!

ANTIPHO:

What's all this?

GETA:

You've freed us all from fear, his friends and allies!
Why am I waiting? I need to throw my cloak around my neck and
Find the man, so he can know what wonderful things have happened.

ANTIPHO:

I can't understand a word he says. Can you?

PHORMIO:

No. Nothing.

GETA:

Off to the pimp's I'll go: that's where they are.

ANTIPHO:

Hey! Geta!

15. Sunium is about 25 miles southeast of Athens.

GETA:

(he still does not see Antipho)

Damn you!

That's the way it always is. When you're most in a hurry, they call you.

ANTIPHO:

Geta!

GETA:

Gods, he won't stop shouting! I don't care how much you hate me,
I'm not going to stop.

ANTIPHO:

Why won't you stand still just for a minute?

GETA:

Go get beaten.

ANTIPHO:

That's what's waiting for you, if you don't stop, scoundrel.

GETA:

This guy must be someone I know: he's threatening me with a beating.
Is he the one I'm seeking? He is. Approach him at once.

ANTIPHO:

What is it?

GETA:

You most fortunate man! Of everyone living, your luck's the greatest.
There's no doubt about it, Antipho: you're the one the gods love.

ANTIPHO:

I'd like that to be true. But tell me: why should I believe you?

GETA:

Is it enough if I soak you through with joy?

ANTIPHO:

You're killing me, Geta.

PHORMIO:

Geta, just forget those extravagant promises, and tell us.

GETA:

Phormio? You were here too?

PHORMIO:

I was. But you're dawdling.

GETA:

Alright. Listen.

After we gave you the money just now in the forum, we came straight
back home.
Meanwhile, the master sent me to your wife.

ANTIPHO:
Why?

GETA:
Skip the details.
As I approach the women's rooms, the young slave Midas comes running,
Grabs my cloak from behind, and jerks me back. I turn. I ask him,
"What's the meaning of this?" He says that no one's allowed to enter.
"Chremes, the old man's brother," he says, "and Sophrona just went in
there.
He's inside with them now." Hearing that, I tiptoed to the doorway,
Ever so softly I went, I got there, stood, and held my breath in.
Moving my ear to the door, I stood like this, and started to listen.

PHORMIO:
Good job, Geta!

GETA:
And then I heard the most beautiful thing you could think of.
So good, I almost shouted for joy.

ANTIPHO:
What?

GETA:
What do you think?

ANTIPHO:
I don't know!

GETA:
Something marvelous: absolutely stupendous! Truly amazing!
Chremes, your uncle, is Phanium's father!

ANTIPHO:
What's that? What are you saying?

GETA:
Once he had a secret affair with her mother, who lived on Lemnos.

PHORMIO:
Nonsense! Why wouldn't she know her own father?

GETA:
Believe me, there must be some reason.
Really, I couldn't get every word: I was listening outside the doorway!

ANTIPHO:

Now that you mention it, I heard a rumor like that.

GETA:

And you'll be certain
After you hear the rest. Meanwhile, I see your uncle go outside.
He comes back with your father: they both say you have permission to
keep her.
I've been sent to fetch you.

ANTIPHO:

Well, then, fetch me! Why are you waiting?
Phormio, farewell.

PHORMIO:

Farewell to you. By the gods, I'm very happy.

Antipho and Geta exit into Demipho's house.

What a stroke of good luck these boys have had, all unexpected! Now is
the best chance for me to trick these old men and take away all Phaedria's
worries about money, so he doesn't have to go begging to his friends. I'll
see that the money that was given to me will be given to him, against their
will. From what's happened, I've found a way I can force it out of them.
Now I have to try out a new role. But I'll go over to this alleyway right
here, and from there I'll show myself to them, when they come outside. I
won't go to the market, where I pretended I would be.

*Phormio hides between Demipho's and Chremes' houses. Demipho and Chremes enter
from Demipho's house.*

DEMIPHO: I feel grateful, Chremes, just as I should, and I give thanks to the
gods that these things have worked out so well for us. Now we need to
meet Phormio as soon as possible, so we can get our 30 minae[16] back before he demolishes them.

PHORMIO: I'll go see if Demipho is home so I can . . .

DEMIPHO: Phormio! We were just going to see you.

PHORMIO: Perhaps about the same matter?

DEMIPHO: Yes, that's right.

PHORMIO: I thought so. Why were you coming to my house?

DEMIPHO: As if you had to ask.

---

16. The money given to Phormio as a dowry for Phanium.

PHORMIO: Were you afraid that I wouldn't do what I said I would? Alas, even though I'm as poor as I am, still I've held on to this one thing: I can still be trusted.

CHREMES: Isn't he a gentleman, just as I said?

DEMIPHO: He certainly is.

PHORMIO: And I'm coming to you, Demipho, to report that I'm ready. Give me my wife, as soon as you wish. I've put off all my other business, as was fitting, once I realized that you wanted this so much.

DEMIPHO: But my brother here persuaded me that I shouldn't give her to you. "What will people say if you do this?" he said. "Once, when she could have been sent away respectfully, she wasn't; now it's shameful for her to be thrown out." In general, he said all the same things that you accused me of to my face just now.

PHORMIO: What arrogance! You're mocking me!

DEMIPHO: How?

PHORMIO: You have to ask? Because now I won't be able to marry that other woman. How can I return to the one I've rejected?

CHREMES: *(aside to Demipho)* Say, "Besides, I see that Antipho does not want her to be sent away."

DEMIPHO: Besides, I see that my son does not at all want the woman to be sent away. But please, Phormio, come to the forum and have that money put back in my account.

PHORMIO: The money I've already handed over to my creditors?

DEMIPHO: Well then, what are we supposed to do?

PHORMIO: If you want to give me the wife you promised me, I'll marry her. But if you want her to remain with you, Demipho, then let the dowry stay with me. It's not fair for you to deceive me. Trusting in your honor I broke it off with the other woman, who was bringing me just as much dowry.

DEMIPHO: Why don't you just go to hell, you arrogant bastard? Do you still think I don't know you and what you're up to?

PHORMIO: I'm getting angry.

DEMIPHO: You'd marry her if she were given to you?

PHORMIO: Try me.

DEMIPHO: Sure, so that my son could live with her at your house—that's what your plan was.

PHORMIO: What are you talking about?

DEMIPHO: Just give me the money.

PHORMIO: No. You give me my wife.

DEMIPHO: Then it's off to court with you.

PHORMIO: I'm warning you, if you two continue to be troublesome . . .

DEMIPHO: What will you do?

PHORMIO: What will I do? Perhaps you think I act as patron only for women without dowries. I also like to help women *with* dowries.

CHREMES: What's that to us?

PHORMIO: Nothing. But I know a certain wife here whose husband . . .

CHREMES: Oh, no!

PHORMIO: Had another wife on Lemnos . . .

CHREMES: I'm finished!

PHORMIO: By whom he had a daughter; and he's bringing her up in secret.

CHREMES: I'm dead and buried.

PHORMIO: I'm going to tell her all about this right now.

CHREMES: Please, don't do it.

PHORMIO: Oh! Are you the man?

DEMIPHO: Look how he mocks us.

CHREMES: Alright. You're off the hook.

PHORMIO: Nonsense!

CHREMES: What do you want? You can have all the money, no strings attached.

PHORMIO: I hear you. Damn it! Why do you two keep mocking me like this, with your silly, childish statements? Yes, no, yes, no. Take her. Hand her over. What's said is unsaid; what's agreed upon is not agreed upon.

CHREMES: How on earth did he learn about this?

DEMIPHO: I don't know. I know I didn't tell anybody.

CHREMES: Damn, it's uncanny.

PHORMIO: *(aside)* I've got them.

DEMIPHO: Damn it! Are we going to let this guy take all that money from us right out in the open, laughing at us? Hercules, I'd rather die. Get a hold of yourself, Chremes, and be a man. Face it: your wrongdoing has been brought to light. You can't keep it from your wife any longer. She'll calm down sooner if we tell her ourselves what she's bound to hear from others, Chremes. Then we'll be able to avenge ourselves on this bastard as we wish.

PHORMIO: *(aside)* Oops! Unless I watch out, I'm stuck. These guys are coming at me with the courage of gladiators.

CHREMES: But I'm afraid she'll never calm down.

DEMIPHO: Buck up: I'll bring you back into her good graces, Chremes, trust me. After all, the girl's mother is out of the picture.

PHORMIO: So that's how you're going to deal with me! Oh, you're really clever, going after me this way. It's not to his advantage for you to rile me up, Demipho. *(to Chremes)* And what do *you* say? You've done what you pleased abroad. You respected this excellent woman so little that you found a novel way of insulting her. Now do you expect to wash your sin away with prayers? What I'm going to tell her will light her up with a fire so fierce, you won't be able to quench it, even if you drip with tears.

DEMIPHO: Damn it! I wish all the gods and goddesses would destroy him! How could anyone be so arrogant? They ought to drag this bastard off to some desert island at public expense.

CHREMES: He's brought me to such a state, I have no idea what to do.

DEMIPHO: I do: Let's take him to court.

PHORMIO: To court? No. If we go anywhere, let's go in here.

He moves toward Chremes' house.

CHREMES: Chase him. Hold him while I call some slaves here.

Chremes rushes into Demipho's house. Demipho grabs hold of Phormio.

DEMIPHO: No! I can't do it by myself. Hurry!

PHORMIO: That's one charge of assault against you.

DEMIPHO: Well, then, take me to court.

Chremes returns with a burly slave.

PHORMIO: The other one's against you, Chremes.

CHREMES: Grab him.

The slave grabs hold of Phormio, who struggles.

PHORMIO: So that's how you want to play, is it? Well, then, it's time for me to use my voice. Nausistrata, come out here!

CHREMES: Shut that foul mouth of his. Damn! He's strong!

PHORMIO: Nausistrata, I say.

DEMIPHO: Will you not shut up?

PHORMIO: Why should I?

DEMIPHO: If he doesn't listen, punch him in the stomach.

PHORMIO: Go ahead, poke my eye out, if you want. The time's coming when I'll make you pay dearly.

Nausistrata enters from Chremes' house.

NAUSISTRATA: Who's calling me? Oh my! *(to Chremes)* Please, dear, what's all this confusion?

PHORMIO: Well, why are you standing there mute?

NAUSISTRATA: Who is this man? Why don't you answer me?

PHORMIO: How can he answer you? He doesn't even know where he is.

CHREMES: Don't believe a word he says.

PHORMIO: Go on, touch him: kill me if he's not frozen stiff.

CHREMES: This is nonsense.

NAUSISTRATA: What is all this? What's he talking about?

PHORMIO: You'll know soon enough. Listen.

CHREMES: Will you go on believing what he says?

NAUSISTRATA: Really, Chremes, how can I believe him, when he hasn't said anything?

PHORMIO: The poor guy's hallucinating from terror.

NAUSISTRATA: There must be some reason you're so frightened.

CHREMES: Me, frightened?

PHORMIO: Sure. Since you're not frightened, and this story I'm telling is nothing, you tell it.

DEMIPHO: Damn you, you think he'd tell it to help you?

PHORMIO: And you—you've really been a great help to your brother.

NAUSISTRATA: Chremes, you're not telling me.

CHREMES: But . . .

NAUSISTRATA: "But" what?

CHREMES: There's no need to tell it.

PHORMIO: True, no need for you to tell it, but there is need for her to know it. In Lemnos . . .

DEMIPHO: Hey! What are you saying?

CHREMES: Will you not shut up?

PHORMIO: Without your knowledge . . .

CHREMES: Oh, no!

PHORMIO: He had a wife.

NAUSISTRATA: What? The gods forbid!

PHORMIO: That's what happened.

NAUSISTRATA: Poor me, I'm ruined!

PHORMIO: And he had a daughter by her, while you were blissfully ignorant of the whole thing.

CHREMES: What's to be done?

NAUSISTRATA: By the immortal gods, that's a cruel and wicked deed!

PHORMIO: *(to Chremes)* Nothing: It's already been done.

NAUSISTRATA: Has anything more foul ever been done? And when they
come to their wives, then they become old men.

Demipho, you I'm addressing. I don't want to talk to *him:* it disgusts me
All those trips to Lemnos, staying so long, was this the reason?
This base business, is this what diminished the profits of all our holdings?

DEMIPHO:

Yes, it's the truth, Nausistrata. He's done wrong, I don't deny it.
Still, he should be forgiven.

PHORMIO:

He's giving a eulogy for a dead man.

DEMIPHO:

Neither neglect nor hatred of you made him do what he did, I swear it.
Fifteen years ago or so, he got drunk, and raped a woman.
She gave birth to this girl, but he never touched her again thereafter.
Now she's passed away: the source of the trouble is no longer with us.
Therefore, I beg you, accept this news with your usual calm and

composure.

NAUSISTRATA:

Calm and composure? Really, I do want to put all this behind me.
What can I hope for, though? Should I believe that he'll be better
Now that he's old? But when he did all this, he was old already.
Or are my age and beauty more desirable now, I ask you?
What guarantee can you give that he won't find some other woman?

PHORMIO:

Step right up, if you want to see the funeral games of Chremes.
Go ahead, if you have in mind to pick a fight with Phormio.
Look what's happened to *him:* you'll get the same if you insult me.
Now we'll see if he can soothe her wrath: I've got my vengeance.
She'll be pounding this into his ears as long as he's living.

NAUSISTRATA:

Well, I suppose I earned this, Demipho. Why should I even mention
How many times and in how many ways I've been good to him?

DEMIPHO:

I know them
All as well as you.

NAUSISTRATA:

Did I deserve this, then?

DEMIPHO:

You didn't.

Now, however, since the past can't be changed through accusations,
Pardon him. He pleads, confesses, explains: what more could you ask for?

PHORMIO:

First, before she lets him off, I'll look after myself and Phaedria.
Wait, Nausistrata, don't respond 'til you've heard this first.

NAUSISTRATA:

What is it?

PHORMIO:

I defrauded this man of 30 minae, and gave them to Phaedria.
He gave it all to a pimp for his mistress.

CHREMES:

What!?

NAUSISTRATA:

You think that's a scandal?
Why shouldn't Phaedria have one mistress? After all, you've got two
wives.
You're so shameless. How are you going to scold him, you hypocrite?
Tell me.

DEMIPHO:

Chremes will do what you wish.

NAUSISTRATA:

No. I have a better idea, so listen.
No pardon yet. I won't promise a thing. I won't answer until I've seen
Phaedria.
He can decide. I leave it to him. I'll do what he advises.

PHORMIO:

You're a wise woman, Nausistrata.

NAUSISTRATA:

Thank you. Will that solution suit you?

PHORMIO:

Suit me? I'm thrilled. It's more than enough—beyond my expectations.

NAUSISTRATA:

Tell me your name.

PHORMIO:

             Mine? Phormio. I'm a great friend to your family and Phaedria.

NAUSISTRATA:

   Well then, Phormio, I'll make a promise to you. I swear by Castor,

   From this moment I'll say and do whatever I can to please you.

PHORMIO:

   That's very kind.

NAUSISTRATA:

        You've earned it.

PHORMIO:

                 Well, then, I can think of something

   You could do right now to make me happy—and vex your husband.

NAUSISTRATA:

   Say the word.

PHORMIO:

       Invite me to dinner.

NAUSISTRATA:

            Why certainly: you're invited.

DEMIPHO:

   Let's go in.

NAUSISTRATA:

     Alright, but where is Phaedria, our judge and jury?

PHORMIO:

   He'll be here in a minute.

CANTOR: [17]

(to audience)

        And you, farewell, and please applaud us.

---

17. The *cantor* was an anonymous performer who entered to deliver the epilogue.